Executing God

Also by Sharon L. Baker from Westminster John Knox Press

*Razing Hell: Rethinking Everything You've Been Taught
about God's Wrath and Judgment*

Executing God

Rethinking Everything You've Been Taught about Salvation and the Cross

Sharon L. Baker

WESTMINSTER
JOHN KNOX PRESS
LOUISVILLE · KENTUCKY

First edition
Published by Westminster John Knox Press
Louisville, Kentucky

Published in association with the literary agency of Daniel Literary Group, Nashville, TN.

13 14 15 16 17 18 19 20 21 22—10 9 8 7 6 5 4 3 2 1

Book design by Drew Stevens
Cover design by Dilu Nicholas

Library of Congress Cataloging-in-Publication Data
is on file at the Library of Congress, Washington, DC.

ISBN: 978-0-664-23810-0

Most Westminster John Knox Press books are available at special quantity discounts when purchased in bulk by corporations, organizations, and special-interest groups. For more information, please e-mail SpecialSales@wjkbooks.com.

To my mother, Helen Crosby,
whose life and love
taught me about the God of love

Contents

Acknowledgments

I express deep gratitude to my colleagues. Their scholarship, expertise, and friendship stimulated, motivated, and encouraged me as I researched and wrote this book. They include Crystal Downing, whose own work in *Changing Signs of Truth* gave me the inspiration and courage to reinterpret my tradition; Eric Seibert, whose own personal theology of nonviolence served as a constant companion; Richard Crane, whose theological prowess continually challenged and provoked my own thought. Many thanks to professor John D. Caputo for his radically provocative thought on the event that has informed my own thinking and to professor Jeff B. Pool, without whose teaching, mentoring, and energized discussion, I may not have written this book.

As always, I thank my students, who contributed to this book in profound ways by asking questions, struggling with the issues, challenging me with the biblical witness, and keeping open minds for productive conversations. I especially appreciate Elizabeth Sobrevilla, who always asked the tough questions and willingly discussed with me issues surrounding the atonement. My special gratitude to Joshua Wood, whose questions and struggles have made their way into the pages of this book. I am also grateful to Christian ministers Raborn Johnson and Leslie King, who read the early manuscript and took time to provide valuable feedback.

I am very grateful for my agent Greg Daniel and for the people at WJK who have contributed to the production of this book. Thank you to David Dobson, Jana Reiss, and Daniel Braden. They made the publishing process a pleasure with their professional expertise, unending patience, and discerning eyes.

My special heartfelt thanks to B. Keith Putt, my closest and dearest friend, for editing this manuscript and proving once again that he knows the Bible better than I do!

Introduction

Execute: to carry out a plan or action, to follow out an intention
Execute: to inflict capital punishment, to put to death in pursuance of
a sentence.

           —*Oxford English Dictionary*

Whan ye thinke eny good thought, execute it.
    —Earl Rivers, tr., *Dictes or Sayengis Philosophhres* (Caxton) (1877)

Two other men, both criminals, were also led out with him to be
executed.

           —Luke 23:32 (NIV)

Once upon a time I was a fundamentalist, Southern Baptist and I had
God all figured out. I knew it all, and delighted in telling people all
about God. Men and women flocked to my Bible study classes. They
sold cassette tapes in the church narthex, and people bought them.
If someone had a question about God, I was one of the first persons
they turned to for answers. I knew what I believed and held onto those
beliefs tightly. I was proud that I spent hours and hours a day studying the Bible and praying, even though I was raising four small boys,
homeschooling one of them, and taking care of a home while my husband traveled for work 80 percent of the time. I memorized whole
books of the Bible and used Scripture as a tool to discipline my sons. I
knew what it said on every topic that confronts us in life, from abortion
to dating, from sexual orientation to marriage, from managing money
to rearing children, and from creation to kingdom come. God spoke to
me personally, and I always listened. I even knew what God was telling other people and had Scripture to back it up. Yes, I had a hotline
to God. I knew with absolute certainty how God acted and why God
acted in certain ways. Then a couple of things happened one right after
the other: two of my children became very sick with an incurable liver
disease, and I went to seminary.

All of a sudden I didn't know everything about God anymore.
In fact, I didn't know anything. The tragedy of two sick sons made
me question all that I thought I knew about God. Learning Greek,

Hebrew, and basic hermeneutical skills made me realize that I had been
so wrong about so much. My whole belief system came crashing down
around me, and I wandered around in the rubble, kicking at the broken
pieces of my absolute certainty. My anger at God and my surprise at
learning about how much I never knew had a strange effect. I started
asking the kinds of questions that good Southern Baptist women never
dare to ask. As time went by we all learned to deal with my sons' liver
disorder, and I continued working toward a PhD in theology and religion. But my questions and my search for answers became bolder, more
numerous, and much more intense. As it turned out, the more I kicked
around in the rubble of my crushed certainty, the more I realized that
in the midst of the destruction one thing remained the same, one belief
stayed firm, one foundation survived upon which I could plant my
feet: that Jesus Christ is Lord and Savior. And upon that foundation I
began to rebuild.

Nagging questions still plagued me: for example, "Is God really
love?" or "Would a loving God send most of the world's population to
burn in an eternal hell for temporal sin?" or "Does God really require
the death of an innocent man in order to forgive sin?" I decided that
if Jesus were to remain my foundation, then I would have to search
for answers and rebuild my faith according to what Jesus modeled and
taught. Then, from there, I would move on to the Old Testament and
then to the letters of Paul, Peter, and others. I did just that, and found
a God of love, compassion, mercy, grace, hospitality, and healing: a
God who forgives unconditionally, who seeks to reconcile with every
person ever born, who desires nothing less than the healing and salvation of all people (and of all creation if you believe Romans 8:18–22).
The answers I found to my questions so completely changed my view
of God that I felt compelled to write about them. Thus the birth of
this book.

Even though I successfully rebuilt my belief system into something
new and more forgiving, my absolute certainty never returned. In fact,
doubt replaced certainty and that doubt gave birth to faith. Strange,
isn't it? I always thought doubt was the opposite of faith. Now I realize that if it weren't for doubt we wouldn't need faith at all. Absolute certainty is the opposite of faith. The more certain we are about
something, the less we need faith, or hope for that matter. So now my
doubt-turned-faith gives me hope for the future, for what God has in
store for us, and for how God will deal with us all as time meanders on
to its end.

In fact, this book is about hope—hope for the healing of our souls and hospitality for all who enter our gates, for reconciliation between estranged parties and restoration of broken relationships, for open minds that lead to open hearts toward differences of opinion or disagreement over doctrine, for love that overcomes evil and mercy that triumphs over judgmentalism. So this book begins with a question, one that deals with the cross of Jesus, one I have asked over and over again, and one that several of my students have asked as well. It is a question that I hope to answer in the following pages. Did God have Jesus murdered? That question, an echo of my own thoughts, came from a theology student during a class discussion about the cross on a chilly autumn afternoon. But the questions and discussion that followed were even more chilling than the weather outside. One of my best students interjected with, "Right! Did God so love the world that God gave us Judas or Caiaphas or Pilate? Were they employed by God to execute Jesus and make it look legal?" I could almost imagine God commissioning one or more of these heavies to take out Jesus. But as sacrilegious as these questions sound, they provoke some extremely troubling quandaries surrounding the crucifixion. For the sake of argument, let's say that God did premeditate the murder of Jesus, knowing the torturous suffering he would endure and needing that suffering in order to fulfill the divine plan. The questions we must ask, then, are these: Does God require the suffering and death of an innocent person in order to redeem? Does God demand the torture and abuse of an innocent man before God will forgive sin?

Some of you may be thinking that this is what we've always been taught. Why question it now? I question it because I have to. I can no longer sit comfortably with my head stuck in the proverbial sand (or my backside sitting in a comfortable pew in an air-conditioned building) and think that the death of Jesus somehow served divine justice. I don't agree that the horrific death of an innocent man somehow "bought" God off so God would forgive sin. The whole deal smacks of blasphemy. I say this with both a sense of satisfaction and fear—satisfaction because I'm finally being honest about my thoughts, and fear because I could be wrong. Maybe you're thinking that I'm the one blaspheming. God forgive me if that's true. I want to portray God in thought and print just as Jesus portrayed God: as loving, compassionate, merciful, and forgiving. I want those who hate God to see and to know God as one who strongly desires to redeem all creation and to restore all people to loving relationships, not only with God but also with each other.

But that's not the only reason for this book on salvation and the cross. Those who believe in and love God may need to reconsider traditional views in order to see God mainly through the lens of mercy and compassion as well. And here's why.

I'm extremely concerned about religious violence; I am worried about the thousands upon thousands of people injured, massacred, or otherwise abused by violence committed in the name of some God or some theological "certainty." Violence in itself is bad enough, but the fact that it's "religious" adds insult to horrifying injury. This type of violence infects our world and poisons our relationships with nations, states, communities, and other people. We don't need scientific evidence for proof; just pick up any newspaper and read. Religious violence wreaks havoc on our world and has done so for millennia. We may wonder why a religion based on the love of God and others so often produces love's opposite—acts of hatred and violence in the name of God. Consumed with some sort of holy fire, divine impetus, or doctrinal justification (we claim), we do horrendous things to each other. Why? What makes us behave in such unloving ways? I believe that for Christianity at least, we can begin with the Old Testament and find plenty of fodder for rationalizing our violent behavior.

In these sacred pages we read about a God who wipes out thousands in one fell swoop, who commands the massacre of entire nations without blinking an eye, and who drops balls of fire on an unsuspecting city with apparent abandon. Although these stories make for exciting reading, they unfortunately incite copycat killings here on earth. Take Jerry Falwell as an example. After 9/11 he opined that we should blow the terrorists away in the name of the Lord—just like God did in the Old Testament.

But, pointing our finger at the Old Testament alone overlooks a major instance of violence in the New Testament. Traditionally, we have called doctrines of the death of Jesus "atonement theory," and we came up with names for these various theories as they were developed throughout Christian history. The four we will discuss in this book are

Christ as the Victor theory

The Satisfaction theory

The Penal Substitution theory

The Moral Example theory

Although each of these theories differs significantly from the others, they all have one thing in common. They hinge upon violence, and divine violence to boot. Jesus is murdered. Moreover, the murder of this innocent man is orchestrated by none other than God. In other words, the cataclysmic event of the Christian religion and of its doctrine of redemption and reconciliation is born from divine violence. The crux of our entire belief system, the one major event that activates the good news of God's grace, requires, and at best condones, violence and serves as a model for us to imitate. If the violence Christians have wreaked in the last two thousand years results from our desire to do as God would do, we may safely say that human religious violence is the child (however illegitimate) of divine violence.

But as I mentioned before, there's another impetus for reinterpreting traditional theories of atonement. Not that divine violence and the consequent copycat cruelty isn't reason enough. Our common theories of atonement may give birth to violence for those inside the faith, but they also act as a repellent to those outside the faith. Many atheists and those who have turned their backs on God cite the cruelty of God as their reason. For example, one woman said, "the main reason I had to reject Christianity was because god killing his son went too far. I could never worship a god that evil."[1] Sad. But if we stop a second and try to see the cross through the eyes of an unbeliever, it does come off looking much like an injustice. Some theologians have gone so far as to call it divine child abuse.[2] I want to redeem God for those who have become disillusioned and have turned their backs on the God who redeems. In addition, one of my former students (I'll call her Lindsay) turned away from Christianity and then from God altogether because of the "mean-spirited, close-minded, judgmental Christians" she knew. She figured that kind of behavior fit right in with a God who would order the death of a beloved son in order to forgive sin. She reckoned she could live without a forgiveness that entailed such retributive and unjust measures. So, I say it's time to rethink not only the image of God but also those made in the image of God—not just God's modus operandi in the world and in the story of redemption, but also our own.

That said, my desire to write a book on salvation and the cross emerges out of a desire to think differently about the workings of God in what we traditionally refer to as the atonement. As a Christian who is stymied and disturbed by religious violence, I want to help other Christians rethink an issue that historically has caused massive pain and suffering. In the desire to take up our own cross and follow Jesus, we have crucified countless others in our zeal to please God and rid the world of heretics. If any of our violent behavior, any at all, stems from traditional theories of atonement—from what we might call "redemptive violence"—then we must begin to reinterpret these theories. In light of the spread of religious violence infecting our societies and cultures worldwide, rather than portraying God as a violent, angry deity, finger cocked in readiness to blast the disobedient with lightning bolts of destruction, we need to emphasize the God of mercy. This God loves enemy and friend alike and desires to transform the world, not through arms and ammunition but through grace and forgiveness. I am not suggesting we throw away two millennia of Christian tradition in favor of the newest trend in theological studies; I am suggesting that, as believers have done for centuries, we reinterpret our tradition so that it remains relevant for our changing world, and powerful enough to transform our world with the good news of salvation through Jesus Christ.

I'll be right up front with you from the very beginning. I am going to privilege certain texts of Scripture. We all do it. For centuries we have privileged the biblical passages that speak of God's retribution, vengeance, wrath, and punishment—just take a close look at our doctrines of hell and atonement, at our theories of just war and capital punishment. We have subordinated the biblical texts that portray God's restorative justice, love for enemies, extravagant forgiveness, and mercy. I will privilege the teachings of Jesus and the Old Testament prophets who proclaimed God's desire for peace, nonviolence, and love of others—yes, love, even to the point of loving the stranger in our gates. Even to the point of loving our enemies. I do this because we have to do something to stem the tide of violence, resisting the shameless call to abuse others in the name of the Prince of Peace. I want to reinterpret our tradition in order to disarm the rulers and the powers that be with the love of God through Jesus Christ.[3] If just one person changes his or her perspective on how God behaves in the world and, therefore, how we should behave, then it will be worth all the criticism a book like this may generate.

As in my earlier book *Razing Hell: Rethinking Everything You've Been Taught about God's Wrath and Judgment*, we will wrestle with our difficult questions and quandaries with conversation partners, people just like us, who have the same struggles, who worry about how to think about God, the Bible, the Christian tradition, and their own faith journey. Along the way, various students will join in the conversation as we journey through rethinking the cross. Some of my more theologically sophisticated students who struggle between faithful adherence to the tradition of the community of faith and the inconsistencies they see in traditional doctrines of faith will enter into the discussion. We'll hear from others who hold to pacifist ways of thinking and who want to interpret the Bible through the lens of a peaceful, loving God. We will consider questions from students whose disillusionment with the theological inconsistencies found in traditional theories of atonement and the portrayal of God as an angry father out for a pound of flesh before granting grace has caused them to question seriously their deeply held beliefs. And I am sure you will relate to Josh's questions. He is a very conservative Christian ministries major who took a number of my courses. I can always count on Josh to ask the tough questions, to hold my feet to the flames so to speak and take the class back to what the Bible says. His questions are pointed, relevant, and he asks them with a humility and open-mindedness that is a rarity in most students. I am hoping that these conversations will help my students and readers to reconstruct their theology in life-giving ways.

So we journey together as we rethink God, salvation, and the cross. We will struggle together as we deconstruct and then reconstruct one of our most fondly held doctrines—the doctrine of the atonement. To keep from feeling too threatened by this exercise, let's just consider it a thought experiment, another way of perceiving what God has done for all creation through the life, death, and resurrection of Jesus Christ. All I ask of my students as they learn the various ways of thinking through their faith theologically is that they give it some thought, chew on it awhile, consider it, much like they'd try a new dish at the dinner table. Then, after careful study and consideration, they can decide what they believe—a decision made from knowledge, not from what a pastor, Sunday school teacher, college professor, or anyone else has told them must be true. As with my students, I ask that readers of this book give new ideas and models a chance. Then you can make up your own minds based on what you yourself have discovered as you struggled and studied and contemplated God and your faith.

WHAT YOU'LL FIND IN THIS BOOK

Every book has a purpose and every author a motivation for writing it. In chapter 1, I will explain my motive and the purpose of the book. Too often our deeply held religious convictions lead to violence. Because that's the case, we need to responsibly explore, deconstruct, and reconstruct our fondly held, yet potentially dangerous, beliefs. We have seen horrific acts of terror committed in the name of God— from wars to massacres to slander. Our perception of God influences how we behave. If we perceive of God as justifiably violent, it becomes easier for us to be violent. I believe that to staunch the onslaught of violence and to ensure a future in which Christians promote peace and justice, we need fresh and relevant interpretations of our central doctrines. So, in this chapter I will build a case for the part religion plays in the world's violence. I will talk briefly about the violence prevalent in Christian history, the need for new ways of being Christian, reading Scripture, and living as productive members of God's kingdom in the here and now.

If we are going to talk about the various models of atonement in the Bible and throughout the Christian tradition, we also have to discuss the wide use of metaphor in Scripture itself, especially metaphors that describe the work of Jesus on the cross. Deep and otherwise incomprehensible truths—truths that human language cannot grasp—can often only be revealed and understood through the word pictures that we are familiar with: that is, through metaphor. So, in chapter 2 we will discuss the use of biblical and cultural metaphors used in forming understandings of God and of the atonement.

In order to construct an alternate way of thinking about a certain Christian doctrine we also need to familiarize ourselves with what has gone before. So, in chapter 3 we will discuss traditional theories of atonement, examining how theologians of the past have explained God's work of salvation through Jesus. We will think about both the positive and negative aspects of these various theories and discuss the theological quandaries they leave us with.

In chapter 4 we will talk about how such traditional theories of atonement have led to a dysfunctional image of God that promotes human violence and abuse. We'll discuss some of the biblical passages that lead us to see God as violent and compare them to those passages that portray God as loving and compassionate. We'll build a case for a compassionate, peace-loving God who abhors violence and wants human beings to live peaceful, loving lives.

If we rethink our traditional theories of atonement, we also have to rethink justice. The model of justice portrayed in traditional atonement theories is based upon a retributive model: Jesus "paid" the debt for our sin or Jesus made satisfaction to merit forgiveness of sin. Our ways of thinking about justice and the atonement also portray God as necessarily violent and retributive, requiring the death of an innocent person in order to forgive sin. Without thinking about the implications, we've considered the divinely required death of an innocent man just. When Jesus died on the cross, suffering an unjust death, our culturally imbedded minds have been taught to believe that something good happened. So, in chapter 5 we will talk about notions of justice in Scripture and in culture, revealing that divine justice is reconciling rather than retributive.

After we've wrestled a bit with the concept of justice, we'll tackle forgiveness. Is forgiveness an economy of quid pro quo? Does God forgive only on the basis of a system of pay back—as when Jesus dies and suffers our punishment, thereby paying God back for the debt of sin? If so, the nature of forgiveness is compromised. In chapter 6 we will discuss the "dilemma of forgiveness"—that if God truly forgives sin, God doesn't require payment in advance through the death of an innocent man. God pardons without the need for divinely ordained violence. Such notions of forgiveness require that we think differently about atonement.

Many might ask at this point, what about sacrifice? If God doesn't need repayment in order to forgive, is the death of Jesus sacrificial? If so, how? The short answer is yes: through his life, death, and resurrection, Jesus offered a costly sacrifice on our behalf for our redemption. In chapter 7 I will tie sacrifice into the notion of forgiveness. Although forgiveness does not entail a violent economic transaction of any sort between Father and Son, the sacrifice of forgiveness is extremely costly. In this chapter we'll discuss just how and why the life, death, and resurrection of Jesus were very much a sacrifice. But that's not all. We'll also discuss the blood.

"Nothing but the blood of Jesus." This theologically loaded hymn has been a familiar and comforting part of our worship all our lives. And as we sing we think of the blood of Jesus that washes away our sin, that provides the payment for our forgiveness, we inadvertently put forth an image of God as violent and retributive, who cannot forgive sin without recompense of some sort. In this case, the recompense happens to be the horrific death of an innocent man. If I take away the notion of payment from the atonement, what happens to the blood of Jesus? What significance does it play in the passion and in the effecting of our redemption? Is it true that "without the shedding of blood there is no forgiveness" (Heb. 9:22)? Could this be metaphorical language, and if so, what is its meaning? We'll find some answers to these questions in chapter 7.

In chapter 8, we'll discuss what Jesus really accomplished with his life, death, and resurrection. I will weave together all the things we discussed in the preceding chapters dealing with the atonement: metaphor, images of God as a loving forgiver, justice, forgiveness, the power of the blood of Jesus, sacrifice, concluding with our "at-one-ment."

In the last chapter, we will construct and consider an interpretation of our redemption in Christ that speaks against the complicity of violence in God's plan to forgive and to redeem creation. We will also consider the profound implications for witnessing to those who don't claim Jesus as savior. If we hold to the view of atonement put forth in this book, we can no longer scare people with a message of forgiveness only through divine punishment of sin, even if we believed that an innocent man suffered the punishment instead of us. This does not mean, however, that we give up preaching the good news. The exact opposite, in fact! We finally begin preaching the good news of salvation through the love and forgiveness of God revealed and accomplished by Jesus. Part of preaching any message, of course, is living it out for family, friends, neighbors, and coworkers to see—the "so what?" of atonement. So in this chapter we will also address kingdom living for those who have been redeemed by God through Jesus.

I hope you enjoy this execution of God and the examination of the cross. And while you read, I hope you'll find new and refreshing ideas and ways of thinking about God that will enable you to tell others about the good news of salvation through Jesus. Take a bite, taste, and see—maybe the Lord's goodness is sweeter than we thought. Let's begin our journey.

1

God Gone Bad?
Religion Gone Bad?

I give you a new commandment, that you love one another. Just as I have loved you, you also should love one another. By this everyone will know that you are my disciples, if you have love for one another.
—John 13:34–35

I like your Christ. I don't like your Christians. They are so unlike your Christ.

—Gandhi

When religion is in the hands of mere natural man, he is always the worse for it; it adds a bad heat to his own dark fire and helps to inflame his four elements of selfishness, envy, pride, and wrath. And hence it is that worse passions, or a worse degree of them are to be found in persons of great religious zeal than in others that made no pretenses to it.
—William Law, "Christian Regeneration"

As he hung in midair, arms outstretched, feet pointing down toward the fiery abyss, Reverend Frank Scott, a passenger on the SS *Poseidon*, shouted out to God these words of desperation and anger: "What more do you want from us? We've come all this way no thanks to you! We did it on our own; no help from you. We didn't ask you to fight for us, but damn it, don't fight against us. Leave us alone!" That he even bothered to talk to God at all was quite surprising, given he had quit believing that God intervened in the world but instead simply left human beings alone to struggle through life and the blows it dealt. After leading a few disciples on a long, arduous, and deadly journey through the bowels of the capsized ship, Reverend Scott found himself staring at the locked door that marked their only way of escape. With death behind him, flames beneath him, and apparently no salvation ahead of him, he ironically—or perhaps not so ironically—reverted to a more traditional way of thinking about God.

For Scott, the only way to gain God's favor, the only way to motivate God to move on his behalf, was through violence; God needed another bloody sacrifice. So many had already suffered brutal deaths in the twisted steel wreckage. Knowing he had little time to act, Scott had jumped through the flames and grabbed the wheel. Suspended in the air, slowly, painstakingly he edged his hands one by one around the wheel, turning it a few inches at a time. After what seemed like an eternity, the hatch opened so the few survivors could finally reach the bottom of the upside down ship and escape. He had helped to liberate his fellow passengers from the ship's iron clad prison, but he knew he would never reach that hatch himself. In anguish, Reverend Scott cried out his last words to God: "How many more sacrifices?! How much more blood?! How many more lives?! You need another life?! Take mine!" And he let go of the wheel and fell to his death.[1]

We may scoff at Reverend Scott's theology, but the fact remains that many Christians believe God required just such a sacrifice in order to save humanity from devil's dominion of darkness in the fiery abyss of hell. We believe that God required Jesus to hang on the cross, suspended in midair, and die a sacrificial, violent death so we could escape the divine consequence: imprisonment in a place of eternal violence. In other words, we believe in a violent God of love.

We also believe that God doesn't blink a divine eye at violence that we consider just. In fact, Christians use God's violence to promote their own agendas. For instance, read about the psalmist who voices the community's prayer for vengeance, asking God to get back at the enemy by dashing their babies heads against the rocks (Ps. 137:9). In more recent times, we saw the violent God image invoked by Baptist pastor Wiley Drake, the former second vice president of the Southern Baptist Convention. A few months after Obama was sworn into office in 2009, Drake exhorted Christians to pray according to the imprecatory Psalms and ask God to kill the President.[2] Fortunately, God didn't answer that prayer.

Some Christians find that belief in a tough, retributive, violent God undergirds and strengthens their faith, even though most would never explicitly express God in those words. Take Mark Driscoll, pastor of Mars Hill Baptist Church in Seattle, Washington, for example: In trying to prove that Christianity is not a sissy religion, he asked a few men to come up on stage and hit him. They refused. Not to be daunted, Driscoll hit himself a couple times and then said that in the book of Revelation, the Bible reveals a Jesus "with a tattoo down His leg, a sword in His hand and the commitment to make someone bleed." He continued with confidence, saying, "That is a guy I can worship. I cannot worship the hippie, diaper, halo Christ because I cannot worship a guy I can beat up."[3] So not only do we need a tough, kick-ass God, we need a Rambo Jesus, too. It's these violent images of God that lead to all sorts of violence on the part of Christians. Christianity is a killer of a religious tradition, as history will attest.

If we could read the headlines of history we might see something like the following: "God Says, 'Christians Kill Thine Enemies!'" And we did. Three million men, women, and children massacred during the two hundred years of terror due to the Crusades (1095–1291). Another one million Christians killed by other Christians in the Albigensian Crusade of the thirteenth century (1208–1229). Seven and a half million more died as Protestants and Catholics killed each other in the Thirty Years War (1618–1648). An additional three million people died in the religious wars between Protestants and Catholics in France from 1562 to 1598. And up to sixty thousand innocent people accused as witches were executed in Europe from 1400 to 1800. Add to those numbers three-hundred thousand to five-hundred thousand people killed in Cromwell's invasion of Ireland (1649–1653). Two-hundred thousand people were killed in Bosnia from 1992 through 1995, and fifteen million indigenous peoples were killed in the conquest of the Americas. And these are just the people killed by Christians over the centuries, not counting that fact that some historians add to the list the six million Jews and their supporters murdered during World War II.[4]

Christianity kills. When it runs off the rails, when it becomes an ideology, it's a dangerous enterprise. Christians have a long history of doing violence against minorities, the poor, women, those who think differently, and the earth itself. If we look at our history, we people of faith have put society and the world at large in grave danger. Although Christianity is held up as the religious tradition that most especially preaches and teaches love and peace, its followers often practice hate and war. Well-known scientist and atheist Richard Dawkins argues that religion is dangerous "because it gives people unshakable confidence in their own righteousness. Dangerous because it gives them false courage to kill themselves, which automatically removes normal barriers to killing others. Dangerous because it teaches enmity to others [who are] labeled only by a difference of inherited tradition."[5] No matter what we might think of Dawkins and his tirade against religion, we have to admit, at least to ourselves, that a quick glimpse of our own Christian history seems to prove him right.

The violent rhetoric and subsequent violent practices of Christianity in the prosperous West are so entirely woven into the fabric of our societies that we consider them normal. When I speak to students in class about the problems associated with Christianity's violent history and the violence intrinsic to some of our dearly held doctrines, they don't understand what I'm talking about. For instance, I point out to them the violence of God built into traditional theories of hell and the atonement, and they fight back with one-liners they've heard from the lips of a pastor or a Sunday school teacher that justify God's violent behavior. They respond with surprise and bit of defensiveness when they realize that there's more than one way to interpret Bible passages that speak of eternal punishment, the meaning of the cross, and the stories of God's violence in the Old Testament. I appreciate the students, like Josh, who ask, "What's wrong with a violent God? God can do whatever God wants to do, right?" Right. But after we do the hermeneutical dance to justify God's violence, we take it one step further: we justify our violence. In this chapter we will see a connection between violent Christian behavior and the image of God communicated through traditional doctrines of atonement. And I hope we'll realize the importance of casting another light on these doctrines and reinterpret the behavior of God implicit in them so that we can transform the way we ourselves act in the world.

Atonement: Reconciliation between God and humans. First used in the early 1550s as "at-one-ment"—to be "at one" with God or others. Atonement came to be known as the means by which humans are brought into an intimate relationship with God.

JUSTIFYING VIOLENCE

"Strike in the name of the cross!" cries one impassioned Anglo-Norman poet geared up for battle in the twelfth century.[6] But calling the masses to arms in the name of Christ or the cross or God was something the people heard quite often in those turbulent centuries. And it seems to have worked. Thousands of men, women, and children rushed to take up their own crosses and kill or be killed for the glory of God, the forgiveness of sin, the defeat of Christ's enemies, and the furtherance of God's kingdom.[7]

When I mention the various instances of Christian violence inflicted upon innocent people, invariably one of my students asks, "Wait! Are you saying that people actually fought and killed others and used Jesus and the cross to justify their actions? Doesn't Jesus tell us to love our enemies? If so, why is Christianity so violent?" An important question.

Granted, much of Christian history can boast of feats of bravery, courage, and love in the face of adversity and crises. The church has cared for the poor and the oppressed through ministries on the local, national, and international levels. But the church has also participated in so much violence throughout the ages that we might want to start asking ourselves why. Why does a religious tradition, obviously founded on the commandments to love God and to love others, including our enemies, engage in such violence against the very others Jesus commands us to love? What arouses such atrocities? And what's the cross got to do with it? Let's see if we can unearth some answers.

VIOLENCE IS . . .

First, we need to think about what constitutes violence. How do we define violence? For the purpose of this book we'll define violence as that which does harm through the misuse of power, hostile forms of aggression, brutality, and the use of force whether or not the victim offers resistance. We'll talk about violence as the antithesis of justice. It insults human dignity and rapes God's good creation.[8] The violence we'll focus on takes various forms, including physical, emotional, and psychological abuse. Think about the various "isms"—terrorism, sexism, racism, militarism, colonialism, classism—as forms of violence that haunt our Christian past and stain our Christian present. As dysfunctional and distant from most of us as all these "isms" seem, the blood of their victims cries out from the ground; the tears of their poor would fill the coffers of the wealthy; the screams of their defenseless children reverberate throughout our neighborhoods; and the pained lament of abused women, blacks, gays, Jews, Muslims, and overpowered, underrepresented people everywhere echoes throughout the world in newspapers, on TV, in hospital hallways, in unemployment lines, sometimes in silence, darkness, often alone, usually without hope.

Now I know we can't blame all of the world's violence on Christians or Christendom or religion in general. And most Christians throughout the centuries were and are peace-loving and compassionate toward others. The majority of the clergy through the ages didn't sanction the crusades and the inquisitions, the genocides, and the political oppressions. And church theologians like Augustine (drawing upon Cicero), for example, worked toward constructing what we now call the "just war theory" in order to alleviate some of the fighting. Though, throughout the centuries, what various rulers and some

clerics considered "just" is usually considered unjust, cruel, and bar-
baric today.

That said, however, we have certainly tangled ourselves up in much
more than our fair share of violence. And that's what I'm concerned
about—the violence that we as Christians initiate, engage in, condone
(even if by our silence), support, or encourage. If even one person suffers at the hands of Christians, then the rest of us have a responsibility
to speak out against it and to rethink the theology that works to justify
it. Untold numbers of innocent people have suffered untold forms of
violence because Christians (albeit a minority in numbers) have used
their theology to rationalize it and it's time we rethought that theology in order to eliminate, or at least minimize, future suffering. That's
what I am doing in this book—rethinking, reinterpreting the theories
surrounding one of most important doctrines of the faith in order to
minimize the future violence these theories may continue to generate.
So, in this chapter we'll meander back and forth through the centuries
of Christian history and try to pinpoint a catalyst for some of the violence that far too many believers have been able to rationalize.

As I mentioned earlier, there are different kinds of violence, each
expressed by inflicting physical, emotional, or psychological harm and
pain upon others or ourselves. As we look at Christian history, we can
see at least three ways that violence has manifested itself in the lives and
believers and their victims: the violence of war; the violence inflicted in
order to increase piety; and the violence of abuse, induced in order to
convert, punish, or to interrogate. So we'll cover these three forms of
violence, but first, let's answer our question about why Christians can
so easily justify violence.

VIOLENCE AND THE BIBLE

To be fair, much of the violence we see committed by Christians springs
from good intentions. Devout believers throughout history thought
they were defending God's kingdom on earth. Of course, that fact
doesn't make them right or excuse their behavior. But most of those
who killed, tortured, or tormented others did so because they thought
God willed it—and they found support for that idea in Scripture and
in the church's doctrines.

Some of us have read the Bible so much and for so long and have
heard it preached and taught over and over again for years in church

that we think nothing of it when we come to passages that describe God doing or commanding violence. Yet, we see God as an executioner who kills Uzzah because he reached out to stop the ark from falling on the ground! He dies for an act of goodwill (2 Sam. 6:3–11). God plays the role of a mass murderer, wiping out thousands of innocent people because David took a census and counted heads—a census that in 2 Samuel 24:1–16, God incited him to take. God goes genocidal in 1 Samuel 15 and commands Saul to massacre all the Amalekites, including the women and children and animals.[9] Nowadays people agonize over the genocides in Rwanda, Bosnia, and Darfur. We criticize people like the late Saddam Hussein or the drug lords in Colombia for killing indiscriminately. Yet we don't question God about the unjust violence executed against the innocent masses in the Bible. In fact, not only do we not criticize or question, we strive to imitate God by doing violence ourselves and calling it God's will.

The violence doesn't stop with the Old Testament. The inaugural event of the Christian faith, our founding story, is the violent death of Jesus on the cross—a death that we typically believe God required, orchestrated, and approved. And we believe that this horrific death justly satisfied God and somehow redeemed us. As we'll see later in this chapter, justifying God's violence in the passion event sometimes leads us to justify our own violence in defense of the cross. If we believe God uses violence to redeem the world, we too can use violence in order to defend God and the kingdom, win converts, make ourselves more pious, and defeat those we consider to be God's enemies.

Often, we read our sacred texts with preconceived notions that lead people to behave in certain ways. We have recently seen examples of this in Islam. Thanks mostly to the media attention, many of my students think the Qur'an teaches that it is faithful to kill, to abuse women, and to torment those outside the Muslim faith. What they don't realize is that we can interpret our Bible in the same way. In the Old Testament, God is much more violent and unforgiving than the God in the Qur'an. A friend and I once had an argument over which religious tradition put the most emphasis on forgiveness. So I went to my digital versions of the Qur'an and searched for the word "forgiveness" in a number of different translations and did the same with the Bible. I was actually quite surprised at the outcome. The Qur'an won, hands down. It had more to say about forgiving others and letting others of different faiths live in peace than the Bible did.[10] But when we study the Bible through the lens of God's grace in Jesus Christ we tend to emphasize forgiveness in our reading of the text. When circumstances suit the occasion, we read the Bible through the lens of a more warlike God, which serves to justify our actions when we think violence is the answer to our problems. Yet, that very violence seems to contradict what we read about the life and teachings of Jesus. And that violence is killing us. So if we want to obstruct the flow of violence committed in the name of God, we must read and interpret the violence of God in the Bible in ways that promote peace rather than in ways that instigate violence. That is, if we want to reduce our chances of blowing ourselves and the rest of the world to bits in the next world war, we need to read the Bible through the lens of peace, grace, forgiveness, and love—through the teachings of Jesus, the Prince of Peace.[11]

But before we move on, let me offer a bit of a confession. Whether we are aware of it or not, all people who read the Bible (yes, *all* of us) do so through a specific perspective that leads us to privilege certain books, passages, and verses of Scripture. We all pick and choose the parts of the Bible we pay most attention to. I am no different, and I want to be honest about it. My concerns about Christian violence, the reasons for justifying it, and my desire to limit it, lead me to privilege Scriptures that speak of God's desire for peace and well-being (*shalom*), for compassion and mercy as seen both in the God of the Old and New Testaments, and in the life and teachings of Jesus. It's not that I ignore the passages in the Bible that portray God as violent—I don't. I am well aware of the Old Testament passages depicting a violent God. Unfortunately, Christians have pulled from those Scriptures the defining image of God, images that have been very destructive throughout history. Those images haven't worked well for us. Christians are guilty of spilling too much blood—we have the blood of too many innocent people on our hands. That said, I want to bring to the forefront the God whom Jesus reveals in the Gospels—to offer an alternative image of God so that as we imitate a more loving and compassionate God, we might be led to do our part to stem the tide of violence Christians have inflicted on others. So let's begin by examining how our earlier traditions have used the cross and our views of atonement to justify violence.

VIOLENCE AND THE CROSS

When I teach atonement theories in class, I write five of the theories on the board along with explanations, Scripture verses, strengths, weaknesses, and the central focus of each theory. Students express great surprise when they see so many different ways of viewing the passion event. Their surprise increases when they realize that four of those models of atonement require divinely sanctioned violence: God requires violence in order to redeem us.

On one occasion, Josh raised his hand and asked, "What's so bad about God being violent? If that's the way God wants to deal with things in order to save us, who are we to question?"

The problem, other than the inconsistencies between the love and compassion of God and the vengeance and violence of God, is that we tend to imitate God, to order our agendas and our notions of justice from our image of God. Then, as history bears witness, we do terrible things to each other. We'll get to the discussion about various theories of atonement in another chapter, but for now, let's see how our traditional theories of atonement and their complicity with divine violence have led to our own violence toward others.

The Cross and the Violence of War

As we take a quick look at the various ways in which Christians participated in violence over the last 1,800 years or so let's also keep in mind that devotion and piety, the defense of the gospel and the furtherance of God's kingdom motivated the different forms of violence that we'll discuss in this chapter. But we need to remember that some, if not many, of the violent methods found support in theological conceptions of the crucifixion of Jesus.

During the first three centuries CE, the Christian churches suffered persecution as a religious and political minority with little power or prestige. As a result, the young Christian communities focused on what gave them the most hope—the victorious, resurrected Christ rather than Jesus dying on the cross. As victims of violence themselves, these early Christians believed firmly in the sinfulness of war and killing.

Although the Eastern churches continued to condemn violence for the most part, the churches in the West four centuries later began to function from a position of power and prestige, and changed their tune. The cross, rather than the resurrection, reigned supreme. After Constantine conquered Rome under the sign of the cross from the fourth century onward, through the Middle Ages, into the years surrounding the Protestant and Catholic Reformations, the Inquisitions, and the various culture wars stretching into the twenty-first century, the different theologies relating to the cross of Christ served in some ways as a motive to go to war. The very event meant to bring peace on earth became the event that brought violence and terror for people living in those times—even for those who professed Jesus as Savior. For Western Christians the idea that eternal salvation stemmed from the victory Jesus won in battle with the powers of evil, thereby bringing peace with God, easily translated into the idea that the earthly armies of Christ must battle for temporal salvation, bringing with the battles a temporary peace on earth. Rulers and many clerics reinterpreted Jesus, the Prince of Peace, to accommodate a warrior mentality. Not only did this image of Jesus justify fighting wars, it also helped mold the ways we view the cross and redemption.[12] Take a quick glance through history and we'll see that Christ was dressed up in knightly attire as a war hero who fights evil and triumphs over his enemies, suffering a God-ordained death in order to accomplish the deed. This warrior-redeemer image resonated powerfully with soldiers of the empire and knights in the Middle Ages, enabling them to justify their wars as God's wars, their killing as God's will. They destroyed the enemy while at the same time laying their lives down to fight God's battles, just as Jesus did.[13] We see hundreds of thousands (possibly millions if you believe some of the websites) of people over centuries of violence tortured and massacred as a result of an image of Christ as a warrior.[14]

During a conversation in class over this very topic, one of my students asked, "I'm not getting the connection between fighting for Jesus and our traditional theories of atonement—how does one influence the other, exactly?"

Although we can't prove a direct connection with absolute certainty, we can look through the pages of history and see some links between the violence of Christian holy war and theories of the atonement. And I'm not in the business of proving these connections with scientific certainty but only in showing patterns of behavior, examples of rhetoric, and models of discourse seen in written works over the centuries that likely served as catalysts in motivating violent behavior in order to accomplish God's (so-called) will.

Empowered by the favor of governments and the influence of church clerics like Augustine, Anselm, Aquinas, and eventually Luther, and Calvin among others, Christian theology turned from blaming the devil for the crucifixion of Jesus to blaming both the Romans and Jews who crucified him. They also believed in the divine necessity for serving justice by unleashing God's vengeance for sin on the innocent man Jesus. According to the most common notions of Jesus' death on the cross, we see that he appeased the just wrath of an angry, offended God who must take vengeance on someone for sin. Through horrific suffering and by dying an unjust, violent death, Jesus placated the Father and paid the unfathomable debt that sinful humanity owed to God. Clearly, according to this view, only the torturous suffering of an innocent man deflected God's vengeance from us and pacified the divine wrath. Violence, the physical suffering of a righteous man tormented with whips, thorns, mockery, beatings, and nails somehow satisfied God.

So, the next logical step for those in power who hold this view is that God's enemies are now the objects of God's wrath and vengeance. Christ's followers can now imitate God and execute God's same vengeance for sin, usually the sin of believing a different doctrine or not believing in Jesus at all.[15] This "warrior Christ" mentality influenced Origen's Ransom Theory of atonement in which the ransom for sinful humanity is paid to God instead of to the devil. God now becomes the one who demands the violence of the cross. Athanasius, a fourth-century theologian, asserted that God, not the devil, demanded the death of Jesus on the cross. So we see a theological turn toward a God who wills the violent death of Jesus. As we discussed above, understanding God as condoning or inflicting violence often allows us to justify human violence in honor of God and according to the will of God. The chances are great that this mentality eventually led to the crusades against Jews and Muslims, along with other forms of violence we believe God wills. In fact, one of the mottos shouted out by popes, clerics, and armies during the Crusade period was, "God wills it!"[16]

Priests praised soldiers who bravely and indiscriminately swung their swords, killing not only unbelievers, but believers as well—often over some doctrinal difference. At the same time, out of the same mouth, they urged their parishioners to be agents of love. They, like us, were unable to negotiate the paradox of following the Prince of Peace and the Lord of Hosts.[17] They believed with all their hearts that the way to defend the Prince of Peace was to fight and kill in his name under the sign of his cross.

The twelfth-century priest Peter the Hermit formed an army for the first Crusade under the cry of "take up your cross!" Eager to heed the call, either to follow Jesus into death or to kill others for his sake, they went forth in the name of Jesus, armed with the image of the cross, and slaughtered over ten thousand Jews.[18] One preacher proclaimed, "I assert that every man was won in battle through the mighty death that Christ suffered on the cross."[19] In the same vein a fourteenth-century aristocrat cries out, "Now war is upon us again, thanks be to Christ!"[20] Incredibly enough, even the celebration of Communion (the Eucharist) fell victim to the Christian warrior mentality. "Peace by the blood of the cross" unified those who shared in Christ's body and blood. Eating the bread and drinking from the cup obligated believers to convert others or to kill those who refused to become Christians. Killing or being killed enabled them to imitate Christ's death and the agony of his self-sacrifice as celebrated in the eucharistic meal.[21] Christians conforming to Christ diverged into conforming Christ to the Christian militia and to militant theories of atonement. In fact, Anselm's theory of atonement so impressed Roger of Apulia, a Norman knight, that he invited Anselm and Pope Urban II to watch the siege of Capua (1098). Both appeared quite at ease watching this cruel violence of war in the name of the warrior Christ.[22] Again, they whole-heartedly believed that they were defending God with God's means and methods.

Although Jesus exhorted his followers to love their enemies and got himself nailed to a cross trying to show us how, we've taken up his cross and with it sanctioned violence and war. From the fourth century on, popular theories of the atonement depicted an angry, vengeful God demanding blood and suffering in order to forgive sin. The understanding of the cross sometimes led to this mentality: the more horrible Jesus' sufferings, the more extravagant our salvation from God's wrath; the more extravagant our salvation, the more we, too, must suffer for Christ; the more we must torture others into conversion, and the more we must win land and lives, through taking lives, for God.[23] Christians have used the supreme example of self-sacrificing love to steal, kill, and destroy, absolving themselves of unethical behavior under the guise of "God wills it."

The Cross and the Violence of Piety

After hearing how political and religious leaders often used the way of the cross to justify killing others, students began to think about other forms of violence they had heard of or read about in Christian history. "Well," a student ventured thoughtfully during a class discussion on the topic, "didn't Christians justify other forms of violence too? I mean, not that justifying war isn't bad enough, but I remember watching the film *The Da Vinci Code,* and that albino priest tortured himself because of a sense of piety, right? Can their interpretations of the cross be linked to the violence of piety, too?"

My students do ask good questions. Yes, views of the cross did result in other forms of violence, especially in the area of personal piety. Not only did artistic depictions of the cross with the dead Jesus hanging on it become more popular beginning in the tenth century onward, but the language about the cross became increasingly gruesome and bloody, filled with vivid imagery describing Jesus' horrendous suffering. Church leaders, such as Abelard, Bernard of Clairvaux, and others romanticized his agonizing torment and death, urging Christians to imitate Christ in his suffering—to take up *their* crosses and follow Jesus. Bernard believed that getting yourself slaughtered served God gloriously and honorably. Torture and abuse were the marks of those who followed Christ with their whole heart. Often, a violent death became a spiritual ideal; and in the church, people venerated martyrs for their union with Christ in suffering. As co-sufferers with Jesus, these saints were burned alive, mauled by wild animals, disemboweled, and flayed alive. At times, devoted monks and priests practiced self-mutilation and voluntarily put themselves in danger's way in order to suffer with Christ. Sometimes these devout Christians thought that identifying with Jesus' crucifixion in suffering unto death led to a spiritual transformation or a mystical union with God, so they justified the violence as sacred. They exemplified the infliction of pain and the suffering of pain as holy acts and actively sought ways to suffer violence for the sake of Christ.[24] Granted, many church authorities roundly rejected practices of self-mutilation, but it still occurred. And this violence against the self could be justified theologically through interpretations of the crucifixion of Jesus.

Hearing stories about Christians treating others (and themselves) so horribly naturally leaves my students feeling a bit defensive. Since they found it hard to believe that anyone would actually think such horrific infliction of pain and death were desired by God, I gave them some examples from history. For instance, Pope Urban II (1095) said, "May you deem it a beautiful thing to die for Christ in that city in which he died for us. . . ." The community led by Peter Damian (1007–1072), an eleventh-century monk, thought that to appear before Christ without evidence that his followers had suffered his wounds would damn them, so they tightened iron bands around their bodies and beat themselves. Others rejected all creaturely comforts, starving and freezing themselves, often dying in the process.[25] Artwork from the Middle Ages depicts martyrs being boiled alive, stoned, beheaded, eaten by wild beasts, tortured on a rack, burned at the stake, pierced with spears, and disemboweled. Crowds would gather to watch the torture sessions and executions, which were sometimes repeated in stories and artistic works.[26]

But that's not all. Men, women, and children also took up arms or sought martyrdom in order to redeem themselves, to appease God, and to escape the fiery clutches of hell. They saw in God's anger toward sin, vividly revealed by the cross of Christ, good reason to imitate Christ's sufferings and save themselves from eternal torture in the afterlife. In order to justify the monks' violence against bands of marauders, Odo, the abbot of Cluny (878–942) exhorted his flock to take up arms as warriors for Christ as a form of piety and charity pleasing to God. In the eleventh century, Pope Gregory VII (1020–1085) exhorted his knights to go into battle "defending righteousness for the name of Christ and in order to win eternal recompense in a holy war so pleasing to God."[27] Many believed that those who fought for Christ would rejoice in heaven, forever united with Christ and the martyrs in glory. The result? The gory massacre of thousands of men, women, and children (yes, children—you can read about the children's crusades in history books or online). Granted, for the most part, leaders believed the violence of war not only purified them as they fought for Christ, but they also thought they were fighting justly in order to defend God's kingdom. The violence is bad enough, but their theology of the cross partially served as a reason to justify their behavior. By valorizing pain, ironically as a beacon of love and piety, large numbers of innocent, well-meaning people killed or were killed for Christ, the Prince of Peace.[28]

What they didn't take into account is that Jesus didn't want to suffer. Jesus tried to get out of suffering. He fought against oppression, abuse, violence, sickness, and all kinds of suffering. He agonized over the prospect of his death and was afraid of pain and torture (Matt. 26:36–46). Jesus didn't embrace death. He embraced *life*! And he gives that life to us.[29]

The Cross and the Violence of Abuse

During a discussion with a student about Christian violence, she began to see our history a bit more clearly and was able to drop her defense mechanism a bit. This led her to think of other instances in which Christians inflicted violence on others. "Gosh," she reflected, "not only did we go to war in the name of the cross and discover a sense of piety through violence, we also tortured and killed people who didn't convert, like during the Spanish Inquisition! We used the cross to abuse people, didn't we?"

Yes. But is it enough if I say "we meant well"? Christians who tortured and killed heretics and unbelievers during the inquisitions throughout history did think they were doing God and those unfortunate people a favor. They considered the horror of torture and death in this world worth enduring if it meant eternal life in heaven in the next world. They had "evangelical" hearts that wanted to see all people saved from the fires of hell. Fortunately, evangelicals today use different methods. But good intentions absolutely do not justify the violence toward thousands of ordinary, decent people who merely wanted to work for a living, raise children, and live life in freedom without fear.

During the various Christian inquisitions, Christ's suffering, his wounds, and his death acted as accusations against unbelievers and heretics. All who did not convert to Christianity were considered guilty of his death and deserving of imprisonment, torture, and slaughter. The violence against these heretics and unbelievers was necessary in order to convert them and therefore was justified in the eyes of God. So from approximately 1184 to 1858, with the ending of the Roman Inquisition, Christians wreaked violence and fanned the flames of fear, destroying the lives of countless Muslims, Jews, pagans, and heretical Christians—all done under the sign of the cross. The sacrifice of Christ, once considered the ultimate act to end the cycles of violence, became the very stimulus for more vengeance and violence.[30]

For centuries and even today, Christians have done psychological and spiritual violence to others through fear-inducing doctrines such as hell and the atonement. We have threatened exclusion from the community and instilled the fear of God into the very people that most need to feel a sense of God's love. All this flies in the face of the message of Jesus, who accepted everyone and challenged the religious and secular authorities whose systems of power were based on fear and intimidation.[31]

I know that most of us have heard the stories and watched the movies depicting the terrible suffering Christians have inflicted on those who thought differently. I also know that for every act of violence rationalized, justified, or glorified due to interpretations of the crucifixion, there are countless other acts of love, compassion, and kindness toward others in the name of the God of love and the Prince of Peace. But it's the violence Christians have afflicted through history, violence committed in the name of Christ, who suffered and died on the cross, that concerns me. If Jesus taught peace on earth and good will to *all* people, how did we get to the place where we thought we could function as the hand of God and kill people who were basically minding their own business and tending to their own lives—and use the theology of the cross in some way to rationalize our behavior?

It all boils down to hermeneutics—how we interpret the Bible.

VIOLENT INTERPRETATIONS OF THE GOSPELS

The Bible does not kill people, the ones who interpret it do. Theologians Rita Nakashima Brock and Rebecca Ann Parker write that "interpreters have used the Bible to aid and abet the enemies of life, just as others have used it to advocate justice and peace. Those for whom the Bible is a sacred text must exercise discernment and wisdom, accepting both power and responsibility. *How believers imagine God's power shapes how they conceive of and handle their own [power].*"[32] And I would add that our interpretation of God shapes how we conceive of and justify our own violence—wars, abuses of others, pain-based piety, and so on. If we study the writings of early Christians, those before the fourth century, we see that they interpreted the Bible through the lens of a Spirit of love, wisdom, compassion, and justice. Later, when emperors and conquerors desired to unify and secure their empires, they turned to religion as a tool of dominion. Christianity became a pawn in the hands of political and religious leaders alike. They had to make their way through the paradox of war and peace, love and truth, mercy and wrath, forgiveness and judgment. So they interpreted (or reinterpreted actually) the Bible, especially the Gospels, in order to validate their wars and abuse of "barbarians," heretics, and unbelievers.[33]

One of the most blatant reinterpretations of the Gospels is a little-known text titled the *Heliand,* composed during the first half of the ninth century. During the eighth century the warlike Saxons were forced into converting to Christianity. In order to make the gospel story relevant to their own context as warrior peoples, scholars believe Louis the Pious ordered the composition of the poem. Even though the *Heliand* communicated the gospel to the Saxons in ways that enabled them to understand it on their own terms, it also served to justify their own warrior mentality. The title translated from Old Saxon into English literally means "savior." They basically made the language of the text fit the Saxon's war-fused perspective, which may also have given them a rationale for continuing their violent behavior as part of their Christian piety. In the text, Jesus is portrayed as a warrior liege lord who commandeers the great army of God. In Mark 1:17, rather than the words "Follow me and I will make you fish for people," the *Heliand* says, "As ye here catch fish, so shall ye both *with the force of your hands* fetch the children of men . . ." (XIV). Throughout the text Jesus appears as the "Mighty Liege," the "Battle-Lord," and the "All-Wielding Christ." The disciples appear as "warriors," and "war-men." Christians are "a holy army and host" (XVI, XVIII, XXVI, LXXI).

The focus of these Christians, once directed toward the resurrection and our life in Christ here on earth, shifted toward a focus on the stories of the cross—the grisly suffering and death of Jesus. This switch led to a central image of God as vengeful and violent, visiting wrath and judgment on any who would go against the grain. But, unfortunately, "the grain" was determined by those in power. And God's violence endorsed and instigated human violence. In addition, theologians like Augustine, Anselm, and Bernard of Clairvaux, along with some of the mystics who gloried in physical abuse, and later, Calvin and Luther, fueled the fire with their theories of atonement. And *voilà*—crusades, inquisitions, wars, and untold physical, spiritual, and psychological abuses.[34]

THE VIOLENCE CONTINUES TODAY

So, have we learned a few things since then? Not really. The Christian religion at times continues to breed violence, with its claims to certainty, its vying for a position of ultimacy in the religious arena, its triumphalistic and supersessionist attitude, and its ardor to ferret out heretics. Faith turns caustic.[35] And it doesn't take a religious fanatic hell-bent on the destruction of heresy to provoke the onslaught of whatever popular form of terror rules the realm. There are many ways to terrorize and do harm: physical, emotional, and psychological violence cause extensive damage. Many of the so called "terrorists" on the loose these days look like ordinary law-abiding citizens. Many of them carry Bibles, hang out in churches, hold positions of leadership, and live next door to you—or worse, in your own house. They may not start wars or bomb the U.N.

building. They may not hide in alleyways waiting for a chance to attack an unsuspecting old lady. But they might keep a woman from ordination because she's not a man; they may tell an abused wife she should stay with her husband; they might teach your children to hate Muslims. They just might vote for the death penalty or carry "God hates fags" signs. They could stand in the crowds at the World Trade Center site and sing about how God hates soldiers and the America they fight to defend. They could even scare your children by preaching about a hell-fire and brimstone God. They could possibly be in high positions of government leadership and start a war. The list of "terrors" could be as long as this chapter. The people I am talking about are normal, nice, well-bred, respected Christians who do not believe they are doing any harm. But, in fact, they are doing harm. Boyd C. Purcell, author of *Spiritual Terrorism,* writes, "they kill freedom, spontaneity, and creativity; they kill joy as well as productivity."[36] They insult human dignity and cause untold numbers of people to live in shame and fear, pain and abuse—people who could otherwise be liberated by the good news rather than enslaved by an oppressive, cheap imitation. What could serve as the significant unifying force in the world instead becomes a force of divisiveness, chaos, violence, and evil. I know this all sounds a bit hyperbolic—unless, of course, you are one who has suffered some form of abuse at the hands of Christians. Then it just sounds true.

We've learned to camouflage our violence and abuse under the guise of just war, perseverance to the end, and submission to the one in power—be they husbands, pastors, administrations, or governments. We may have clothed our violence in more civilized attire, looking at our reflection and admiring our new look, our more humane way of life. But someone needs to tell the emperor that he isn't wearing any clothes. We still abuse, kill, or destroy those who don't think the same way we do. And if we are ever going to fulfill the mission of Jesus—to bring peace on earth, to function as ministers of reconciliation, as a sweet aroma of Christ everywhere we go (2 Cor. 2:15; 5:18, 20), then we are going to have to start loving God and others more than we love the violence and vitriol. Now, I know that not many people, even those in power, even those we've read about in this chapter, love violence. But regardless of whether Christians have fought, killed, mutilated themselves or others for reasons they could justify and for purposes interpreted to be useful in defending, promoting, and participating in God's kingdom, we just can't seem to get away from its cycle of tyranny. Whether out of fear, a lack of imagination, or a thirst for power over a nation, a community, a family, or a person, our violent ways persistently continue to function as the norm.

For instance, I recently met a woman whose husband continually beat her. She was told by her priest to rejoice in her sufferings because they bring her closer to Jesus. He told her to accept her beatings and bear them gladly, just as Jesus bore the cross. Fortunately, by the time she told me the story, she had gotten some good advice and had separated herself from the man. I've heard story upon story of women and children encouraged and even ordered to stay with abusive husbands and fathers because that's what "taking up your cross" is all about.[37]

When I lived in Dallas, a pastor well known for taking part in getting seminary professors fired for imagined doctrinal faux pas committed a few faux pas of his own. He was exposed for sexually abusing women in his large congregation. It had been going on for years, and the women never felt like they should come forward and report him. One reason for their silence may just be because of their interpretation of the passion event. Feminist scholars argue that sexual relationships between a male minister and a female parishioner imitates the relationship between a patriarchal God who demands recompense and the self-sacrificing Jesus who takes the place of a sinful humanity. This language refers directly to interpretations of the cross that may serve as the motivation for allowing abuse to continue. The abuser plays the part of God, and the abused plays the part of Jesus. For instance, one woman, an incest victim, explained that her church taught her that "you must sacrifice your own needs and wants, you mustn't resist, mustn't stand up for yourself, must serve God, mustn't be your own person with your own ego."[38]

Spiritual terrorism runs rampant in our churches, in counseling sessions, in Bible studies, in sermons preached from the pulpit. We are encouraged to endure; to persevere; to rejoice, and, therefore, unwittingly, to condone domestic and social abuses served up in the name of Jesus in imitation of his cross. But the abuse of the cross to justify violence against others exceeds the boundaries of families and home life, infecting behavior on social and national levels. And speaking of national levels, as a citizen of the United States, I am particularly concerned about the violence that helped build the American nation, violence often couched in theological terms surrounding the crucifixion and the name of Jesus. A quick spin through some sample events in American history reveals that our violence contributed greatly to the building of the United States as a nation. For instance, white

Americans benefited substantially from Manifest Destiny and the stealing of Native American lands, violent acts executed in the name of Christ, the mighty victor.[39] During the American Civil War, the Northern states used the language of God's vengeance, God's "terrible swift sword" while the Southern states referred to themselves as being "baptized in blood"—a direct reference to the cross. The Ku Klux Klan often recruited its members from the clergy. They read Bibles and planted crosses in the ground to mark their violence against Blacks, Catholics, and Jews. The Klan, believe it or not, is still active today. After September 11, 2001, religious leader Jerry Falwell told a CNN reporter that the United States should blow all the terrorists away in the name of the Lord. President George W. Bush used "crusade" language to describe the United States' commitment to fight terrorism. He glorified the idea of sacrifice, saying in a *Meet the Press* interview on the war in Iraq that "[e]very person that is willing to sacrifice for this country deserves our praise. . . . We're in a war against these terrorists who will bring great harm to America, and I've asked these young ones to sacrifice for that."[40] National politicians make use of religious rhetoric to help motivate our young people to action. And our churches are no different.

Just take a look at the words to a still-popular Christian hymn, "Onward Christian Soldiers." Do you remember singing this song in church? They still sing it in my Baptist church in Florida in celebration of July 4th, marching down the aisle with American flags held high:

> Onward Christian soldiers, marching as to war,
> with the cross of Jesus going on before.
> Christ, the royal Master, leads against the foe;
> forward into battle, see his banners go!

Our history, the world's Christian history, with its countless acts of ruthless violence and wars, hides God under the cover of hatred, judgmentalism, and arrogance rather than revealing God openly as the light of the world, as loving, redemptive, and reconciling.[41]

CAN RELIGION BE SAVED?

Often, I sit next to someone on an airplane or in a coffee shop who asks what I do for a living. When I tell them I teach theology and religion at an evangelical college they immediately want to discuss their problems with religion—with Christianity specifically. So many people who would otherwise be attracted to the love of God in Jesus Christ have turned away from God because of the mean-spirited Christians they know. I know many, many Christians who appear "mean-spirited" to people who believe differently than they do. But these same people are also very loving and compassionate to people whom they don't perceive as a threat to their faith. What makes us so hateful sometimes?

I think I know the answer. I'll explain with a true story. When *Razing Hell* first came out, a pastor in upstate New York, whose church I visited many times while there on vacation, reviewed the book on a popular website. He is a very intelligent, kindhearted pastor who has a heart for preaching the gospel and for reaching people with the good news. He does not habitually promote violence or killing or the abuse of others. And I've heard him preach about the love of God. Yet he packed his review full of vitriol and ad hominem attacks, accusing me of heresy, ignoring Scripture, and leading my students astray. His review dripped with sarcasm and hatred. Why? Not because he's mean-spirited and out looking for a fight. But because I had challenged his belief system, the tenets of the faith that he holds to firmly and with great conviction, doctrines that he believes with all his heart are God's truths. Most of us have beliefs that we hold to firmly, as if we had absolute certainty, almost as if God had given us an exclusive interview and said, "Here is The Truth." But we might need to keep in mind that sometimes our strongly held beliefs turn our faith in God through Jesus into hardened, absolute, unbending dogma to the point that we lose sight of the love for others that God calls us to. Often, along with that dogmatic hardness comes a hardened heart toward others.

We also believe God calls us to defend our conceptions of divine truth, whatever the cost. Consequently, we easily justify violence toward any person who challenges that "truth," community that believes differently, or nation that opposes that "truth" (Mark 9:38–41). We believe with all our hearts that we are standing up for God's ways and plans. We develop a "divine-know-it-all attitude and relentless claims of exclusivity." With such absolute certainty in our arsenal, we absolve ourselves from our own violence out of a sense of blind obedience to God.[42] We forget that the image of God fully revealed by Jesus exhorts us to the obedience of love. We forget to stop and think about the core message of Jesus—not just to love God and others, but to love our *enemies*. And I don't think that by loving them, he meant kill them or abuse them or terrorize them or insult them. We forget that following Jesus is not about signing a creed or believing in the "correct" confession of faith (Mic. 6:6–8; 2 Cor. 3:6). It's not about whom we exclude from our doctrinal club, but about whom we include in our lives with care and compassion. Being Christian doesn't mean we recite the "right" liturgy or sing the old hymns. It doesn't require us to believe in hell or in penal substitution. It doesn't hinder us from asking questions and from doubting our faith once in a while. But being Christian does mean we follow Jesus' command to love God and others; to walk in truth—and Jesus boils the whole truth down to one thing—*love* (Matt. 22:36–40). If we are judging or excluding or excommunicating or fighting or abusing others, then we aren't loving them. And we aren't following the single most important command Jesus gives us.

My students often ask, "So, now what? Are we doomed to endless violence until . . . well, until the end?"

Yes, if we don't change our image of God and start reading the biblical texts in ways that promote peace, in ways that focus on the merciful, compassionate, loving, restorative, and just relationships between God, humanity, and all creation. God refused to let David build a house of worship because David had too much blood on his hands. And might that refusal due to David's violence apply in some way to us? Do we hinder God's kingdom through our own violence? Could God's words to the king of Tyre in Ezekiel 28:12–16 apply to us when he tells the king that he has lost his place in the garden of God because of his violence toward others? Have we, too, lost our place in what could be paradise on earth because we have resorted to violence in order to bring "peace"? Could God be speaking to us in Ezekiel 45:9, saying: "Put away violence and oppression, and do what is just and right"? Will Christianity remain an abiding cause of terror and violence or will it become the greatest hope for peace, for overcoming violence in our war-ravaged world? Will we offer a sword or an olive branch to our enemies?

I realize that other faith traditions also embrace violence and therefore assume just as much guilt. But "the time has come for judgment to begin with the household of God" (1 Pet. 4:17). It's time we cleaned our own house, taking the log out of our own eye before attempting to remove the speck out of, say, a Muslim's eye, or an atheist's.

Instead of hanging our hats on Bible passages that speak of God's vengeance and wrath, we should rest on verses such as Isaiah 11:6, where natural enemies like the wolf and the lamb lie down together, where the leopard sleeps with the kid, where the calf and the lion and the bear and the cow eat a meal together (not a meal of bear eating beef!). A small child will play with the desert's most dangerous snake and not be harmed. In other words, peace shall reign—a peace God desires and tried, through Jesus, to inaugurate here on earth. These verses (and there are more) do not point to some utopian age in the world to come. They are for now, today, for the kingdom of God that Jesus ushered in here on earth—metaphorical language that reveals the beauty of life lived under the reign and in the realm of the Prince of Peace.[43] Religion—specifically Christianity—should be the greatest unifying force in the world. I say, let's get about the business of our God and serve as ambassadors for Christ, as ministers of reconciliation, and as a sweet aroma of Christ wherever we go (2 Cor. 2:14–17; 5:18–19). A good place to begin changing our perspective and, therefore, our behavior is with rethinking the cross and our traditional, violent theories of atonement.

2

Truth in Metaphor

"The reason I speak to them in parables is that 'seeing they do not perceive, and hearing, they do not listen, nor do they understand.' With them indeed is fulfilled the prophecy of Isaiah that says:
'You will indeed listen, but never understand,
    and you will indeed look, but never perceive. . . .'
But blessed are your eyes, for they see, and your ears for they hear."
—Jesus, Matthew 13:13–14, 16

Metaphors have a way of holding the most truth in the least space.
—Orson Scott Card, *Alvin Journeyman*

Every religion is true one way or another. It is true when understood metaphorically. But when it gets stuck in its own metaphors, interpreting them as facts, then you are in trouble.
—Joseph Campbell, *The Power of Myth*

Students often take issue with the idea of interpreting some of the language in the New Testament as metaphorical—particularly the language surrounding Jesus' death and resurrection. Although they know that the Bible is filled with metaphors that we shouldn't take literally, they can't figure out how to interpret it in any other way. They find it hard to understand how metaphor actually enriches the meaning of the biblical text, how it creates profound and significant word-pictures that deepen the meaning and reveal God's message to us. So, many of them ask, "Why use metaphors? What do they accomplish that ordinary, literal language can't? Metaphorical language just complicates things."

I understand their frustration with figurative language and the problems involved in trying to understand the meaning of metaphors. When teaching theological concepts to students in an introduction to theology course, I always start the course with a little lesson on the problem of language. You see, language doesn't always say enough. And sometimes it says too much—especially when we try to talk about a complicated subject, like God, in this case. Try to explain how God speaks to us and the way we hear God's "voice" (itself a metaphor). Try to make someone else understand the Trinity by putting it into words. We stumble around looking for the most accurate language. "Well, let's see. . . . We can think of the Trinity as water, ice, and steam. Or how about in terms of a daughter, sister, and mother—one person can be all three" (all metaphors, by the way). We don't have adequate language to talk about something as complicated as God, the Trinity, the sacrifice of Jesus, or how we experience God. So we resort to metaphors—figures of speech that help us to comprehend something otherwise incomprehensible or very difficult to express in literal language. At the same time, the metaphors never really nail it—we still don't completely understand the Trinity by speaking of it in terms of water, ice, and steam. In this case, language doesn't say enough.

Yet, the Trinity is not literally water or ice or steam. It isn't wet and we can't drink it. We can't drop it in a glass and pour tea over it. The same cup of water can exist in all three forms (liquid, solid, and air) at different times but not at the same time, which isn't true of the Trinity. The Trinity isn't male or female; and it certainly isn't all in one person as a daughter, sister, and mother! So, interpreting our metaphors literally makes our language say more than it wants to say about God. Consequently, interpreted incorrectly, metaphorical language about God says either too much or too little. It can confuse us rather than enlighten us. Nevertheless, despite the dangers of misinterpretation, we need metaphorical language to help us understand the complicated, many-faceted, mysterious God.

We don't just use metaphor to talk about God, however. In fact, we are so entrenched in our cultural norms and perspectives that we don't always recognize the fact that we constantly use metaphors in our everyday language to help us understand something too complicated to put into words in their literal sense. If we explore the meaning of metaphor and the reasons for using that specific form of speech, we can better understand their use in the Bible.

THE MEANING OF METAPHOR

The Bible contains many different figures of speech with varying labels for each type—the ones we'll talk about fall into the basic category of metaphor. All of these figures of speech transfer meaning from one "thing" to another "thing," or the meaning of one thing carries across to the meaning of another thing. For instance, the Bible tells us that Jesus is the good shepherd (John 10). By doing so, it transfers the meaning of "shepherd"—one who cares for his flock, protects his sheep, keeps them from harm, and makes sure they have food and water—to Jesus. We understand how Jesus cares for us by transferring the meaning and function of a shepherd to the meaning and function of Jesus. In this way, figures of speech, like this one, serve as tools that not only help us understand our world (and the world of the Bible) better, but they also play a significant role in shaping our everyday lives, how we think, speak, and even act.[1] We'll talk about these figures of speech in terms of metaphor, even though some of the examples might better be labeled similes or analogies.

Linguistic scholars trip all over themselves trying to define the word "metaphor." In fact, we can find over 125 definitions, some of them very complicated.[2] This is what the word "metaphor" literally means: "meta" denotes "transfer" or "substitution" or "across," and "phor" means "the bearer of." So, literally, a metaphor is a figure of speech that bears meaning or carries meaning across from one category to another. For instance, we might talk about the category of "hard work" with words from the category of machines: "He's a virtual *steam engine* today!" Or, "She's really *grinding out* work today!" We use language usually associated with machines to express good old human elbow grease (another metaphor).

The ancient philosopher Aristotle dealt with metaphor at length in his *Poetics*. He said that metaphor is "the application of an alien name by transference."[3] Aristotle is trying to say that metaphors tell us "something" that words used in their literal sense cannot. Usually that "something" is new—an idea, event, or action that we've never quite encountered before but that we can grasp more easily by using words from other ideas, events, or actions that we do understand.

Metaphors say what cannot be said in any other way.[4] They are a lens we look through in order to see and to understand something that we wouldn't have noticed without that specific lens.[5] In other words, metaphors disclose something that literal language can't literally describe. For instance, back in the seventeenth century, mathematician and philosopher René Descartes, in his work *Principles of Philosophy*, described the universe as a machine. Of course, just as we know humans aren't really machines, Descartes knew that the universe isn't actually a machine. But in trying to explain the order and finely tuned movement and operation of the cosmos, Descartes resorted to metaphor. He took an image from everyday life and language that everyone would understand and transferred it into the realm of God's creation.

We often do the same thing. Metaphors are pervasive in our lives. In fact, some linguists argue that our entire conceptual system, all of our language about the world, the universe, and even God, is metaphorical. For instance, we talk metaphorically when describing our feelings. Happy is up and sad is down, as in "You are feeling *up* today!" or "I'm in *high* spirits!" or "I'm really *down* today." We often use "building" metaphors to talk about ideas. For example, "That theory is without *foundation*." Or "You need to *buttress* that idea a bit more. It's *on shaky ground*." We describe romantic desire with metaphorical language drawn from insanity or war images: "I am *crazy* about you" or "Now that I've *conquered* him, I'm no longer interested." Another is "She really *gained ground* with him last night." Many common sayings use metaphorical language: "You're making a *mountain out of a molehill*." Or "It's *pouring* outside," when really it's just raining water from the sky. Or an *ace in the hole*, meaning, "that's a sure thing." Or "he has *ants in his pants*" for someone who can't sit still. We say "*you are barking up the wrong tree*" instead of "you've got the wrong idea" or "it's going to get you in trouble." At any rate, you've got the message (another metaphorical expression). And metaphor comes into play (yet another metaphorical phrase) when we talk about God.

For instance, if I say, "God loves us," what does that mean? Do I mean the same kind of love as my love for ice cream? Or am I talking about the kind of love we might have for our children? Or for our cat? Or for a spouse? The literal sense of the word "love" needs more linguistic help in order to understand the speaker's or writer's intended meaning. So, we might come up with a metaphor, an image taken from one area of life and translated into another in order to understand God as love more fully. For instance, we might speak of God in terms of a father who loves his children (Jer. 31:9; Matt. 7:7–11; Rom. 8:15). Consequently, we know more about God by transferring the image of a loving, human father into language about God. We might try to communicate the love of God with imagery from spatial or architectural relationships such as the height and depth of divine love (Rom. 8:39). The Bible also uses imagery from a very common occupation in those days—that of a shepherd, in this case one who goes to find the single lost sheep out of a flock of one hundred—to explain God's love (Luke 15:4–7).

We know that, literally, God is not a father the way we think about fathers in our lives. God doesn't watch TV or cook dinner or physically conceive children the way our earthly fathers do. And we know that love can't literally be measured with a yard stick in order calculate height and depth (Rom. 8:37–39). We know that God is not literally a shepherd who watches his flocks by night (Ps. 123; John 10:11). But these images come from very familiar aspects of daily life, are easily understood, and help us to understand the unfamiliar and the complicated. Put simply, the biblical authors explained difficult concepts about God, Jesus, salvation, righteous living, heaven, and hell through the use of familiar linguistic patterns and common images from their own cultures and social norms, just as we do.

THE BIBLE IN METAPHORS

A friend said to me the other day, "Mike has a bit of an Eeyore perspective when it comes to feeling better." I knew immediately what she was saying about Mike. Why? Because I know who Eeyore is. Do you remember Eeyore—the donkey in the Winnie the Pooh stories? He always took a dim view of life. So I knew my friend was saying that Mike takes a dim view of things when he is trying to recover from illness—he had just gone through back surgery. How about this example: "Please sit in the broccoli chair." By itself, this sentence has no logical meaning. In order to understand it we need some context such as where the statement was said and why. What was happening at the time? If you know the context, the statement makes perfect sense. In this case, one of my sons loves broccoli. The other three sons don't. So when I made dinner for them one night, I put broccoli on one son's plate and peas on the others. *Now* it makes sense—I told my son who likes broccoli to "sit in the broccoli chair," the chair in front of the plate of broccoli. I had to take you into my kitchen to help you understand that metaphor.

J. W. von Goethe (1749–1832) once said, "anyone who wants to understand a poet must go to the poet's country."[6] And that's true of understanding Scripture, too. In order to interpret and comprehend the Bible we need to go to the Bible's country; we need to understand the cultures and societies within which the authors wrote. So we ask ourselves questions such as, "how did the people who first heard these metaphors understand them? What were their shared beliefs and customs that enabled the metaphors to make sense to them?" In other words, we need to know the context out of which the metaphors emerged. As soon as a reader realizes that one thing is being spoken of in terms of another thing, a metaphor is born.[7] In other words, as soon as the disciples understood that when Jesus spoke of being the good shepherd he was really talking about how God cares for every person and doesn't want any of them to remain outside the kingdom, the metaphor was established. We now don't even think about what that statement means. We don't have to explain it. We understand the metaphor without consciously thinking.[8]

We need to remember, however, that just because we imagine God or Jesus or the work of Jesus in terms of metaphor doesn't mean that we forfeit the truths or the reality that lie behind the language. The metaphor enables us to grasp that truth or that reality in ways we wouldn't have otherwise. For instance, we talk about the church as the body of Christ. A metaphor? Yes. But still true.[9] We picture the Holy Spirit as a breath or a wind (actually the literal meaning of the words in Greek and Hebrew), but is the Holy Spirit literally a breath or a wind? No. Yet, through the metaphor we learn that the Spirit, like the wind, infiltrates all of creation as an invisible force.

Metaphors disclose something new and real that can't be put into literal language. For instance, in the saying "Jesus is the lamb of God," we have no doubt that the phrase is metaphorical. Jesus is not a young sheep. Just as lambs were sacrificed on the altar in Jesus' day, he's telling us that he sacrifices his human life by suffering the consequences of being a man. Or Jesus indicates in John 6:35–59 that he is the "bread of life," that his body is somehow bread we should eat. We also know that Jesus isn't a loaf of bread. He is using metaphorical language to make the point that through him we find the spiritual nourishment that gives us life. The metaphor, although not literally true, discloses something real and true. Just as the sentence, "There is an electrical *current flowing through* this wire," is metaphorical language. Although it isn't literally a flowing current of water, the electricity in the wire is something real. We are merely implementing one category (water) to explain another (electricity).[10] So all metaphors refer to something real, especially those in the Bible.

We can think of quite a few of these figures of speech that we use to talk about God and Jesus. For example, we see God described as the security of a rock, a bird caring for its babies, a potter, a judge, and a king. God is the source of life as Father. We borrow from the category of human qualities in order to explain God. So we imagine a God who exhibits parental care, gives affection, hands out discipline, exercises authority, maintains family unity, and participates in mutual love—all figures of speech that transfer meaning from one arena of life into the life of God.

The same linguistic exercises hold true when we talk about Jesus as the lamb, the bread, the vine, the shepherd, as Lord, as the Word, as a Suffering Servant, or as a teacher. Paul piles on the metaphors, using images from agriculture, stadium games, bookkeeping, experience of darkness and light, and military accoutrements. All of these figures of speech served and continue to serve the community of faith.[11] They give us language that helps us understand difficult concepts about God, the work of Jesus, and our life as Christians.

In the same way, traditional language describing Christ's work of redemption served specific communities of faith. The New Testament explains Christ's life, death, and resurrection as economic, substitutionary, militaristic, sacrificial, and priestly.[12] Borrowing from the Old Testament story of the exodus, the New Testament often describes redemption using metaphors from slavery (Luke 1:68; Rom. 3:23–24; 6:17; 7:14ff; 1 Pet. 1:19).[13] The figurative language pointing to the cross expresses the significance of Jesus' death and how it accomplished salvation. The biblical writers take words commonly used in religious, familial, legal, commercial, economic, and military relationships and transfer them into the divine arena in order to identify the creative activity of God in the world that works through Jesus to reconcile and restore broken relationships.[14] The New Testament overflows with figurative language, revealing the creative energy at work as members of the new community of God sought to explain the person of Jesus and the meaning of his life, death, and resurrection. This language became the starting point for our theories of atonement, themselves explained through metaphorical language.[15]

CROSS TALK IN METAPHOR

Although the New Testament mixes its metaphors, using the language of sacrifice, ransom, and expulsion to explain the work of Christ, these metaphors were taken from ideas and everyday occurrences that the people of that culture could understand. If read and understood as correspondent truth, in a literal manner, these images stand in tension with one another. If we combine all of the metaphors that the Bible uses to explain the cross, they don't make sense—all of them can't be true at the same time.[16] For instance, mixed within the atonement language in Scripture we see a God that is both just and merciful, producing a tension between justice and mercy. God forgives freely yet at the same time demands a substitute to take away the debt, compromising the nature of forgiveness as complete pardon. A just God finds satisfaction in Christ's unjust death, therefore raising the question, Is injustice ever just? Conceptions of the Father demanding the death of the innocent Son pit the persons of the Trinity against one another, portraying an image of God against God.[17]

Can all of these motifs be literal, concrete cosmic transactions that take place between God the Father and God the Son with God the Holy Spirit? Or might these motifs be metaphors, language employed for the purpose of helping God's community to understand the extent of divine love and the extravagance of divine forgiveness?

Although the New Testament adopts language from daily life in various arenas and transfers that language into many different images that describe the atonement, we will spend the rest of this chapter discussing three of the most common metaphors for the cross found in the Bible.

Metaphor of Victory

Although we'll discuss the *Christus Victor* model for the cross in more detail later, let's look at its foundational metaphor first. The idea that Jesus won a victory for us through the cross draws its strength from metaphors found in Scripture. For example, Colossians 2:11–20 uses a whole string of metaphors to describe the work of Jesus in securing our salvation. Paul draws from Jewish religious rituals, baptism, death, law, Roman military life, and the human body, all in a few short verses. But he expresses the victory of Jesus through the imagery of the Roman triumphal procession (2:15). We can probably give the ancient church fathers Irenaeus and Origen credit for our interpretation of this verse as a cosmic battle fought and won by Jesus through the imagery of a victor parading conquered rulers through the streets. Even so, we gain a bit of insight into what Jesus accomplished on the cross. He somehow won a great victory over our enemies. He disarmed them. Other biblical metaphors explain the cross in terms of a victory over the devil. Jesus destroys the demonic forces of evil and releases us from slavery to its power (Luke 10:18; 13:16; John 16:33; 19:30; Rev. 5:5). Although our victory over evil still remains a struggle, ultimately the battle is won for us in Christ (Rom. 8:39; 1 John 5:4). In Matthew and Mark Jesus gives his life as a ransom, winning the victory over the powers of darkness and retrieving us back into the kingdom of God (Matt. 20:28; Mark 10:45; Col. 1:13ff.). Jesus has victory over temptation in Luke 4. According to Luke, Jesus and his ministry achieves the divine victory over evil. Although Hebrews uses metaphors drawn from the activities of the priesthood, it also spills over into the language of victory. Through death, Jesus rendered the devil powerless to hold us in slavery to sin (Heb. 2:14–15). In 1 Corinthians 15, Jesus wins the victory over death and sin (15:54–56).

Remember, however, that if we take the metaphors too literally we run into theological trouble and miss the major point. Early church fathers made that mistake and turned themselves inside out trying to answer questions that the metaphor never intended we ask. For instance, early theologians interpreted the victory metaphor in which Jesus becomes a ransom very literally (Matt. 20:28; Mark 10:45; 1 Tim. 2:6). They fought over questions such as: Who paid the ransom to whom? Did God need to pay the devil off with Jesus's blood? Does that debt owed to the devil put God in a position of being less powerful than Satan? Does it give the devil too much autonomy?[18] Over the centuries scholars have either answered those questions or revised the various renderings of the victor models of atonement so that God comes out on top. But they muddied up the main issue—that the life, death, and resurrection of Jesus victoriously transforms us from slaves to sin to servants of God.[19]

Metaphor of Law

In the Old Testament, the law was connected to God's covenant with the people and with the sacrificial system. God gave this law as a gift for the community, as a way to carry on relationships with God and with each other. The law regulated relationships. At the same time, the law portrayed God as a judge who admonishes the wicked, who defends the weak, guards the orphans, and advocates for the nation (1 Sam. 24:15; Pss. 9:4; 43:1; Prov. 23:11; Isa. 50:8–9; Jer. 50:34; Mic. 7:9). Even Job imagines his problems with God in terms of a court of law, demanding that God justify the divine case against him. Since the law worked to right social and relational wrongs, Job knew that through God's legal system, justice was served and truth preserved.[20]

The New Testament writers used lawcourt metaphors, not because of a preoccupation with litigiousness, but because they sought and found truth and justice through the context of law (Rom. 3:24; 5:9, 17–21). So, it was natural for them to explain the work of Jesus on the cross through a metaphorical legal lens: if the law led to the discovery of truth and the serving of justice, then what better way to articulate the truth of justification and salvation through the sacrificial death of Jesus?[21]

As Christian communities began to articulate their faith in more structured ways, they used metaphors both from Scripture and from their own societies. These metaphors served important functions and were often very convincing to the people who heard them. Our church fathers, many of whom served as lawyers themselves, also interpreted Scripture passages dealing with law and sacrifice not through the lens of God's relational covenant but through their own system of laws based on guilt and punishment. They described God's relationship to humans in legal terms—sin as a transgression of God's law and salvation as freedom from the consequences or penalties imposed by the law. This leads to a very impersonal and non-relational interpretation of our redemption. So, whereas the Old Testament law was more personal, relational, and based on God's love for God's people, Christian theologians interpreted its metaphorical use in the New Testament as more formulaic—in terms of human legal obligations to an angry God who demands vengeance in order to forgive sin. Our traditional satisfaction and penal substitutionary theories of atonement emerge from this perspective.[22]

These models of atonement interpret the metaphorical language too literally and make God appear as a judge in a court of law rather than as a God of love. The traditional theories of the cross fail to do justice to the personal, relational aspects of divine reconciliation with a straying human race. Instead, redemption degenerates into a mathematical balancing of accounts. Jesus bears evil as a counterweight to ours. In addition, legal language taken literally also turns on notions of retributive justice—God requires obedience to the law first from Jesus and then from us.[23] Taking these metaphors too literally portrays God as more interested in legal rather than relational ramifications of the cross. God's act of redemption appears as an exercise of power over and above that of love. Little focus is given to the place of reconciliation, forgiveness, and a renewed relationship with God. Seen through a more legalistic lens, a transaction occurs between God and Jesus, external to us, in a different place and time.[24]

The Metaphor of Sacrifice

The Bible virtually bleeds with the language of sacrifice. In the Old Testament the people literally sacrificed animals to God, not as a substitutionary offering meant to placate an angry God, but as a symbol of a life given over to God in total submission. When we move to the New Testament, the language of sacrifice is metaphorical when used of Jesus (e.g., Rom. 3:25; 1 Cor. 5:7; Eph. 5:2; Heb. 9:26). The metaphorical language surrounding the sacrifice of Jesus doesn't mean that it's not real; Jesus' death really is a sacrifice, but not in the same sense as the Old Testament slaughter of animals—the New Testament is referring back to the Old Testament sacrifices only by way of metaphor. The people living during the time of Jesus and of Paul would have understood the metaphor without the retributive and penal baggage we attach to it today.

We can understand the sacrifice of Jesus in the sense given to us in Psalms 51:17: "The sacrifice acceptable to God is a broken spirit; a broken and contrite heart, O God, you will not despise." Or in the sense of Psalms 27:6, where the psalmist's sacrifice is a heart and voice lifted up to God in praise (Ps. 107:22). In Amos 5:21–24, serving justice serves as the sacrifice God desires. Obedience rather than the death of bulls and goats is the true sacrifice in 1 Samuel 15:22. And Hebrews notes that Christ's obedience counted as his sacrifice to God (5:8–9). Also in Hebrews we see that Jesus "has appeared once for all at the end of the age to remove sin by the sacrifice of himself" (9:26). Clearly this is a metaphorical use of language—there is no altar. There's a cross instead. Jesus is killed by Roman soldiers, not by Jewish priests. And on top of that, there is no provision in the Old Testament for human sacrifice; in fact God forbids it (Lev. 18:21; Ezek. 20:31). How then, I wonder, can we even begin to think God requires the literal human sacrifice of Jesus?

We'll take that up in a later chapter, but for now let's focus on how metaphor functions. The metaphor of sacrifice transfers meaning from the Old Testament sacrificial system into the discourse surrounding the death of Jesus in order to help readers and hearers understand a mystery. Although the New Testament writers describe the death of Jesus with the help of a metaphor, it still contains the reality of a sacrifice, but not in the literal sense we see performed in the Old Testament.[25] In fact, the Bible itself supports the idea that the sacrificial language surrounding the death of Jesus is metaphorical by stating that "it is impossible that the blood of bulls and goats should take away sins" (Heb. 10:4). The literal blood of animals does not rid us of sin. Neither does the literal blood of Jesus. But the metaphorical sacrifice of Jesus "purifies our conscience from dead works to worship the living God"—by offering our bodies as living sacrifices on the metaphorical altar (Rom. 12:1; Heb. 9:14). These verses take the ideas surrounding sacrifice and transfer them as metaphors to express Jesus' (and our) obedience to God. Obedience is a sacrifice. Jesus obediently lived a life here on earth. That obedience took him to his death.

Jesus himself never used death-centered metaphors, never employed the language of atonement, never theorized about substitutionary death. Yet, when New Testament authors write about sacrifice as a metaphor to express Jesus' obedience and to explain his life fully given, *sacrificially* given to God, we tend to take it literally and believe that God required a human blood sacrifice in order to forgive sin. What other New Testament authors *metaphorically* call a sacrifice offered to God, if taken literally, really amounted to a gross miscarriage of justice in that God required a human sacrifice of an innocent man in order to redeem humanity.[26]

Yet, metaphors of sacrifice do help us to understand that within the trappings of a horrific, unjust death, Jesus transformed the wickedness of the act into a vehicle for the renewal of our relationship with God. In the same way, Paul gives his life to God and to believers as the same sort of metaphorical sacrifice when he writes about being poured out (a blood metaphor) as a libation (Phil. 2:17; 2 Tim. 4:6).[27] Interestingly, Paul exhorts believers to offer the same sacrifice in Roman 12:1 by saying, "I appeal to you therefore, brothers and sisters, by the mercies of God, to present your bodies as a living sacrifice, holy and acceptable to God, which is your spiritual worship." Is Paul telling us to offer ourselves as a human sacrifice *literally*? No. He's using metaphorical language throughout in order to teach us something important—first about Jesus, then about himself as an apostle, and afterwards about how we should live as followers of Jesus.

WHAT'S THE POINT?

The church's worship and life find purpose and meaning in the confession that through Jesus God acts to bring all people into a restored relationship with God and with others. These metaphors help to reveal the way of God in the world—the way of love, obedience, mercy, compassion, peace, justice, hope, reconciliation, and joy. Through the atonement metaphors we see divine action happening within the human sphere, within the human heart, affecting the human condition. They show us that through the life, death, and resurrection of Jesus, a real change takes place in the human relationship with God. We can understand these metaphors as expressions in language of the significance of the life of Jesus, born, crucified, risen, and ascended. He came *from* God *into* the life of all humans. These metaphors reveal that Jesus affects and interacts with the whole world.[28]

So the Bible provides us with metaphors that enable us to get a glimpse of a divine reality, not in its entirety, but in part. In so doing, the biblical writers deepen our understanding.[29] Yet, because these metaphors describing God's redemptive work through Christ only provide us with one small piece in a much bigger picture (notice the use of metaphor here), we can't construct a dogmatic, definitive theory of atonement based on one, or even a few, of these figures of speech. Throughout history we have taken these metaphors and reified them into absolute truth, into dogma that we must defend at all costs—often at the cost of destroying someone's life or turning them away from God.[30] But metaphors weren't meant to function as instruments and accomplices of literal-minded, dogmatic, theological constructions. As we've seen, the Old and New Testaments use metaphorical language in order to teach a truth that is otherwise difficult to comprehend. Metaphors abound, depicting God as a rock, an eagle, a compassionate mother, a strong tower, a shepherd, a king, a servant, and many others. Jesus taught profound truth through parables—storytelling using metaphorical language that helps the community of listeners comprehend the mind, heart, and actions of an incomprehensible God. He tells his listeners to cut off the hand or poke out the eye that makes them stumble with metaphorical language not meant to be taken literally (Matt. 5:29–30).

The language used to explain the redemption of the human race through Jesus Christ is also metaphorical language. Paul and the other writers of the New Testament books interpret the saving life, death, and resurrection of Christ in ways that their own communities could understand and apprehend through the use of figurative or metaphorical language, borrowing well-known images from the social structure such as military life, cleansing rites, sacrificial rituals, shepherding, judicial practices, and others. Throughout Christian history we see the community of believers grow in their knowledge of God. They reinterpreted old, out-of-date, culturally conceived ideas and transformed them into new ones that enabled them to make progress in their spiritual journeys without abandoning their appreciation and indebtedness to those who had gone before.[31] Just so, our contemporary Christian community has the responsibility to continue the tradition through reinterpreting these divine truths, to make them relevant for the world in which we all live. For instance, Jesus calls people to faith in him by saying, "I am the gate. Whoever enters by me will be saved. . . ." (John 10:9). A metaphor that the community understood. Back in the days of the early church Peter calls people to salvation by saying, "repent and be baptized" (Acts 2:38). Baptism itself is a metaphorical action that points to the reality of identifying with the death and resurrection of Jesus. And baptism was a very common practice in those days—outside in rivers where all could see it. Paul used the language of "believe in your heart . . ." when he called his readers in Rome to salvation (Rom. 10:9). Knowing the heart as the seat of the emotions and passions, his readers understood the message. Now, we have taken the same ideas and use metaphors we can relate to such as, "ask Jesus into your heart," or "walk the aisle," or "come forward in church," or "receive Jesus as Savior." The early church would not have understood any of these metaphors. They had their own and as cultures and language evolved, the church evolved along with them. When we go about the task of reinterpreting it will serve us well to remember that the Christian tradition always reinterprets the Christian message so that it remains understandable and relevant to the communities it's trying to reach.

Back in the fourth century, theologian and churchman Gregory of Nyssa spoke and wrote metaphorically about the life and death of Jesus using a fishing analogy that spoke volumes to the people during his time period. He said that Jesus was the bait that God used to trap the devil. We no longer use that imagery to explain the death of Jesus, but have employed several others that apply directly to our own culture and circumstances. So let's move on in our quest to reinterpret the cross in terms of the extravagant grace of an unfathomably loving God.

3

Traditional Doctrines—the Good, the Bad, and the Ugly

He himself bore our sins in his body on the cross, so that, free from sins, we might live for righteousness; by his wounds you have been healed.
—1 Peter 2:24

I will not and cannot continue to conduct services in praise and worship of this angry and petulant old man in whom you believe. You turn your backs on the God of love and compassion and invented for yourself this cruel senile delinquent who blames the world and all that he created for his own faults.
—The Reverend T. Lawrence Shannon from
The Night of the Iguana by Tennessee Williams

Violence has no place in the character of God.
—Diognetus, *The Epistle to Diognetus*, VII

THE JOY OF THEOLOGY

I love teaching theology. Students come to class more engaged in theological topics than in other topics, such as history or English or mathematics. I'm not saying that math is boring—well, not directly anyway. But most of my students find theology exciting, yet scary. Most of them have invested their lives in the theological issues we discuss during a semester. They come to class thinking they already know it all—they've been in church for nineteen or twenty years and have sat in Sunday school classes and listened to sermons week after week. What more do they need, right? After about two weeks of class they experience a rude awakening and realize they have a lot to learn. Most of them embrace their new theological experience with enthusiasm and also with a bit of trepidation.

One student in particular comes to mind. On the first day of class I always ask students to tell me what they expect to learn from the course. When it came to Steven's turn, he sat there slumped in his chair with his arms crossed and said: "I don't expect to learn anything—I already know what I believe and don't need to learn anything more."

48

He did, however, need the three credits; so, I knew he would remain in the course. For the first three weeks Steven challenged most of the varying viewpoints we discussed in class—except, of course, for the ones he held. Then, he quit talking. For the rest of the semester he sat, listened, took notes, and never said a word. On the final day of class students handed in a research paper in which they wrote about their own personal theological beliefs. They had to support their beliefs with Scripture and with other theologians from the Christian tradition. Steven handed me his paper and said, "Dr. Baker, thank you for this class. It has been absolutely wonderful and very educational. You have opened my eyes to the vast diversity within the Christian tradition!" Quite surprised by his words, I responded, "Well Steven, I'm very pleased that you benefited from the class! But I'm curious about one thing. You began the semester contributing to the discussions and voicing your objections to many of the viewpoints held throughout Christian history. And then you stopped talking. Why?" He laughed and said, "I realized that I really didn't know anything about theology. So I had to stop talking and start listening."

Talk about making a professor's semester. Steven had spent his life in church and had developed his belief system according to what others—pastors, youth directors, Sunday school teachers, and parents— had told him to believe. They instilled in him a rich legacy, which is wonderful, up to a point. Until he entered college to receive an academic education, he didn't have the opportunity to learn for himself or to think through theological issues enough to decide what to believe or to make his theology his own. The fact that he wrestled with the tough theological topics, considered the evidence for the various ways of thinking about God, the Trinity, Jesus, atonement, salvation, creation, and so on and then discovered what he himself believed made Steven stronger in his faith and enabled him to make his faith his own—rather than his parents' or pastor's. He left class that final day not only knowing what he believed, but also why he believed it. Did his beliefs differ from his parents or pastor? Probably a bit—but still within the realm of what Christians historically claim as orthodox. The joy of discovery aroused in him a new enthusiasm for his faith that would stimulate his journey for the rest of his life. And that's what I hope this discussion on atonement will do for us. When considering theories of atonement we take Scripture, tradition, and life experience (always culturally and socially conditioned) in order to construct a logical, hopefully coherent, explanation of the life, death, and resurrection of Jesus.[1]

Most of us hold to a certain model of atonement, of what Jesus accomplished by living, dying, and rising from the dead. We have our favorite theory. Many of us probably don't know that there are different ways to talk about the cross and how it affects us. As we saw in the last chapter, the Bible itself explains the cross in metaphorical language, using imagery from all sorts of situations and circumstances common to readers and hearers during the times those Scriptures were written. Christians throughout the ages have taken these metaphors, translated them into images, and interpreted them into atonement theories according to what they are familiar with in their own cultures. Now, we have a worldwide web of differing models of atonement that find support in the Bible and in tradition, often in tension with or even in contradiction to one another.

Needless to say, however, these various metaphors, images, and theories have a profound influence on our theology and function as stories that motivate our morality, spirituality, and eventually, our behavior. This somewhat confusing genealogy of discourse reveals to us the significance of the life, death, and resurrection of Jesus. Let's look at four of the most common theories that have developed throughout Christian history.

POPULAR THEORIES OF ATONEMENT

We glean most of our ideas about the atonement from the New Testament. The problem, of course, is that we must interpret it. The fact that the New Testament describes the cross event with so many diverse metaphors and images makes interpretation a tricky task. Part of the reason for this is that the text we have already assimilates a multitude of traditions. We'll see some of these as we continue our study. So we have to navigate through these images and try to understand what the people of those times might have understood about the atonement when they heard them or read them. We should also take into consideration that the earlier church did not develop a doctrine of redemption or of atonement. Early Christians adopted the New Testament language without attaching any doctrinal statements or theories to it. Using the language of "sacrifice" and "redemption," they worked their ideas about the atonement into their devotional practices, their music, and their preaching without attaching to it any formal doctrinal significance. Even so, we can still spot theological tendencies that later helped to construct church doctrine.

Christus Victor or Ransom

Although the Swedish bishop Gustaf Aulén coined the official title, the *Christus Victor,* or Victory of Christ, model of the atonement harkens back to the early church's understanding of the cross. Early theologians thought of it more in terms of paying a ransom to set sinners free from the devil's grasp (Matt. 20:28). Influential church fathers such as Justin Martyr, Irenaeus, Origen, and Augustine favored this view and made it popular in their time periods. *Christus Victor* models of atonement use the image of a cosmic battle between Jesus and the devil and evil. In other words, the devil tempted humans to sin—a temptation we succumbed to—thereby provoking a battle for souls between the two opposing forces of good and evil: God and Satan. Although these and other theologians explain this theory in various ways, we can pinpoint common features that will give us a very basic understanding.[2]

God created us with a free will for intimate relationships with both God and with each other (and with all creation). We, in essence, belonged to God and to God's kingdom. Yet, we willfully chose to turn our backs on our relationship with God, and we fell into sin. Because of our sin, the devil stole us from God's kingdom and holds us captive in his domain of darkness (see Eph. 2:1–3 and Col. 1:13ff.). At the same time, sin causes spiritual death (Rom. 3:23), so not only are we held captive to sin in the dominion of evil, we are also held captive to death (1 Cor. 15:56). In other words, Satan (or evil) holds us in slavery to sin and death; we can't set ourselves free.

Out of compassion for us, God sent Jesus to rescue us from evil and to bring us back into God's kingdom where God created us to belong (Col. 1:13–14). Because Jesus, as God's son, never sinned, he doesn't deserve death as his wages. But the devil orchestrates the death of Jesus, thinking he has won the victory over us and over God. Because Jesus, as God, never sinned, death cannot hold him in the grave. So Jesus rises from the dead, proving and proclaiming his victory over sin and death. When Jesus rises from the dead, a couple things happen. First, the devil realizes his grave error in killing God's son. Second, because Jesus never sinned and therefore didn't deserve death, he wins the victory over sin and death for all humanity. So, just as through the first Adam, the representative of all humanity, sin and death applied to all humans, through Jesus, the "second Adam," and representative of all humanity, the victory is applied to all humanity. The devil loses the cosmic battle—and boy, is he ticked! (Just watch the final few scenes of Mel Gibson's *The Passion of the Christ*.) God wins the battle for our souls, and we are released from sin, spiritual death, and the devil. Victory in Jesus! (1 Cor. 15:54–57).

Of course, theologians throughout the ages have tweaked and nuanced the theory, some leaving the devil out of the equation. Others have talked about our release from the power of evil as a ransom paid by Jesus to the devil and, later on in our tradition, a ransom paid to God.

When I present different models of atonement to my students, I want them to consider each one carefully and choose for themselves one that resonates with their own interpretation of Scripture and their own spirituality. In order to make an educated decision, they need to consider the strengths and weaknesses of each. Understanding the strengths of a theory helps to affirm our view and gives us confidence in our own theological stance. Awareness of the weaknesses allows us to come to terms with what we choose *not* to believe as well as what we choose *to* believe. When we admit to these weaknesses we gain a sense of humility. Considering the faults of our view helps us to realize we don't have a corner on the truth and therefore we could be partially wrong.

All of the variations of the *Christus Victor* model of atonement have their pros and cons, a few of which are important for our conversation in this book.[3] First, let's explore the major strengths of this theory. The theory deals with sin objectively and on a cosmic level. In other words, the life, death, and resurrection of Jesus effected a universal or overall change in the status of all humanity (and, according to Romans 8: 20–22, all creation). We move from a position of captivity to sin to one of liberation from sin. We need only to grasp through faith the victory and liberation that God in Christ has already won for us.

Christus Victor theories place significant emphasis on the reality of evil and the idea that in some way these evil forces influence activities on earth; in other words, whatever form evil takes, there's a real battle going on here. At times, the theory helps us to recognize that evil may not always be totally our fault. It sometimes takes on a reality all its own that is bigger than any actual sin. Jesus wins the victory over that type of systemic evil as well as over personal sin.[4]

The theory also finds strength in the fact that it focuses on liberation from death, sin, and the devil. It emphasizes the resurrection, whereas many of the other models emphasize the death of Jesus almost to the exclusion of the resurrection. Additionally, some of its nuanced forms stress the importance of the life and teachings of Jesus as well as the passion event. Through his obedience to God, Jesus repaired the damage done by the first Adam (Irenaeus called it recapitulation). Through faith, we partake of the healing and participate in a life of obedience as well. Many in the early church—those nearest to the actual happenings—favored this theory.

Now, let's look at some of the weaknesses. The *Christus Victor* theory of atonement splits the universe into dual realms, one good and one evil, smacking too heavily of Manichaeism (or the ancient Zoroastrian tradition). The cosmic battle takes place between unseen angelic and demonic creatures fighting an invisible war. A battle with the devil for our souls, if you will. Consequently, the devil plays too prominent a role in some forms of the theory and for some theologians.

Along those same lines, depending upon which version of the story we read, God deceives the devil in order to win the victory through Jesus. Or, as some have it, God must pay the devil a ransom to get us back. Either way, the devil enjoys a good bit of power over the fate of creation and God must be complicit with deception in order to win us back. God must also contradict the concept of justice by requiring the death of an innocent man in order to win the battle with the devil. Even in our own justice system we consider it unjust to make an innocent person suffer for someone else's crime. Moreover, pacifist theologians believe that this model of atonement portrays God as needing the violent death of Jesus in order to win the victory over sin and death. This makes God not only involved in an injustice but also puts God in collusion with violence.

Another possible weakness points to the diminished role of forgiveness. Although liberation includes forgiveness, it is not explicit in the diverse forms of the *Christus Victor* theory. The theory by itself attenuates forgiveness by emphasizing instead the victory of liberation from sin, death, and the devil. Forgiveness and its more relational aspects are overshadowed by the story of a cosmic battle between Satan and God.

Finally, in forms of the *Christus Victor* theory that theologians tie in with the idea of victory through a ransom paid to God, many have taken the theory too literally, causing debate over who paid what to whom—did God pay the devil off with Jesus' blood? Did the devil hold so much power over God that God couldn't gain our release from sin in any other way? Or did Jesus pay God in some sort of domestic charade?

Scriptural Support

We find support for the *Christus Victor* theory of the cross in various passages. We don't even have to stretch the meaning of the verses to fit our theory like we do with some of the others we'll discover later in this chapter. For instance, Colossians 1:13 says that "He has rescued us from the power of darkness and transferred us into the kingdom of his beloved Son. . . ." The language of rescue denotes victory. Another passage in Colossians tells us that God disarmed the rulers and authorities and triumphed over them through the cross of Christ (2:15). My favorite is 1 Corinthians 15:54b–57: "'Death has been swallowed up in victory. Where O death is your victory? Where O death is your sting?' The sting of death is sin, and the power of sin is the law. But thanks be to God, who gives us the victory through our Lord Jesus Christ." And in Hebrews we see that Jesus claimed the victory over temptation—a victory that also belongs to us (2:14–18).[5] For those who like to add the ransom theory to the mix, Matthew 20:28 and Mark 10:45 support that view.

The thought of demonic cosmic forces were very real to the people during this time (and still are today). It was commonplace in many of the surrounding cultures to believe in the personification of evil and to think of redemption in terms of a cosmic battle between good and evil. In addition, the cosmic battle imagery that the *Christus Victor* model depended upon harmonized with the social conditions of the struggling Christian communities. They suffered persecution at the hands of political and religious leaders, which mirrored to some extent the battle between God and Satan in the cosmic realm—the devil against God and the Roman Empire against Christians. So, until around the sixth century this view of the atonement flourished as the early church's favored explanation of salvation through Christ.

The *Christus Victor* theory still remains popular today. Theologians, such as J. Denny Weaver with his narrative *Christus Victor* motif, have adopted the early theory, reinterpreted it for contemporary society, and solved some of the weaknesses involved in its more ancient renderings. In fact, Weaver's book, *The Nonviolent Atonement,* eliminates the need for divinely sanctioned violence surrounding the death of Jesus and places the blame for the violent death where it belongs—on us.[6]

Satisfaction

In the fourth century, Christianity won the favor of the Roman emperors and, therefore, no longer struggled with persecution by the Roman authorities. Christians enjoyed the perks of political and religious prominence to the point that the cosmic battle between God and Satan no longer mirrored the social conditions of the church. Consequently, the *Christus Victor* model of atonement diminished in significance, and eventually new ways of defining the passion event took its place as the favored theories. One of these views, still popular in some form or other today, is the satisfaction theory of atonement expressed by Anselm of Canterbury in the eleventh century and later by Thomas Aquinas in the thirteenth century.

In 1098, Anselm, the archbishop of Canterbury, wrote a book titled *Cur Deus Homo* (Why the God-Man?), in which he denied that the devil had any rights over us or that Jesus had to pay some sort of ransom to Satan in order to free us from sin and death. As we just learned, these were some of the theological inconsistencies surrounding the *Christus Victor* and ransom theories favored by the early church. Anselm's view of God wouldn't allow him to believe that the devil could possess enough power to capture and keep us in his domain or to force God's hand in sending an innocent man to die in order to win us back (book 1.7). So he had to reinterpret the Bible and his tradition in order to reconstruct a theory of atonement more in line with his view of God and more relevant to Christians living in Europe in the eleventh century. So he made use of metaphors from his own culture, images with which the people would be very familiar.

During Anselm's lifetime, the feudal system operated as the popular form of government. Vassal lords lived in castles surrounded by the village folks who paid homage in words, deeds, and the payment of money or of goods. In return, the lords offered protection against roaming bands of vandals or other lords seeking to add to their lands and wealth through war. The lords kept the community in order and maintained justice and the rights of the people. Yet, if a villager defied the lord through words, actions, or by withholding payment, he would offend the lord's honor and incur a debt. Only by paying the debt could the villager restore the lord's honor. If he didn't pay, he would be punished.

I'm not saying that Anselm deliberately decided to take images from his own culture or that he even thought to himself, "I need to make atonement theory more relevant to people, so I'll borrow ideas from the feudal system." As is true for all theologians, Anselm gleaned his theological ideas and framed his theological beliefs according to what was most familiar and natural to him—the worldview of his culture and society. Like most of us entrenched in our own culture, he may not even have been aware of its influences on his theology. In other words, Anselm naturally saw God and the atonement through the eyes of the ordered structure of the feudal system as he formulated what we know as the satisfaction theory of atonement. This model, tweaked and built upon in various ways by learned clergy from the eleventh century on, especially by Thomas Aquinas, has profoundly influenced what we believe today about the cross.[7] So let's move on to the basic premises of the satisfaction theory of atonement.

God, as the sovereign Lord, created the universe to exist in perfect balance, according to a certain divine order. God created us to trust, love, honor, and obey God as Lord (book 1.9; book 2.1). Yet, we disobeyed God in the garden and by doing so offended God's honor and knocked the once perfectly balanced order of the universe out of whack. Moreover, these unbalancing actions broke God's law, and variations of this view stress the legal obligations dictated by God's law. For instance, an offense against God is also an offense against the law (1.13, 15, 19). We, therefore, have broken the law, set the order of the universe spinning out of kilter, and dishonored God. In order to escape eternal punishment, we must satisfy the debt due God's offended honor so God can restore the normal order of the universe. So, for Anselm, the clincher is this: we must satisfy God's honor or suffer eternal punishment for the offense—satisfaction or punishment (1.9, 15, 19).

We've got a major problem though. We cannot ever hope to satisfy God's honor. For Anselm, an offense against an infinite God equals an infinite offense, which cannot be satisfied by a finite creature—us. Only another infinite person can satisfy the infinite offense against the infinite God and restore God's infinite honor. If this doesn't happen, we are doomed to suffer infinite punishment for our finite sin (1.4, 19).

But, since only an infinite person can make the necessary satisfaction for God's offended honor and since only God is infinite, God must make satisfaction. The problem with this is that God didn't offend God's honor, human beings did. So only a human being should make satisfaction (2.5–6, 8, 18).

So, since only God could make satisfaction and only a human should make satisfaction, God sent the God-man Jesus to do it for us (1.24–25; 2.6–9). By dying on the cross, Jesus, as a man, satisfied God's honor. As God, he provided the infinite payment necessary to satisfy an infinite debt. Jesus satisfied God's honor so that we do not have to suffer eternal punishment. Satisfaction eliminates the need for punishment (2.18, 19). The order of the universe is now restored. And we who trust and obey God through the work of Jesus on the cross will enjoy eternal fellowship with God. As we've seen, every theory has its strengths and weaknesses, and despite its popularity, the satisfaction theory is no different. So, let's consider some of them now. Keep in mind that although I critique this and other models of atonement, I am in no way suggesting we discard the theory. I am saying, however, that we consider the strengths and weaknesses and determine if there might be alternative ways to think about atonement, ways that contribute to being the peacemakers that God calls us to be. In addition, when I talk to students about strengths and weaknesses of any Christian view or doctrine, I do so in order to teach them how to think critically, to be aware of the positive and negative sides of each doctrine they hold. An educated faith is a stronger faith. That said, here are the major strengths of this model.

The satisfaction theory deals with sin in an objective way, on a cosmic level. Through his death Jesus solves the problem of our disobedience and sin in a manner that affects all of creation for all time. By satisfying our debt for offending God's honor, Jesus restored order to the universe, which changes our status on a cosmic level. We are back in God's good graces if we will only grasp those good graces through faith.

Most people like logical explanations and the satisfaction theory provides us with a logical, systematic explanation of what Jesus accomplished on the cross and why God deemed such a death necessary. It makes sense to our human perceptions of right and wrong, guilt and innocence, punishment and pardon. In that way, the satisfaction theory provides a psychologically plausible way for us to deal with guilt.

Now for a few weaknesses. The satisfaction theory of atonement makes God seem subservient to the order of the universe. An offense must be punished or satisfied for the universe to remain ordered and in harmony with itself and with God. For order to resume, God requires satisfaction and, therefore, must redeem humans through the death of the God-man Jesus—the only one capable of repairing the offense. There's no other way, according to the laws that God set in motion at the creation of the universe. Because the satisfaction theory hinges on the notion of "we did something bad to God, so God must make us suffer in return," our redemption through grace seems more of an economy of quid pro quo: You offend, you pay. You pay, God redeems. In this case, however, an innocent person pays the debt—shouldn't that alone set the order of the universe out of kilter?

Along those same lines, in order to redeem us, God must have the satisfaction of someone's torturous death. Someone must die a violent death in order to satisfy our Lord's offended honor. Only after God is satisfied does God forgive sin. Consequently, this theory compromises the nature of forgiveness. God can't forgive sin without first getting something in return—the blood of the innocent (sinless) Son of God. Jesus must balance the cosmic accounts before God will forgive. But what is there to forgive if the debt has been paid and the books balanced? More on this later.

The death of Jesus was extremely violent and painful. Thomas Aquinas actually calls it a crime, a result of evildoing. Taking that idea a step further, some contemporary theologians argue that requiring the torturous death of an innocent man makes God complicit with the evil and violence of those who killed Jesus. If the death of Jesus was a crime and God required the death, didn't God also, then, require a criminal act? Although God doesn't directly kill Jesus, God is the one who needs it, ordains it, and sees it through to the end. For some of us, it's very difficult to swallow any theory that aligns God with evil and violence.

Moreover, theologians interested in portraying God as peace-loving and compassionate believe that the satisfaction theory privileges retributive justice over restorative justice. By doing so, it takes the focus away from the Bible passages that speak of God's unconditional love, mercy, and forgiveness, leaving us with a one-sided impression of God as retributive and violent.

Scriptural Support

Unlike the *Christus Victor* theory, it's difficult to find Bible verses that directly support the satisfaction theory of atonement. But if we stretch the meaning and don't take into consideration the language and historical context, we can find some passages that fit.[8] For example, Hebrews talks about Jesus as the high priest offering a blood sacrifice in the heavenly temple once and for all. In this way Jesus secures our redemption (9:7, 11–12). We find another passage in Romans that tells us that God put Jesus "forward as a sacrifice of atonement by his blood, effective through faith" (to read in context see 3:21–26). But as we'll see later in this book, neither of these passages ever mentions Jesus making satisfaction for sin. In the Greek, these and other passages don't even allude to such a concept.

Students don't put up too much resistance when I outline the weaknesses of the *Christus Victor* theory on the chalkboard. But when it comes to discussing the weaknesses of the satisfaction model of atonement, they get very uncomfortable. Maybe that's because this and penal substitution are the theories they're most invested in. They've heard satisfaction and substitution language preached and taught in church; they've sung about it in hymns and choruses. To think differently makes them feel like they're doing something wrong. Or if they begin to critique what they've always been taught, they worry it will have a snowball effect and get out of control. And then, where does it stop? If we critique and possibly change one thing we've always believed, what's next? Do we start questioning Jesus as savior? Or as God? Will we find out it's all a sham and we're fools for having faith? Then doubt sets in.

I understand the fear. Been there, done that; got the T-shirt, as the saying goes. We like certainty. Ambiguity makes us uncomfortable, and doubt shakes us up big time. But contrary to what most of my students think, doubt isn't a sin. Doubt and faith go hand in hand; they are roommates. We need faith because we *do* doubt. If we had absolute certainty we wouldn't need faith—we'd know with certainty. Yet, at the same time, we need to understand our faith, what we believe, and why we believe it. The only way to do that is to study the traditional ins and outs, to explore the theological possibilities, to consider the interpretive options. That's exactly what this book asks us to do surrounding the issue of atonement. That's what Anselm was doing when he developed the satisfaction theory. But questioning and considering the loopholes in a specific doctrine, such as the cross, doesn't mean our entire belief system will implode. Just the opposite. As we wrestle with the questions and the critiques, we'll formulate consistent and solid theological beliefs, each part harmonizing with the next. We'll strengthen our faith and live the Christian life more fully. So hang in there as we continue our exploration of atonement.

Moral Example

In protest of Anselm's satisfaction theory of atonement, Peter Abelard (1079–1142) developed a model more in tune with the ideas of courtly love that were popular in his day. He objected to the idea that Jesus' death paid for or satisfied God's offended honor. For Abelard, we didn't need to assuage an angry, affronted God. Jesus didn't need to die in order to change *God's* mind about punishing us. Instead, Jesus lived, died, and rose again to change *our* minds about rejecting God. Rather than perceiving God as angry, judgmental, and retributive, Abelard wanted his listeners to think about God as loving, compassionate, and merciful. Consequently, Jesus lived, died, and rose again in order to reveal God's love to us. Everything Jesus said or did served as an example not only of how God behaves, but how we should behave too. Abelard reminds us that God's love for us motivated God to send the Son to redeem us from sin. Further, Jesus lived and died not only to show the depth of God's love for us but also to convince us that we must love God (and others) in return.[9]

Students have a bit of trouble understanding how redemption works if Jesus lived and died merely to reveal God as love and to set an example for us to follow. One of them came to my office one afternoon after class with a confused look on her face. "How does God save if we hold to the moral example theory? Jesus doesn't seem to deal with sin on an objective or cosmic level, does he? So how does God save us?"

These are great questions and they raise one of the major criticisms of this model of atonement. Let's first go over the basics of this view, and then move on to the strengths and weaknesses.

We sinned and separated ourselves from God's love. Because of sin, we lost sight of how to live according to God's will. But God sent Jesus to demonstrate God's love and to give us an example of how we should live. Jesus served as the perfect example by fully revealing God's love to us. By dying on the cross, Jesus demonstrated the extravagance of divine grace and the lengths to which God will go to in order to redeem us. Abelard directly refutes any thought that leads us to believe God holds someone else accountable to suffer for our sin. In no way would God allow Jesus to suffer our sin in our place. In Abelard's view, that is not justice.[10]

When we look upon the cross of Christ and see God's incredible love for us, we desire union with that love. Our desire acts as an invitation to the Holy Spirit who then infuses us, fills us, and empowers us. Through the Holy Spirit, God pours the divine love into our hearts

(Rom. 5:5) and by doing so, justifies us and saves us by forgiving our sin.[11] Because of the power of God's Spirit, we then live our redeemed lives in imitation of God's love revealed in Jesus.

The moral example theory has a few strengths. Rather than focusing on the death, it embraces the life, teachings, death, and resurrection of Jesus. It helps us to focus on God's love rather than on the retributive nature of God that we see in some of the other theories. God does not need to punish the innocent Jesus in order to forgive. Neither does God need any sort of satisfaction to appease God's offended honor. But through love, God forgives our sin if we receive God's love through the Holy Spirit. Forgiveness, then, truly is unconditional, given freely without the need for pay back first. Moreover, if we live our lives intent on following Jesus in the way of love, we will treat others the way God asks us to—loving them, even if they are enemies. Finally, the theory places a significant emphasis on the work of the Holy Spirit, an emphasis that was unusual for the early twelfth century.

Now for the weaknesses. Many argue that this view does not deal with sin in an objective way, on a cosmic level. In other words, the Holy Spirit infuses those who ask on an individual basis, but nothing has happened on a universal level as in the other theories we've discussed. This seems to make the moral example theory too subjective. Some theologians even argue that any good person could have died, and as long as we follow his or her example, we can secure our own redemption. In other words, it's very easy to misrepresent the moral example theory as a works based salvation when in actuality salvation occurs through the power of God as we receive the Holy Spirit. Granted, salvation takes both God's grace and our acceptance of that grace. In other words, it takes two.

One of the most important weaknesses and one that the moral theory has in common with the other models we discuss in this book is that Jesus still must die a tortured death in order to demonstrate God's love and provide an example for our behavior. And God still requires that Jesus die in this manner. So, although it's not retributive or penal, this theory still makes God complicit with violence. God still needs the death of an innocent man in order to give us an example to follow and a motivation to love.

Scriptural Support

It's easy to find Bible verses that tell us Jesus came as an example for us to follow (John 13:15; Phil. 2:1–11; 1 Pet. 2:21–25). But 1 John 3:16

says it best: "We know love by this, that he [Jesus] laid down his life for us—and we ought to lay down our lives for one another." We also see support for the salvific effect of the Holy Spirit in Romans 5:5 that says ". . . God's love has been poured into our hearts through the Holy Spirit that has been given to us."

I have a great appreciation for Abelard's attempt to refute Anselm and the idea that divine justice requires an innocent person to suffer in order to redeem us. Anselm's take on redemption doesn't seem just at all. Abelard's new focus on the love of God as a means of salvation and as a way of life for those who follow Jesus point us in the right direction, not only for changing our own behavior, but also for rethinking how God acts in the world.

But Abelard doesn't go far enough, and he's a bit too subjective. That, and the fact that God still needs the horrific death of an innocent man, drive me to keep looking for an interpretation of the cross that portrays God as more restorative, reconciling, and just. I continue to seek a model in which God does not require violence and that deals with sin in a concrete way and on a cosmic level. Let's see if the next theory of atonement fits the bill.

Penal Substitution

Although theologians over the centuries allude to what we now know as the penal substitution theory of atonement, John Calvin (1509–1564) formalized it and made it popular. Again, as with all theological developments, Calvin's social context significantly influenced how he expressed his theology. In Calvin's day, there was a gradual shift from the feudal system with its emphasis on paying a debt to a focus on criminal law and the punishment of the guilty. With the growth of the nation-state in the thirteenth and fourteenth centuries, judicial power was transferred from the local community to the state. This change in venue for trying criminals engendered the prison system as punishment for crime. In their own culture, one obsessed with sin and guilt along with the institution of newer civil laws, the reformers, such as Calvin, interpreted the atonement through the lens of punishment and justification. Calvin expressed the legal ramification of sin, using language characteristic of the criminal law theory common in his community. He called God a "stern judge, a strict avenger of sin" and said that God will punish all sinners who disregard God's law.[12] Thus, the "penal" image served as an explanation for the cross.

Penal substitution language haunts our hymns, liturgy, sermons, and even our everyday conversations with Christian friends. In my own evangelical tradition, this image of the cross was and still is the most popular. In fact, when I decided I'd better take measures to escape the clutches of hell, this is the model that made the most sense to me at the time. If this is your theory of choice, you might feel a bit defensive and maybe a bit fearful or angry when you read the section on its weaknesses. Remember, though, you are merely considering a different point of view. Either or both of us could be mistaken. I merely want readers to consider the options and the ramifications of each model. Let's ask ourselves the question, Does this model enable us to justify our own violent behavior toward the enemies we are commanded by Jesus to love? My concern is that all too often the answer is and always has been yes.

Although there are many variations of the penal substitution theory, it begins with the idea that all of us have sinned and fall short of the glory of God (Rom. 3:23). The penalty for sin is death. Because of sin, we deserve eternal punishment (for many people this punishment takes place in hell). But out of extravagant love for us, God desires to save us from that punishment, sending Jesus to suffer our penalty for sin on the cross. Jesus acts as our substitute, taking on our sin and suffering our punishment so we don't have to.[13] Those who have faith in Jesus and his substitutionary death are saved. One variation is that strict Calvinists believe that God elects only a small number of us for salvation, relatively speaking. In their view, Jesus died only for the elect, whose faith is already preordained by God. So if you are not one of the elect, you go to hell.[14]

Of course, there are two main strengths of penal substitution. First, it deals with sin in a concrete way and on a cosmic level. The heavenly accounts for sin's debt have been balanced. Like the satisfaction theory, this is a nice cut-and-dried system that explains the work of Jesus on the cross. Many of us like the neatness of the penal theory. Similar to the mindset in Calvin's society, we also like the fact that it satisfies our psychological thirst for retribution or pay back for sin and helps us deal with our guilt and shame.[15]

But there are far more weaknesses to the theory of penal substitution. First of all, according to this theory, God requires the violent death of an innocent man before God can forgive sin, casting salvation as more of an economic transaction between God the Father and God the Son. Furthermore, the penal substitutionary model appears to assert that Jesus must save us from God, or, in other words, that God the Son must save us from God the Father, pitting two members of the Trinity against one another. God (the Father) punishes God (the Son), and then God (the Son) appeases God (the Father). It also pits God against us as God's enemies. Yet, Romans 5:8–10 tells us that even though we were God's enemies, God loved us and sent Jesus to reconcile us.

In addition, God the Father needs the sacrifice to forgive sin, but God the Son does not. Jesus forgave sin long before he died on the cross (Matt. 9:1–5). In fact, while hanging from the cross Jesus asks the Father to forgive us.[16] If God can't forgive until Jesus pays the price for it on the cross, what does that say about the nature of forgiveness? According to the penal model of atonement, God will not forgive unconditionally. Someone must first take the hit for sin, and that someone is Jesus the Son.

Just like with the satisfaction theory of atonement, the penal theory makes God seem complicit with evil. Theologian Gregory Love criticizes the model for this very reason: "God works in and through evil human hearts and deeds to bring about the divinely-willed effect—the salvation of the world." It seems, therefore, that God desires human beings to do evil so that God can accomplish the divine purpose—in this case, the redemption of the world. Shall God will evil that good may come? May it never be! But that's not the end of it. Some theologians and psychologists believe that the penal theory contributes to instances of women and children continuing to live in abusive situations. As we discussed in chapter 1, well-meaning pastors, husbands, relatives, and friends encourage victims of abuse to stay with their abusers under the guise of "God supports the sacrifice of innocent people" or "we all deserve to suffer so you are suffering like Jesus did on the cross" or "this innocent suffering will end up saving your abuser by the love you show for him or her."[17]

Scriptural Support

Just as in the satisfaction theory of atonement, the Bible doesn't explicitly support the penal substitution model of the cross. But if we stretch Scripture a bit and read it through the lens of John Calvin we can find verses to fit this theory. For instance, 1 Thessalonians 5:9–10 says that "God has destined us not for wrath but for obtaining salvation through our Lord Jesus Christ, who died for us, so that whether we are awake or asleep we may live with him." But there's nothing here that speaks of punishment. Here's another one: "Whoever believes in the Son has eternal life; whoever disobeys the Son will not see life, but must endure God's wrath" (John 3:36). Those who support the penal image of the cross assume that if we aren't destined for wrath because Jesus died for us, then Jesus must have suffered the wrath. They equate "wrath" with "punishment."

Although we can find other verses to squeeze into this mold, they require a bit more of a stretch. They also speak more about our redemption, reconciliation, and restoration to God than they do about a penal model of the cross. For instance, 1 Peter 1:18–19 tells us that we were not redeemed with "perishable things like silver or gold, but with the precious blood of Christ, like that of a lamb without defect or blemish." Although Christ's blood is mentioned as the vehicle of redemption, there's nothing in this verse that remotely indicates either satisfaction or penal images of the cross. Although at first glance, these verses might appear to be talking about substitution at most.

But keep in mind that we tend to read into scripture what we've always been taught. Let's try, while reading this book, to look at Scripture and its interpretation from another, valid perspective. The verses in 1 Peter tell us that the blood of Jesus redeems us and that he is like a perfect lamb. So we have two images working together—that of the Old Testament sacrificial system with the lamb and that of the shed blood of Jesus. As we'll see later, the Old Testament sacrifices were not penal or substitutionary in any way. They actually signified a life given over to God in total submission with blood as a symbol for that life. But keep that thought in mind and read on—it will become more clear as you read the chapter on blood.

WHAT'S THE PROBLEM?

As I mentioned earlier, when we decide upon a certain theological position, in this case a model of atonement, we also decide not to believe certain other things. There's a lot at stake in theories of the atonement, because they show us certain things about God. The very nature of God is expressed in how we interpret the life, death, and resurrection of Jesus. For instance, if we hold to the *Christus Victor* theory of atonement, then we will, at the same time, believe (consciously or unconsciously) that God practiced deception in order to liberate us from slavery to sin. So, just as the devil practiced deception to enslave us and subject us to sin, God practices deception in order to win us back! That may not bother some of us. Others, like Anselm, for instance, couldn't believe that God would deceive in order to save. So he studied Scripture and the traditional interpretations and reinterpreted the atonement, leaving the devil and his deception out of the equation. But if we believe Anselm, we must imagine God as retributive, requiring violence in order to forgive. We must believe God considers it just to kill an innocent man to satisfy for someone else's sin. If we buy into Calvin's theory, then we have to believe that God must punish someone for sin before forgiving it—even if the one suffering the punishment never sinned. In addition, God already punished Jesus for humanity's sins, yet unfathomable numbers of people will burn in hell for all eternity as a punishment. So God punishes twice for the same crime—an injustice in our own courts of law. Also, because Calvin's view draws a huge chasm between justice and love, we must also believe that retribution takes precedence over mercy. So each of these theories damages God's reputation in one way or another. Each of these theories provides us with the justification to take part in acts of violence against others. In order to stem the tide of religious violence, I am committed to rethinking, reinterpreting, and reconstructing our fondly held theories of atonement in favor of a model that will motivate us to love our enemies, that will reveal the true nature of God's extravagant, unconditional forgiveness even in the face of our most heinous sin.

The penal substitution and satisfaction theories of atonement do the most damage to God's reputation. Because of the image of God they portray, those of us who advocate for a God who abhors violence and who acts according to restorative justice with mercy, compassion, and love, believe these theories border on blasphemy. Here's an earthly example of how we say God functions in the act of saving us from sin, if we hold to penal or satisfaction theories of atonement. I once read a story in the *New York Times* about the activity of former drug cartel members in Mexico. They demand "protection" payments from local businesses, doctors, taxi drivers, street vendors, and even school teachers. Pay or die (much like some feudal lords in the middle ages might demand payment for protection). In fact, one nightclub owner refused to pay for his protection and the street thugs burned the club to the ground, killing the fifty-two people trapped inside.[18] These former drug dealers required payment in order to protect the innocent from them, the very ones demanding payment! Easy solution here, right? If they stop their terrorist killing habits no one needs protection from them.

I'm not saying that God is a former drug cartel member turned terrorist killer. But the logic is the same. According to Calvin, Jesus paid God to protect us from damnation and hell. Or in other words, God protects us from God by taking payment from an innocent man. For some of us that's extremely troubling. The commonsense solution for this problem is to eliminate our need for protection. If God has the authority as the sovereign creator of the universe to make the rules and the fathomless love of a divine father to forgive, God can also take away the threat of damnation and hell by simply forgiving sin—no need for payment through the execution of an innocent man. Now, as you'll see later on, I am not espousing a cheap grace here. Grace is never cheap. And by forgiving sin, it does "cost" God something.[19]

Since all of the models we have discussed in this brief synopsis have weaknesses, all the models also require us to believe something in particular about God. The consequences and theological implications of holding some of the above views are profoundly significant. If what we believe about God affects how we behave, as I have argued earlier, then what we believe about God matters; in fact, it could be a matter of life and death. It was to those who suffered torture and death during the crusades or the various inquisitions or the numerous genocides, even in recent history. So what do we believe about God if we hold to any of the views we've discussed so far? We'll discuss that in chapter 4.

4

The Problem of God in the Atonement

"For God so loved the world that he gave his only Son, so that everyone who believes in him may not perish but may have eternal life."

—John 3:16

True Christianity, with its doctrine of humility, of forgiveness, of love, is incompatible with the state, with its haughtiness, its violence, its punishment, its wars.

—Leo Tolstoy, *The Kingdom of God Is within You*

We are not to hold the Scripture terms of vicarious sacrifice, as importing a literal substitution of places, by which Christ becomes a sinner for sinners, or penally subject to our deserved penalties. That is a kind of substitution that offends every strongest sentiment of our nature. He can not become guilty for us. Neither, as God is a just being, can he be any how punishable in our place—all God's moral sentiments would be revolted by that. . . . How often has the innate sense of justice in men been mocked by the speculated satisfactions of justice, or schemes of satisfaction made up for God.

—Horace Bushnell, *The Vicarious Sacrifice*

We've discussed the basic assumptions of four traditional theories of atonement that gained popularity for certain communities of Christians living in particular social structures. For early Christians suffering persecution for their faith, the *Christus Victor* model of atonement gave them hope for present and future victory over the evils of the world. Through his undeserved death Jesus wins the victory over sin, death, and evil. For Anselm, the classical theory of satisfaction provided a restoration of order in line with the feudal system of his day: Christ pays our debts and restores God's offended honor. For Abelard, Christ suffered and died in obedience to God in order to reveal the extent of divine love. By living a self-sacrificing life of love and dying a violent death unjustly, Jesus serves as an example of how we should live our lives in total obedience to God out of love. For Thomas Aquinas, the love of Jesus revealed in his selfless life and death brought us salvation through satisfaction. God was so pleased with Christ's offering of himself for humanity in payment for a debt owed to God that his merit saves us. For John Calvin, the passion of Christ vindicates the law that proceeds from God's righteousness. Christ bears our punishment for sin and balances the divine accounts. Martin Luther's theory of atonement uses the language of satisfaction in which Christ takes our place in a divine/human transfer of punishment for sin. Jesus suffers our punishment and we enjoy justification through his righteousness.

I always present these theories in theology class, lining up the details of each across the chalkboard, emphasizing theological details, cultural context, and strengths and weaknesses. "Atonement Day" always generates lots of discussion and even more surprise as students realize there are more views out there than just the one they've been taught all their lives. After I presented these various atonement theories in a class one afternoon, Josh, one of my students who always asks the hard questions, spoke up with a couple of good questions: "These theories have served us well for centuries. Why fool with them? What's so wrong with them? I mean, if it ain't broke, don't fix it!"

Many of my students feel this way. They would rather not rock the theological boat for fear of falling overboard into the choppy waters of shipwrecked faith, only to drown in the sea of relativism. But where would we be if theologians like Irenaeus, Athanasius, Martin Luther, Karl Barth, Gustavo Gutiérrez, James Cone, or Rosemary Radford Ruether had decided not to rock the boat? If we want contemporary society to understand and relate to the gospel message, we must continue reinterpreting it, rethinking it, and rearticulating it—especially if what we believe about God affects our actions toward others. As we saw in chapter 1, if we can use Christian history as an example, traditional atonement theories, with their image of a God who at best condones violence, and at worst participates in it, seem to have played some part in motivating us to justify violence toward others.

I'm not advocating that we discard twenty centuries of the Christian tradition surrounding the cross. I am suggesting that we also consider alternate ways to understand it. Then maybe we will imitate God in Christ by loving our enemies rather than killing them or abusing them either physically or psychologically. When I explained this in class, Josh nodded his head and was ready to listen, which is all I am asking my readers to do. So let's see how these traditional models of atonement portray God. In other words, what do we believe about God when we hold to these theories?

DIVINE VIOLENCE: WHAT IT SAYS ABOUT GOD

For the most part, we like to think of God as love (1 John 4:8), as compassionate (Ps. 86:15), as patient (2 Pet. 3: 9), and, as one whose mercies are new every morning (Lam. 3:22–23). And most of us know that God calls us to imitate Jesus with the same attitudes and actions (Eph. 5:1), to love others as God loves us (1 John 4:7), to show mercy (Luke 6:36), to be patient toward those who irritate us (1 Cor. 13:4–5), and to be at peace with everyone (Rom. 12:18). On the other side of the coin, however, many of us like having a kick-ass God, who either fights our battles for us (2 Kgs. 19:1–37), or who commands us to go and massacre entire communities, women, children, and animals included (1 Sam. 15:3).

I know that proving a definitive causal connection between doctrine and Christian violence is difficult, but if history serves as an example, it seems that we see God's violence and use it to justify our own. Unfortunately, we have interpreted the one defining event for the Christian faith, the cross of Jesus, through the lens of divine violence. As we saw in all four models of atonement, God doesn't just need the horrific death of an innocent man, but God specifically needs the death of the only begotten son, Jesus. If we step back for a minute and think through what we believe when we hold to any of these doctrines of atonement, we might be able to see the inconsistencies between a loving God, who desires the salvation of every person (2 Tim. 2:4) and a retributive God, who requires a bloody death in order to forgive.

If God required the execution of an innocent man before God could save us, then what does that say about God's power? Or God's goodness? Isn't God powerful enough to forgive sin without an unjust execution? Isn't God good enough to desire to use divine power to save us without violence? If we think in terms of "ransom," in which Jesus pays God for our release from eternal death, then God saves through bribery. These thoughts about God's actions should upset our moral equilibrium—the morality that God instilled in us. When we hold to our traditional theories of atonement we choke out God's compassion, grace, and power to heal and save us and compromise love with the divine necessity for retribution.[1]

Granted, the *Christus Victor* and moral example theories of atonement do not hinge upon notions of retribution or upon God needing someone innocent to suffer punishment for our sin. Yet, in some of their forms they still require the death of the innocent, sinless Jesus.

These theories still implicate God in the need for a violent death in order to secure salvation, whether that death serves as an example or generates victory over sin and death. I focus mainly on the satisfaction and penal substitution theories of atonement in the remaining chapters of this book due to the fact that not only do they implicate God in a violent death, they also compromise the nature of forgiveness with an economy of exchange: Jesus takes the fall for sin so that God can forgive the rest of us. And only after sin is punished or the debt of sin is satisfied will God forgive. But God's grace is more extravagant than that and God's forgiveness more unlimited and sacrificial.

Rebecca Adams and Robin Collins, colleagues of mine, detected a disconnect between the teachings of Jesus and our traditional theories of the cross. So they rewrote the story of the Prodigal Son through the lens of the satisfaction and penal models of atonement. The story reveals to us how the father might have behaved toward his wayward son had he believed the way most of us do about the cross:

> There was a man who had two sons. The younger said to his father, "Father, give me my share of the estate." So the father divided his property between them. Not long after that, the younger son went off to a distant country, squandered all he had in wild living, and ended up feeding pigs in order to survive. Eventually he returned to his father, saying, "Father, I have sinned against heaven and you. I am no longer worthy to be called your son. Make me one of your hired servants."
>
> But his father responded: "I cannot simply forgive you for what you have done, not even so much as to make you one of my hired men. You have insulted my honor by your wild living. Simply to forgive you would be to trivialize sin; it would be against the moral order of the entire universe. For nothing is less tolerable in the order of things than for a son to take away the honor due to his father and not make recompense for what he takes away. Such is the severity of my justice that forgiveness and reconciliation will not be made unless the penalty is utterly paid. My wrath—my avenging justice—must be placated."
>
> "But Father, please . . ." the son began to plead.
>
> "No," the father said, "either you must be punished or you must pay back through hard labor for as long as you shall live, the honor you stole from me."
>
> Then the elder brother spoke up. "Father, I will pay the debt that he owes and endure your just punishment for him. Let me work extra in the field on his behalf and thereby placate your wrath." And

it came to pass that the elder brother took on the garb of a servant and labored hard year after year, often long into the night, on behalf of his younger brother. And finally, when the elder brother died of exhaustion, the father's wrath was placated against his younger son and they lived happily for the remainder of their days.[2]

Fortunately, the Bible records a different story, a story about a father who forgives without payback, without causing either of the sons to suffer first (Luke 15:11–32). In fact, in the real story, the father, watching for his younger son, sees him coming from a long way off and runs to meet him. He *runs*—quite an undistinguished and unworthy activity for a wealthy father in those days. Did the father run to meet the son because he couldn't wait to punish him? I don't think so. It seems he ran to meet his son in order to show his forgiveness, to take him back into the familial fold without any prerequisites. He had already forgiven his son even before his son decided to come home. He didn't need to punish him first.

But we have constructed our doctrines of atonement more according to how Rebecca and Robin wrote the story. We think of God as retributive, subject to an economic sense of justice that requires payment in order to forgive sin. In effect, we believe that God will not restore us into a right relationship until someone dies a violent death. That someone is not just anyone; he is the Son of God, a member of the Trinity. So within the Godhead, the father has the son beat up so that God then can forgive the rest of us. Would you ever punish one child so that you could forgive another? Would most parents consider that fair treatment? Of course not. But we seem to think God can and does, and we call it "justice." When we think about God requiring Jesus to take the hit for our sin, to suffer our punishment, we also imagine God's justice as retributive and violent, and at that point theologian Peter Schmeichen says that "the *wondrous* cross becomes a *horrendous* cross!"[3]

Throughout Christian history, theologians have often noted the discrepancy between the various images of God we see in the Bible. The Scriptures portray God as both violent and loving, retributive and compassionate, judgmental and merciful. I want to point out that our traditional theories of atonement pit the God of wrath against the God of love. Think about it. Satisfaction and penal theories depend upon the image of God as retributive, requiring a pound of flesh from those who disobey the divine commands. This is a God who holds to the letter of the law rather than one whose Spirit freely gives life to all people out of grace. If the Bible tells us to be ministers of the Spirit because the letter of the law kills but the Spirit gives life, would God stick to the letter of the law and ignore the life-giving Spirit (2 Cor. 3:4–6; Gen. 1:1–2)?

But if we look at the life and teachings of Jesus we see a vastly different image of God. We see a God of love and peace, who freely forgives sin without first balancing the cosmic accounts. As the fullest revelation of God, Jesus never demands retribution. He never talks about his offended honor. He forgives and heals and saves unconditionally. He is the Prince of Peace who reveals to us the true nature of God and tells us so when he says, "whoever has seen me has seen the Father" (John 14:9).[4]

In justifying God as violent and at the same time loving, we twist ourselves into knots trying to harmonize the tension between the God of love and the God of war. I'm not denying the fact that the Bible tells stories that portray God as violent and vengeful. It does. But we also see other images of God in Scripture, and those are the ones I am encouraging us to focus on. If we imagine God as mainly loving, compassionate, and forgiving, maybe we will behave in like manner more often than not. Maybe we'll find it a bit more difficult to justify our own violence in God's name.

Most of the stories that reveal God's nonviolent nature come from the New Testament and the actions of Jesus. If we believe that he most fully reveals God to us, then we will have no trouble applying Jesus' actions and attitudes to God. The next step of course, is applying them to ourselves.

DIVINE ECONOMY: WHAT IT SAYS ABOUT FORGIVENESS

Although each of these atonement theories entertains various nuances that are more complex than I have indicated in our brief interaction with them, one thing remains clear and common to all: God would not simply wipe sin's slate clean, write off the loss of honor or debt owed, and forgive sin. Instead, God needed some sort of violent recompense or payback before forgiving our sin. In addition, all four theories assume God's complicity in a violent death in one way or another. The penal and satisfaction theories teach that God must either inflict punishment or assume punishment or satisfy an offense in order to forgive sin. Consequently, satisfaction and penal models of the cross compromise the entire foundation of forgiveness. In these theories, we can receive salvation only through some sort of economy of quid pro quo. Lurking behind these theories is the ghost of a punitive father, haunting the image of forgiving grace, a cruel tyrant who demands the blood of an innocent person, finding the death of his own son an agreeable way to forgive and to save the world.[5]

But is that true forgiveness? A parable in Matthew 18 reveals to us the nature of forgiveness: A king wished to settle all the debts owed to him. One man owed him an indescribable amount of money. So the king was going sell the man and his family into slavery. But the man begged the king for mercy. The king responded by releasing the man and forgiving his debt. The man didn't have to pay it. It was forgiven, written off, pardoned in full. The king took the loss (Matt. 18:23–35). During the same class period on atonement, Josh again raised his hand and retorted, "God still forgives. Jesus died so God can forgive us. How is it compromised?"

That initially sounds logical, but let's think about it like this. Mike owes me one hundred dollars. I tell him he has to pay me back or I'm going to break his legs. Because he is a bit attached to his legs, he pays me the hundred dollars right away. And I say to him, that satisfies me; I forgive you. But, have I truly *forgiven* him?

"Well, if you put it like that, no, if Mike paid the debt there's nothing to forgive," Josh admitted. "But what if I pay Mike's debt?"

Okay, let's say that Mike owes me a hundred dollars, but he can't afford to pay and he doesn't want me to break his legs. Out of compassion and love for Mike, Josh pays me the money for Mike's debt. I say to Mike, "I am satisfied with this payment. I forgive you." Have I really *forgiven* Mike's debt?

A period of silence while Josh thought this though. Finally he said, "No. I suppose not. If you have been paid back for the debt, no matter who pays it, you aren't forgiving it. It's been satisfied, paid in full."

Exactly. In the same way, if God has been paid back for the debt our sin incurred, then God hasn't truly forgiven it. If God cannot forgive us until the scales are balanced and God's anger is appeased, then God isn't forgiving anything. Strangely enough, the Bible tells us to love our enemies and to forgive seventy times seven (Matt. 18:22), which in those days meant over and over and over again. It says nothing about punishing them or receiving restitution before forgiving our enemies. But many of us have interpreted the Bible to say that God promises to torment God's enemies, without compassion or mercy for all eternity, with no forgiveness in sight.[6] That means, no forgiveness, no mercy, no redemption—ever. We must unconditionally forgive our enemies, but God refuses to do the same—unless someone suffers first and pays the debt.

"Hold it!" Josh exclaimed. "But God paid God, right? It's like taking money from one of your bank accounts in order to add money to another account."

Many of my students raise the same question—and I love these questions because it gives us an opportunity to think through these issues together. But think about it. God paying God is fraught with problems. First, it pits God against God. There's conflict and angst within the Trinity. It also separates God the son from God the father. God the father needs satisfaction, but God the son doesn't? God the father is too holy to forgive in the midst of sin, but God the son isn't (Luke 5:20; 23:34)? For instance, Jesus forgave the paralytic man lowered through the roof well before he made atonement for us by suffering on the cross. And what kind of charade is God playing by killing an innocent man? If atonement merely means God taking from one account to balance another account in order to forgive, why does God need the transfer of funds if God already has the money needed to make the transfer? Why go through the motions of a bloody, torturous passion play?

Again, a bit of thought-filled silence then Josh very quietly commented, "Hmmmm, . . . so not only do these retributive theories of atonement compromise the nature of forgiveness, they also compromise the love relationship within the Trinity." That's it exactly. Not only do the persons of the Trinity have different requirements for forgiving sin, but one must see the other die a terrible death in order to forgive sin. Although the son forgives freely, without condition, the father does not. In fact, the father needs the death of the forgiving son before he can forgive us.

The next step that students usually take in considering the pitfalls of rethinking their views on the atonement deals with justice. This same student, Josh, said that he's concerned about justice. "If God forgives without restitution of some sort, what does that do to the concept of justice? How is justice served if God just up and forgives sin?" he asked.

That's the next logical question. So let's move on to what traditional theories of atonement say about divine justice. We'll talk more about the topic of forgiveness later.

DIVINE RETRIBUTION:
WHAT IT SAYS ABOUT JUSTICE

Traditional explanations for the cross see justice through a retributive lens. Someone must take the hit for sin. Someone must suffer the punishment in order to serve justice. And many cultures construct their laws within a retributive justice system. If you commit a crime and get caught, you must pay your debt to society by sitting in prison for a certain length of time. For the most part our criminal justice system centers around retributive rather than restorative justice. Criminals don't get thrown in prison in order to restore them to society or to their victims.[7] They go to prison as a punishment for their crimes. That's why it's called the *penal* system. But even in our own penal systems of justice, we select juries who cast judgment on whether or not an accused person is guilty, and elect judges who hand down a sentence that fits the crime. If a judge sentences you to thirty-three years in prison for a crime I committed, no one would leave the courtroom that day saying justice was served. That would not be a just sentence.

Yet when God sentences Jesus to thirty-three years in a human body and then to a horrific execution on the cross for *our* crime, we say that divine justice is served. Does a different sense of justice apply to God than applies to us? Even if we are called to imitate God? Or does that imitation not extend to justice? Or maybe, with our favorite models of the cross we are projecting onto God our own sense of justice as retributive.

"Wait a second," we might quickly say, "We forget that God is God. God's ways are higher than our ways and God has the right to use a different scale of justice."

That sounds good. And it's hard to refute an appeal to "divine mystery." But think about it. If God's ways are higher, and I'm not disputing that, wouldn't the higher way of justice accomplish the desires of God's heart—the salvation of all people (1 Tim. 2:4)? Our lower way needs retribution, punishment, suffering, vindication. But if God truly desires reconciliation and restoration, then it seems that divine justice wouldn't lower itself to our level and demand retribution. God's justice might just take the high road that leads to restoration—that's restorative justice (2 Cor. 5:18–21).

WHY DOES IT MATTER?

As we discussed in the first chapter, our traditional theories of atonement have caused all sorts of problems in society. We've thought of God as a punishing God, as a God who demands a rightful pound of flesh in order to balance the scales of justice. We've conceived of God as one who requires satisfaction to restore offended honor, retribution in order to reconcile, an innocent death in order to defeat evil. The concept of God as a tribal God who must punish at all costs, or as a divine child abuser who requires us all to accept abuse in the name of Christ, advances an image that promotes punishment as positive, as part and parcel with God's mercy and justice in a divine (and thus human) system of domination. Consequently, to love is to punish, to punish is just; retributive justice sets all things right, and violence is justified. But then, we really don't see love and punishment as bed partners in the teachings of Jesus. Many difficulties lie in this paradigm, the least of which is that it creates an artificial tension between divine mercy and divine justice, divine power and divine humility. And this tension matters because it might affect the way we treat others.

As we saw in chapter 1, all these beliefs about God have infected the structures of the world's governments, courts of law, and familial relations. Just ask the philosopher Friedrich Nietzsche. Blaming the Christian concept of salvation for centuries of bloodshed, he writes, "Every evil the sight of which edifies a god is justified. . . . The gods conceived of as the friends of cruel spectacles—oh how profoundly this ancient idea still permeates our European humanity! Merely consult Calvin and Luther," who made the traditional penal model popular.[8] According to Nietzsche, society continues to inflict a cruelty (through the penal system, through war, and through abusive family structures) that is validated by religion, specifically by God's penal actions, especially seen in the cross of Christ. Consequently, because we strive to imitate God and to confuse our agendas with what we think is God's agenda, the "church has contributed both to the mentality in which people make war, and to vengeful attitudes towards offenders."[9]

Penal and satisfaction theories of atonement communicate more than ways of salvation through Jesus Christ. They give us a glimpse of divine character and behavior and, therefore, give us a framework for social action. In other words, theories of satisfaction and penal substitution have provided a subtle yet profound justification for capital punishment and for retributive punishment generally. Public surveys reveal that Christians tend to favor capital punishment more than non-Christians.[10] Is this because the traditional preaching of the cross with its penal and judicial notions worships Jesus as the icon of punishment and the justification for its legality? Can the same be said for the justification of war as governments exert power, even "God-given" power, to exact retribution for acts of violence?

Our traditional theories of atonement may be used to support the idea of suffering love. There's nothing wrong with suffering love. But if it turns masochistic, our highest ideas of love seem close to perversion. For instance, a friend of mine lived with an abusive husband. She never knew when he would fly off the handle and start slinging curse words and fists around. When she went to her pastor for advice, he told her that she needed to stay with her husband and love him even in the middle of his fits of temper. He encouraged her to "take up her cross and follow Jesus" down the path of suffering. How else would he see the love of God? And, of course, she wouldn't be alone in her suffering: she had Jesus as her example who suffered plenty out of love for her. Unlike the woman in chapter 1, my friend stayed with her husband and suffered willingly at his hands. She actually became quite pious about it. As crazy as it sounds, this happens much more often than we realize.

Another person came to me complaining that her pastor told her that if she wanted to be a good witness to her boss, she should graciously put up with his verbal and emotional abuse without complaint. He said she needed to show him love and compassion in return. "This is your cross to bear right now," he told her. I'm just not sure that God wants us to carry that kind of cross.

Along similar lines of thought, feminist theologians fear that theories of atonement in which God is an abusive father who finds satisfaction by punishing his innocent son places child abuse at the center of the Christian faith. In addition, they argue that the image of innocent suffering at the hands of God encourages abused and oppressed people to passively accept suffering as a way of taking up their cross and following Christ.[11] These theologians claim that Christianity and its views of atonement as penal or as a satisfaction motivate attitudes that lead toward acceptance of abuse, communicating the message that suffering is redemptive. In this view, to be a good follower of Jesus we must accept senseless suffering and even at times seek it out.

Furthermore, some biblical scholars and theologians, such as Stephen Finlan, J. Denny Weaver, and Perry Yoder, among others, hold that doctrines of atonement that advocate penal or satisfaction theories are not true to the biblical witness. Rather than endorsing retributive readings of the New Testament, they say we should interpret Jesus' life, death, and resurrection as a theology of divine protest against violence and a divine movement toward restoration and reconciliation. "God was in Christ reconciling the world to himself," so that all people might be reconciled to God through the cross, having by the cross put to death the enmity between God and humanity.[12] The heart of the New Testament witness seems to indicate reconciliation rather than retribution, reconciliation as justice and mercy, rather than punishment or satisfying an offended deity.

When the cross is seen in terms of payment, payback, satisfaction, or retribution, the death of Jesus becomes all about retribution, appeasing an offended and angry God who must, absolutely must, have a pound of flesh before God can forgive. That's not the story Jesus told, or that Paul told. In their theology, the cross is about love, not punishment. Not appeasement, not retribution, but *love*. Jesus wasn't paying God back for our sin. He was revealing how to surrender a life to God in submissive love. He revealed the extent of divine love and the extravagance of divine forgiveness while showing us true kingdom-of-God living.

Again, I am not saying that we do away with our favored traditional theories of the cross. What I am saying is that in order to change our worldview and therefore our behavior, we might want to start privileging a different model of atonement. One that portrays God as loving, compassionate, truly forgiving, and desirous of reconciling and restoring all creation to a perfect relationship with God and others.

The question now becomes, Are some of these problems with classical theories of atonement enough of a deal breaker that I have to reinterpret and possibly change my view of atonement? Most of my students consider all of the angles of their favorite theory of atonement. Some decide to tweak their theology a bit, change their views based on the evidence in tradition, Scripture, reason, and experience. But many decide to hang in there with what they've always been taught. Okay. At least they now know exactly what they believe and why they believe it: the good, the bad, and the ugly. But most importantly, they all took time to think critically through their fondly held beliefs—that's all I ask from my students.

THE NEED TO REINTERPRET ATONEMENT

What we believe about God matters. Why have the satisfaction and penal models of atonement persevered over time? Why do we continue to hang on to them even after we realize what they say about God? It boils down to tradition and our traditional interpretations of Scripture. Because our theology emerges from worldviews inherent in our societies and cultures, they relate well to the human condition.[13] They appeal to our own sense of justice and our desires for vindication that align so well with our criminal justice systems. But when we have used our theology for abusive ends, there comes a time when we need to reinterpret our tradition in order to promote peace and to maintain a relevant Christian message.

We are not alone in this endeavor. We see throughout Christian history faithful theologians reinterpreting the cross according to their contemporary situation. For example, Irenaeus, one of the earliest advocates of the *Christus Victor* theory, lived in conflict with the social structure of his day. Christianity was a persecuted, offshoot cult accused of cannibalism. And for the majority of citizens, Caesar, not Jesus, was lord. These Christians needed a theology that communicated the future victory of their Lord Jesus, a victory that would give them hope. So Irenaeus related the earthly conflicts between Caesar and Christianity to a cosmic battle between celestial powers in which Christ wins for all time.[14]

Anselm's satisfaction theory interprets the atonement according to the feudal system prevalent in his age. Abelard interprets the atonement according to the notions of "courtly love" and the new humanist culture just becoming popular in his society. With the assimilation of Aristotle, Aquinas interprets the atonement according to and in harmony with the philosophical categories and ethical principles of his day. By the fifteenth and sixteenth centuries, judicial power had largely transferred from the local community to the state. This change brought about a focus on punitive measures and the popularity of penitentiaries. In a culture concerned with sin and guilt along with the institution of newer civil laws, the reformers interpreted the atonement through the lens of punishment and justification.[15]

The liberal social theologians reinterpreted atonement according to the Enlightenment's positive humanistic attitudes and the new scientific discoveries that appeared to undermine faith in an invisible, non-verifiable God. Realizing that the world was not slowly moving toward a utopian society after all, theologians like Karl Barth, a neo-orthodox thinker who wrote after the devastation of two world wars, reinterpreted atonement for a world reeling from profound suffering and disenchantment with humankind. Then beginning in the 1960s liberation theologians, concerned with making the gospel of Jesus relevant for innocent people oppressed and murdered by empires, wars, and crooked governments, reinterpreted the atonement for their suffering communities.[16]

The layers of reinterpretation in both the biblical texts and in the history of Christian doctrine lead to the realization that the tradition *is* to reinterpret the tradition. We reinterpret continually, with a repetition of reinterpretation that preserves the relevance of the living and active Word of God. Without the continual reinterpretation of our tradition we fall victim to a stagnant traditionalism that sucks the life out of our faith. In fact, well-known theologian Jaroslav Pelikan wrote that "tradition is the living faith of the dead; traditionalism is the dead faith of the living."[17] So, the responsibility to reinterpret the character and heart of God, from being violent to antiviolent, looms before us as we work toward a theology of peace, reconciliation, and restoration through the gospel of Jesus.

Unlike some contemporary theologians, I do not want to discard the tradition. Our Christian tradition richly expresses the community's efforts to understand the divine mind and hands down to us valuable insights that we can continue to treasure and to remember. At the same time, we need to reevaluate, continually putting tradition to the test of time, preserving what enriches and serves the community and reinterpreting those portions of the tradition that no longer speak relevantly to the contemporary situation.

Unfortunately, tradition does not always come to us in the form of a rich heritage. The New Testament word commonly translated "tradition" (*paradosis*), which means "to hand down" or "to hand over," is also translated as "to betray" in the story of Judas who betrayed Jesus to the authorities, *handing him over* to be crucified. According to this double-meaning, tradition either enriches us or betrays us with the wisdom of the past. Tradition, then, needs to be wisely rethought so that we can identify any points of betrayal.

Yet at the same time, attempting to sift through the tradition handed down to us with the intent to reinterpret might make us appear arrogant by thinking we have all the answers regardless of what's been thought and taught before us. But nonetheless, if the violence of Christians past is an indication, our tradition needs help in order for us to live less like the children of wrath and more like the Prince of Peace. T. S. Eliot hauntingly expresses both the potential folly of clinging to the wisdom of old traditions and the need for the wisdom of humility and then he writes,

> The only wisdom we can hope to acquire
> Is the wisdom of humility: humility is endless.[18]

With the wisdom of humility, we can realize that there are instances in which our tradition is folly, in which it has betrayed and deceived us. When we discover these betrayals we can reinterpret the scriptural and theological events in ways that redeem and preserve the tradition so that it can remain relevant for our own communities. We reinterpret, however, with a mind and attitude of wise humility, knowing that the tradition we set in motion through our reinterpretations may require further reinterpretation in the future. My goal, therefore, is to reinterpret the tradition by reading Scripture through the lens of a peace-loving, antiviolent God, preserving the language of sacrifice and satisfaction, justice and mercy, forgiveness and love, with a mind and an attitude of what I hope is wise humility.

5

What Is Justice?

When I discuss in class the penal and satisfaction theories of atonement and particularly the issue surrounding the divine need for someone either to satisfy God's offended honor or to suffer punishment before God will forgive, many of my students raise significant questions. Josh, whom you've already met, and who's taken a number of my classes, always asks the tough questions. I can always count on him to hold my feet to the proverbial fire by pointing out relevant Scripture references or just by questioning the validity of views he's never encountered before. This one afternoon in class he commented, "God is a just God. He can't off-the-cuff forgive everyone. Justice must be served. Sin must be punished, and Jesus took that punishment so God could forgive us."

If we think of justice only in the retributive sense, then, yes, Josh has a valid argument. Retributive justice hangs on notions of quid pro quo, a tit for a tat. It says, essentially, "you did me wrong, so I must do you wrong back; however, my wrong to you will be right because you did it first and I am only seeking justice." But other forms of justice seem more just—especially when we think about God as love, who desires the salvation of all people (2 Tim. 2:4). So let's look at another form of divine justice touted not only in the Bible but also by none other than William Shakespeare. This brief detour into the secular will help us to understand the sacred. We'll see a form of divine justice that doesn't hinge on retribution.

IMAGES OF JUSTICE FROM SHYLOCK TO SHOAH

In *The Merchant of Venice*, the merchant, Antonio, owes the money-lender Shylock a substantial sum. Suffering from financial difficulty and possible ruin, he can't repay the debt. A scornful Shylock demands justice before the royal court. He wants his pound of flesh in payment for Antonio's debt. Appeals to Shylock to show mercy, to forgive at least a portion of the debt owed by Antonio, fall on deaf ears. No amount of pleading or persuasion moves Shylock from his resolve for justice; he will not forgive the debt, and he shouts vehemently, "I crave the law!"[1] Since Shylock must have justice, the court demands that Antonio repay the debt in full. Unfortunately for the heavily indebted Antonio, he doesn't have the cash. Shylock will take his payment by cutting off a slab of Antonio's flesh equal to the amount owed. As Shylock prepares to raise the knife to cut off a pound of Antonio's flesh, the clever heroine Portia, posing as a male lawyer, reminds him that justice must be served, the law upheld. He can take his pound of flesh, as the law dictates, but he must take his pound of flesh *only*, nothing more. Since the law requires that Antonio pay *only* with his flesh, Shylock must take it without shedding one drop of blood. Otherwise, justice will be demanded from him as well for taking more than his due. If that happens, he will lose all he owns and be thrown in prison. Shylock is reminded here of Portia's earlier words comparing mercy and justice: "Therefore, [Shylock], though justice be thy plea, consider this, that, in the course of justice [as retributive], none of us should see salvation."[2]

Outraged, horrified, and scared, Shylock has a quick change of heart and withdraws his demands for a pound of flesh. Since he has already required the court to serve justice, however, the court remains firm and only pauses to inquire of Antonio, who has now been granted half of Shylock's wealth, "What mercy can you render him?"[3] Shylock, the one who minutes before demanded justice instead of mercy in his dealings with Antonio, stands trembling with humility before the same Antonio, hoping against hope for mercy instead of justice.

Do we not all stand in Shylock's place? Do we not all hope against hope for divine mercy rather than divine justice? But by seeing them as two different concepts and actions, we actually put justice and mercy in polarity as opposites. Are divine "justice" and "mercy" polar opposites? Are they mutually exclusive acts on the part of God? Have they anything in common at all? Shakespeare sheds some light on these questions.

Earlier, in the midst of the courtroom scene, Portia insists that Shylock show mercy, to which he responds, "On what compulsion must I?" In true Shakespearian form, Portia expresses the nature of justice from the heavenly perspective:

> The quality of mercy is not strain'd,
> It droppeth as the gentle rain from heaven
> Upon the place beneath: it is twice blest;
> It blesseth him that gives and him that takes:
> 'Tis the mightiest in the mightiest: it becomes
> The throned monarch better than his crown;
> His sceptre shows the force of temporal power,
> The attribute to awe and majesty,
> Wherein doth sit the dread and fear of kings;
> But mercy is above this sceptred sway;
> It is enthroned in the heart of kings;
> It is an attribute to God himself.
> And earthly power doth then show likest God's
> When mercy seasons justice.[4]

According to Shakespeare, in order for justice to be most like God's, it must be infused with mercy. Mercy and justice are not opposites—they complement each other. Working together in harmony, they reveal God's character. For Shakespeare, and for God, mercy and justice do not live in tension, butting heads in a contest over how to render to us our just deserts. Any antagonism between the two actions results from a human construction of justice. Our human justice is retributive, quantitative, and destructive of relationships. But as we'll see, God's justice is restorative, qualitative, and builds relationships. Although Shakespeare is not a theologian or a biblical scholar, his concept of justice resonates with the biblical witness.

Some of my students object to restorative justice on God's part because they think it makes God seem less powerful or too easy. But during the Holocaust, the German businessman Oskar Schindler saw it differently. During World War II, through his business dealings with the Germans, he found his way into the company of top Nazi officials. At the same time, Schindler found a way to save over 1,100 Jews from certain death in concentration camps. In the film *Schindler's List* (Universal Studios, 1993), during a conversation with the Nazi commandant Amon Goeth, a notoriously vicious killer of the Jews, Schindler expresses the greatest form of power, which also describes restorative justice. He tells Goeth that people fear the Nazis because they have the power to kill arbitrarily. Schindler says that a man who commits a crime should know better. When he gets killed for his crime, we feel much better about the situation, and even better if we get to kill him ourselves. He continues, saying: "That's not power though. That's [retributive] justice. It's different than power. Power is when we have every justification to kill and we don't."

> Goeth: "You think that's power?"
> Schindler: "That's what the emperor said. A man stole something. He's brought in before the emperor. He throws himself down on the ground and he begs for mercy. He knows he's going to die. And the emperor pardons him. This worthless man—he lets him go."
> Goeth: "I think you are drunk."
> Schindler: "That's power, Amon. *That* is power."

We could say, that's forgiveness. That is restorative justice at work. And that's more powerful than any display of retributive "power" or violence. I also believe that's how God acts in the world. How about us? Do we believe and act more like Goeth, who thinks retributive justice is power, or Schindler, who believes restorative justice in the form of pardon is power? Or Shakespeare, who thinks about justice infused with mercy, or Shylock, who chooses justice over mercy? Is there a problem with either?

THE PROBLEM WITH JUSTICE

If we read through the Bible in search of justice, we see it sketched out for us in various forms. For instance, if we imagine God primarily as a judge who punishes evildoers, we will focus on the Scriptures portraying God as retributive. Those verses support our own ideas of justice. Some of us imagine God primarily as loving, compassionate, and forgiving, and therefore concentrate our attention on Scriptures that portray God as restorative. The difficulty lies in the fact that the Bible talks about God as retributive *and* as restorative in the execution of justice. Well, we might ask, which form best expresses God's character?

In many cases, the passages that portray God as retributive appear to contradict the passages about God as restorative. For instance, remember God's prophet Elisha? While taking a trek on foot to Bethel, forty-two young boys followed behind him, mocking him. Not to be outdone, Elisha cursed them *in the name of Lord* and immediately two bears came out of the woods and massacred all those boys (2 Kgs 2:23–24). Obviously, Elisha had the power of God on the tip of his tongue—he curses and God uses creation's resources to strike. But then, we read about Jesus telling his disciples to love their enemies, to pray for those who persecute them (Matt. 5:44). We read about Jesus saying, "Let the little children come to me, and do not stop them" (Matt. 19:14). So does God orchestrate the death of children or does God embrace them and love them, even if they misbehave?

In another passage, God promises to punish children for the iniquity of their parents for three generations; but, in the next line, God promises to show steadfast love for a thousand generations (Exod. 20:5–6; Deut. 5:9–10). In one scene we see God wreaking havoc on innocent people because of something David did, and in another scene we see God as one whose compassion never fails, whose mercy never ceases (2 Sam. 24; Lam. 3:22–24). Which one of these examples (and there are many more) characterizes God most accurately? Which image of God should we imitate? How do we choose? It seems from these passages that mercy triumphs over retributive justice (Jas. 2:13). As someone concerned about religious violence, who truly wants to present God as loving, compassionate, and just, I focus on the passages that reveal God as restorative. I prefer to do so because that's what Jesus taught and that's how he lived. As the one who most fully reveals God, we need to make his life and teachings the lens through which we interpret the Bible, imagine God, and construct our theology.[5]

My students often make astute comments when we discuss the varying, and seemingly contradictory, images of God in class. Josh, as usual, voiced his questions out loud: "Well, we can't say something isn't just when it concerns God. God's ways are higher than our ways. The Bible portrays God as retributive, so whether we like it or not, we have to take it at face value, knowing we may not understand God's reasons for taking vengeance on people."

While I agree that God's ways are higher than our ways, I also argue that we must take the verse in context. In Isaiah 55:9 the prophet utters the words of God, saying: "For as the heavens are higher than the earth, so are my ways higher than your ways and my thoughts higher than your thoughts." But a quick reading of the surrounding verses gives us the context of those words. The prophet lets us in on God's gracious invitation to come drink of the divine waters that lead to forgiveness and mercy. So according to these verses, God's ways are higher than our ways in the context of forgiveness, pardon, and restoration. It's as if God expects the people to respond to the invitation by saying, "What? God will simply forgive—no retribution?" And Isaiah says, "Who would have thought it?! God's ways are higher than our ways! We expect retribution and God says, 'I will forgive you' and invites us into a relationship." God's "higher" way, the heavenly way, then, is not our low or earthly way. We want retribution. God wants to forgive—it's beyond our simple understanding.

When we look through the Bible for glimpses of God's type of justice we also must think about the genre of a book or passage of Scripture. The Bible verses that give us a retributive view of God often come from prophetic literature or narrative in which the author wants to make an important point. Usually those passages are packed full of hyperbole and metaphor. The people who first heard and later read these texts were used to the rhetoric, dramatic flair, and judgmental tone. For example, God gave Jeremiah the daunting task of pronouncing divine judgment against many different nations and people. In one passage God says through Jeremiah, "For I have set my face against this city [Jerusalem] for evil and not for good. . . . It shall be given into the hand of the king of Babylon, and he will burn it with fire" (Jer. 21:10). You will find many other examples of violent prophetic rhetoric in the books of Isaiah, Ezekiel, Hosea, Nahum, and others.

Then look at the Psalms, which are packed full of hyperbolic violent rhetoric. If I listed all the Scripture references, it would take up at least the rest of this chapter. But, because of their culturally structured, preconceived ideas about God, they expected to hear language about divine retribution and vengeance. Many of the judgment passages that depict God as retributive are rhetorical devices commonly used and acknowledged by the people. We use this form of speech quite a lot by saying things like, "I'm dying of hunger"; "I'm so hungry I could eat a cow"; "I am freezing"; or "I'm going to kill you!" Biblical scholar Stephen Finlan writes that "the judgmental rhetoric was intended to awaken the people and turn them away from making choices that would lead the nation to doom by undermining the only thing that gave Israel and Judah a unique role in the world."[6]

In addition to the context and the genre, some scholars believe that the understanding of God evolved throughout the Bible and is still evolving today.[7] Jesus disclosed the progressing nature of interpreting God and Scripture in his Sermon on the Mount. He tells his hearers, "you have heard it said . . ." and then says, "but I say to you. . . . ," as he goes on to reinterpret the Old Testament text in favor of a new way of thinking and acting (Matt. 5:21–22, 27–28, 31–34, 38–39). He also challenged the law and reinterpreted it when he and his followers picked grain on the Sabbath and were scolded by the Pharisees (Mark 2:23–28). So when we ourselves set out to reinterpret biblical texts that speak of judgment and violence in order to make them more relevant to our context, we are following Jesus' example just as he followed the example of the rabbis and biblical writers before him. We reinterpret the tradition.

Of course, most Christians believe that the final revelation of God, according to Hebrews 1:1–3, is Jesus. Those of us who believe Jesus fully reveals God and God's ways read the Bible through the lens of what Jesus taught and how he acted. As the beginning, center, end, purpose, and focus of our faith, we should read *all* Scripture through the interpretive lens of Jesus—the fullest revelation of God we have (Luke 10:22; John 1:18; 5:39; Col. 1:15, 19). In fact, the great Baptist minister Charles Spurgeon said, "O you who open your Bibles and want to understand a text, the way to get into the meaning of a text is through the door, Christ."[8] The Bible scholar Peter Enns gives us insight into why Jesus should provide the interpretive lens through which we read Scripture—both the Old and New Testaments. He points out that Jesus *is* the Word of God—the living Word, the incarnate Word. Why, then, would we interpret the written Word in any way other than through Jesus, the living Word? In a similar vein, Martin Luther asserted that any discussion on the character of God in biblical interpretation must begin with the selfless, dying Jesus or we not only miss the point, we also miss God. Any understanding of God that does not harmonize with the teachings and actions of Jesus is what we might call a conceptual idol.[9]

Think about it. If Jesus heals the sick, would God do less? If Jesus welcomes the outcast, eats dinner with the sinners, touches the untouchable, talks to women, pulls children onto his lap, and embraces all those whom others shun then wouldn't God behave in the same way with grace, compassion, and loving-kindness? If Jesus forgives sin without payback, wouldn't God do the same? If Jesus loves his enemies, doesn't God love them too? If Jesus seeks restorative justice, as we see in his prayer for our forgiveness while hanging on the cross, would God do any less? Of course not! Consequently, to try as much as possible to avoid conceptual idolatry, we will study and interpret the written

Word of God through the lens of the living Word, Jesus. When I read
Old Testament texts, I do so in light of the overall redemptive message
of the Bible and interpret divine justice as restorative, reconciling, and
infiltrated with divine love—even for enemies.

As much as many of my students desire to believe in divine justice as
restorative rather than retributive, they also want to square with Scripture their inclination to favor that perspective. They ask questions like,
"Isn't privileging one form of justice over another like having your own
canon within a canon? We ignore one part of Scripture in order to justify
an opposing belief or action that we find in another part of the Bible?"

I do privilege the teachings of Jesus. So, yes, I have my own canon
within a canon, and I admit it openly. But even though many Christians don't admit it or don't even realize it, they too have a canon within
a canon. They privilege the law in legalistic traditions. Or they hold to
verses that speak of hell over those that speak of God's unconditional
forgiveness and desire to save all people. Some readers focus on verses
that support predestination and ignore those that support human freedom to choose or not to choose God. Others read Scripture and interpret it through the lens of God's liberation of the poor and oppressed,
pushing into the background passages in which God rewards the righteous with power and wealth. In other words, we all read the Bible
through an interpretive paradigm that significantly influences how we
think about God, salvation, and other people. Jesus had his own canon
within the canon, or interpretive paradigm, of the Old Testament.[10]
In Luke 4:18–19, Jesus stands in front of the congregation and reads
from the prophet Isaiah (Isa. 61:1–2a). But he stops mid-verse, closes
the book, and sits down. The part he leaves out? He omits "the day
of the vengeance of our God." It doesn't harmonize with the message
he's been preaching and teaching. He ignores one part of the Bible and
favors another part. Jesus reinterprets the age-old Jewish tradition in
order to reveal a bit more of God's heart and to remain relevant to his
changing culture.

Like Jesus, we need to find a way to assimilate later developments in
our knowledge of God into our Christian theology. We can reinterpret
our tradition in order to remain relevant to our contemporary culture
without despising earlier traditions. We can value them for their service
to the kingdom of God, yet allow the Spirit of God to grow in us and to
lead us into a life of love, compassion, and joy in imitation of Jesus. So
with that in mind, let's take a quick tour through Scripture to see what
it has to say about God's justice as restorative rather than as retributive
and reinterpret a bit—as Christians have always done.

REINTERPRETING DIVINE JUSTICE AS RESTORATIVE

In our societies and cultures past and present, we most often think of justice as retributive. We may not call it that, favoring other labels such as punishment, paying a debt to society, or getting what "they" deserve (we usually don't want what *we* deserve unless it's something good). But whichever way we slice it, our sense of justice boils down to some sort of retribution. Naturally then, as we discussed above, we project that form of justice onto God. We read the Bible through that lens. But the Bible says more about restorative justice than we realize.

I have read all the verses in the Bible that speak about justice and interestingly enough, many of them in one way or another critique violence. Human violence counteracts, eliminates, and opposes justice. Over and over again, we see God decrying violence, warning us against it, rebuking us for it, and predicting its dire consequences. In fact, Psalm 11:5 actually says that God's soul hates those who do violence! In Ezekiel 45:9 God tells the people to stop doing violence and injustice and start practicing righteousness and justice. Their violence will lead to their demise. Verse after verse reveals to us that where violence flourishes justice dies out.[11]

The Bible also connects justice to righteousness and mercy. In fact, these three actions are so closely intertwined in Scripture that we might refer to them as a trinity of utility. If we want to live according to God's will, in imitation of Jesus, we will utilize the three practices: justice, righteousness, and mercy.

Interestingly, the Hebrew word for "to do" most always accompanies the words "justice," righteousness," and "mercy." That little word (*'asah*) that we translate "do" adds significant meaning in our application of our trinity of utility. Justice, righteousness, and mercy aren't merely abstract concepts that we toss around lightly in our vocabulary. And they don't just express an inward condition of our hearts and minds. Coupled with "doing," these words turn from talk to walk, from the internal to the external. We *do* justice; we *do* righteousness; we *do* mercy. In other words, we live those values as we act them out in our lives and we direct those actions toward others out of love.

This perspective on justice and its marriage to righteousness and mercy don't leave room for retribution. They are energized and animated by love. Psalm 33:5 tells us that God loves righteousness and justice. And because God loves them, the earth is filled with God's loving-kindness. The Psalmist connects justice, righteousness, and mercy directly to God's love for all the earth and its inhabitants—even enemies. Isaiah 30:18 makes the same connection between God's justice and love. Here, God's justice culminates in God sitting in the heavens longing to show us grace and love. Divine justice results in grace and love, and we are called to the same sort of justice (c.f. Hos. 2:19).[12]

We don't just *say* we love our enemies, we *show* them love through acts of compassion, serving the cause of justice by serving others. For example, justice and righteousness acted out, according to Scripture, include loving compassion for others, taking care of the oppressed, the marginalized, the outcast, and even the enemy.[13] According to Zechariah we do justice, righteousness, and mercy by taking care of the widow, the orphan, the poor, and by showing compassion to each other (7:10). We feed the hungry, rescue the oppressed, and try our best to make peace with others (Deut. 10:18; 24:17; 27:19; Pss. 140:12; 146:7; Isa. 1:17; 42:1–4; Jer. 22:3). God's righteousness—God's carrying out right actions—is an extension of God's justice, which does not include violence or retribution, but instead demonstrates mercy and loving compassion even for the enemy.[14]

We also see that divine justice is redemptive—it saves us (Ps. 119:156; Isa. 1:27; 59:11).[15] God promises Jeremiah that the day will come when God will do (*'asah*) justice and redeem the people (Jer. 23:5–6; 33:15). In other words, it appears that redemption is the result of doing justice. To redeem, therefore, is to *do* justice. We see a beautiful picture of justice as redemptive in Amos 5:24. It describes justice as cool, fresh water flowing over a dry, parched land. As we know, water in an arid land brings life, new growth, and quenched thirst for all those dwelling in the desert. It cools and refreshes, cleanses and nourishes—and Amos compares it to divine justice. In other words, the imagery of justice as a continual flowing stream over the land imposes upon us a beautiful picture of something redemptive, restorative, and life-giving that satisfies the longing of those in need.[16]

JUSTICE, JESUS STYLE

The restorative justice we've seen in the Old Testament harmonizes with the justice Jesus taught and practiced. He forgave his enemies and exhorted us to do the same (Matt. 5:43–48). In fact, Jesus directly connects loving our enemies to being holy, just like God is holy. We might conclude from these verses, then, that divine holiness means we love even our enemies—just like God does. And it doesn't seem possible that loving our enemies includes exacting retribution on them, even for God. In addition, if we interpret certain verses in Isaiah as pointing to Jesus, we see that Jesus brings justice to the nations and establishes justice on the earth. The Bible heralds the justice of Jesus as a light for all people and connects it to our salvation (Isa. 42:1, 3–4, 6; 51:4; 56:1). Along those same lines, Jeremiah (33:15) believed that God would execute justice on earth through the righteous Branch of David. For most Christians, this refers to Jesus, and the justice of Jesus redeems and restores.

In the New Testament, Jesus proclaims justice. He leads justice to victory. And he reveals to us the justice of God through love (Matt. 12:18, 20; Luke 11:42). From our reading of the New Testament, how does Jesus execute and establish God's justice? Not by violence, that's for sure. He loves and forgives, even from the cross.

The justice of Jesus not only forgives enemies, but breaks down boundaries between Jew and Greek, slave and free, male and female. It brings together Samaritan and Jewish travelers, tax-gatherers and disciples, shepherds and angels, wise men and peasants. It repairs (restores) those relationships through love.[17] So as we reinterpret justice from retributive to restorative, we see it as antiviolent, as righteousness and mercy in action en route to redemption. Restorative justice in action stops the cycle of violence and oppression, retribution, and vengeance, bringing *shalom* (peace, wholeness, and health) to the entire earth.[18]

Retributive justice sticks to the letter of the law, requiring its pound of flesh, demanding compensation, an eye for an eye, in order to forgive sin. Conversely, divine restorative justice requires neither payment nor retribution. Instead, it seeks restoration, peace, and the fore-giving of pardon so that restoration and qualitatively new relations can take place between offended parties. In other words, divine justice is steeped in mercy. It lights the way to forgiveness and restores without violence. Richard Rohr, in his commentary on the book of Job, writes that "[t]he general belief in the scriptures . . . is that God's justice is not achieved by punishment, but by the divine initiative we call grace. . . ."[19]

Charles Moule, who works in the field of criminal and civil justice, also argues that divine justice—the deepest level of justice—is restorative rather than retributive. Whereas retributive justice seeks to fit the punishment to the crime, attempting to control wrongdoing through punishment, restorative justice forgives the crime and seeks to redeem wrongdoing through a repairing of the relationship. He states that "the first great step towards justice at the deepest level is, paradoxically, when the victim abandons quantitative justice, waives the demand for 'just' retribution, and begins to become ready to forgive—that is, to meet the damage by repair."[20] The Gospel accounts of Jesus reveal to us a God who meets the damage by repair through forgiveness. Take for example the woman caught in adultery (John 8:1–11). Guilty, ashamed, and afraid, she stands before the scribes and Pharisees knowing that the law commands she be stoned as the penalty for her crime. But they ask Jesus what he would do. You know the story. After driving home the point that no one is without sin, Jesus doesn't command her death; he pardons her. He sets the woman free and asks her to sin no more —the ultimate example of restorative justice. We see other instances of restorative justice when Jesus heals and forgives the paralytic whose friends have just lowered him through the roof (Luke 5:17–26) and when Jesus dines with the corrupt tax collector Zaccheus and saves him. Why did Jesus save (heal, forgive) Zaccheus instead of condemn him to the outer darkness? Because God gave him the mission to restore people to a relationship with God. Jesus says, "For the Son of Man came to seek out and to save the lost" (Luke 19:10). Jesus didn't come to exact retribution or mete out punishment. He came to forgive the lost, reconcile them, and restore them to a loving relationship with God.

Understandings of divine justice as restorative and qualitative rather than as retributive and quantitative carry significant implications for theories of atonement. The justice Jesus reveals to us in the New Testament moves us away from the pursuit of retribution, vengeance, and retaliation and draws us toward forgiveness, restoration of relationship, and new life together in the community of God. Paul, too, takes part in that movement away from retributive justice as we see in 2 Corinthians 5:19: "in Christ God was reconciling the world to himself, *not counting their trespasses against them*" (italics mine). What does it mean when God doesn't count our trespasses against us? It means that God forgives them. The words and actions of Jesus reveal God's justice at work to forgive and to redeem, to repair and to restore—definitely not retributive justice at work.

Through the actions of Jesus during his lifetime, death, and resurrection, we gain an understanding of the divine response to retributive violence and conceptions of human justice. Rather than shouting threats of retaliation in the name of God, Jesus set in motion the ultimate expression of divine justice and its restorative character by asking God to forgive us in a moment that may have instead provoked vengeance and retribution.[21] As revealed in the life, death, and resurrection of Jesus, the process of forgiveness, reconciliation, and restoration without retaliation demonstrates the most profound level of justice.[22]

SO WHAT'S THE PROBLEM?

Human beings tend to have difficulty accepting the possibility that God forgives sin unconditionally since, from a human viewpoint, forgiveness of such magnitude is not only impossible for God, but also unjust. Many of us have trouble accepting an infinitely loving God who forgives without the use of violent power or punitive measures. We often seem to prefer a God who exacts justice through violence, through sending the wicked to eternal punishment without a hope for reconciliation with the God who created and loves them.[23] We cling to human notions of justice that tally up all the wrongs done and then demand restitution as retribution. Divine justice as restorative and redemptive, however, does not keep accounts with records of retributive actions or satisfaction. It is unaccountable. God applies the unaccountable justice through forgiveness.

But what about those who suffer horribly at the hands of an oppressor? Sometimes their only source of hope comes from the belief that God will vindicate them by punishing the ones who have hurt them. These protests are valid and we need to respect and address them. Those who live under the abuse and violence of unjust governments, who have suffered much at the whims and agendas of political oppressors, or have been victims of violent crimes, need to believe that, when all is said and done, God will vindicate them; their oppressors will be brought to justice.[24] The hope of vindication understandably enables victims to retain their faith in a good God even in the midst of profound suffering. Yet, the exhortation to love our enemy includes loving those who cause extreme suffering. Divine justice in the form of restoration, however, still vindicates the oppressed and calls the guilty to account. I'll explain how. Doesn't it seem that restorative rather than retributive justice more effectively and completely reveals the love of God and God's desire to save all of creation? Let me offer a hypothetical illustration that occurs in the "throne room" of heaven in the presence of God. Hitler (a typical stand-in for someone very evil) comes before God to give an account of his life. Trembling in terror, expecting the equivalent or more in punishment, he explains his motives and deeds done while alive. He knows without doubt that the sentence will be harsh and eternal, and he hates God and God's justice. Much to his astonishment, instead of receiving the expected eternal death sentence, he is confronted with extravagant, unexpected love and forgiveness, and promised a place in God's kingdom as if he were God's own son. Unnerved by such an unorthodox approach, Hitler realizes completely the depth and depravity of his own sin. Filled with remorse and repentance he falls on his face before God, completely undone, horribly and inconsolably grief-stricken over the suffering and injustice he has caused others. No amount of eternal torment in the fires of hell could have filled him with such remorse and sorrow. It took coming face to face with the extravagant, unfathomable love of God to make Hitler realize the tremendous, egregious pain he caused others and bring about his accompanying grief and repentance. His victims see and understand his unimaginable remorse. Yet, forgiven by a just God, Hitler finds redemption and restoration. He is transformed by divine justice and can now be reconciled with God and with those he has victimized, terrorized, and marginalized.[25] I can almost hear some of you thinking, "wait a minute, does everyone always respond the same way to the overwhelming presence of the loving God? Does God still respect free will?" Those are good questions that I address in my book *Razing Hell*. But let me ask you a couple of questions. You are standing before God, knowing your sinfulness, waiting for your punishment, knees trembling, heart beating outside your chest, paralyzed by fear. Then the fearful presence of God begins to burn away your unrighteousness and sinfulness. With them go the rebellious, unrepentant attitudes, the anger, and the resentment. God's purifying fire leaves you pure and righteous, basking in the love of God you so took for granted or completely rejected all your life. Then God speaks. "I love you with an unfailing love. I forgive you all your sins. Will you enter the joy of the Lord and be reconciled and restored to me?" The choice is yours. What will you answer? What would any righteous, sinless, person with a free will say in return? Would any truly righteous person turn away from God? I think anyone's answer to God's question would be, "yes, oh my God, yes!"

Now, restorative justice doesn't just work in hypothetical stories, but in real life, too. Maybe you remember the 2003 trial of Gary Ridgway. Authorities believe he murdered close to seventy-one women. At one point during the trial, the victims' families were allowed to speak to the murderer. One after the other stood in front of Mr. Ridgway and expressed their feelings of hatred and their desire to see him rot in hell. They understandably wanted retribution. Gary Ridgway glared at them with a stern, hard look of hatred, showing no remorse whatsoever. Then Bob Rule stood up to speak. He told the man who had ruthlessly murdered his daughter that he didn't hate him. That he didn't want retribution. He said, "I forgive you." At that moment, Gary Ridgway began to cry. In the face of such grace, his hatred and anger gave way as he realized the significance of his crimes. He later wrote a letter of apology to his victims' families and expressed deep remorse for his horrific actions. But it wasn't the retributive attitudes of most of the families that made him acknowledge his sins and feel remorse. It was Bob Rule's decision to set aside retributive justice and seek restorative justice through forgiveness instead.[26]

In another case, a man named Darrol arrived home and found that someone had broken into his house. The thieves stole expensive pieces of equipment and damaged family heirlooms. The authorities caught the culprits shortly after the crime, discovering that they were mere boys who had burglarized other homes in the neighborhood as well. Instead of demanding retribution, Darrol went and talked to the boys, expressing his sorrow and his forgiveness. Recognizing their remorse, he invited them to a neighborhood dinner at his home so they could meet the community they had terrorized with their crime spree. He bought the food and the boys cooked it and personally delivered invitations to the neighbors. At one point, Darrol gave one of the boys money to buy party supplies. But after getting the supplies from home, he returned the money to Darrol. The neighborhood now holds yearly block parties. Rejoicing in the restoration of relationships within the community, Darrol writes, "we can do something other than buying bigger fences and bigger locks. Hatred cannot be met with hatred. It has to be met with love." If Darrol had set his heart on retribution, restoration might not have taken place in that neighborhood.[27] Justice born from love restores; justice born from hatred breeds and seeks retribution.

So we see that the kind of justice that leads to non-retaliatory forgiveness may have profound consequences for the one forgiven with such sacrificial abandon. In fact, the expenditure of forgiveness often results in a response of repentance that proves just as costly. Thomas Aquinas comments that "an equal gift of grace means more to the penitent who deserves punishment than to the innocent who has never incurred it."[28] In other words, God's extravagant grace more profoundly tears at the heart of a person who has committed the most horrible sins than it does the person who has sinned little. In the same light, according to theologian Gil Bailie, "Jesus seems to have understood that the only real and lasting contrition occurs, not when one is confronted with one's sin, but when one experiences the gust of grace that makes a loving and forgiving God plausible."[29] Reconciling justice and non-retaliatory forgiveness form two sides of the same coin that call the guilty to account and yet redeem peacefully with love.

Justice, therefore, does not mean "getting let off the hook," or "getting away with murder." Instead, it means realizing the shameful magnitude of our personal sin by coming face to face with the one who has the right and the power to punish but who instead loves and forgives. Love and forgiveness instead of anger and punishment bring repentance and redemption. And of course, we all know that the one who has been forgiven much, loves in even greater measure (Luke 7:47). In this manner, justice is served.[30]

The biblical witness testifies to this picture of divine justice that casts out fear of judgment and punishment through forgiving love:

> So we have known and believe the love God has for us. God is love, and those who abide in love abide in God, and God abides in them. Love has been perfected among us in this: that we may have boldness on the day of judgment, because as he is, so are we in this world. There is no fear in love, but perfect love casts out fear; for fear has to do with punishment, and whoever fears has not reached perfection in love. We love because he first loved us.
> (1 John 4:16–19; compare with Rom. 5:8–10).

Justice embraced by divine love, mercy, forgiveness, and restoration removes the fear of punishment with the extravagant outpouring of love, which in turn kindles repentance and love in the guilty person. This kind of selfless love seeks to restore a relationship in spite of an offense.

Raymund Schwager beautifully expresses this process of divine restoration that still manages to redeem in the face of human hatred and hardness of heart. He says that on the cross "the law of revenge became the law of redeeming love. The curse was repaid with blessing. The conspiracy of hatred was answered with an outpouring of love."[31] Seen in this light, love redeems us, not by winning a victory over us, but by winning us over, filling us from the source with love for God. God's love and the resulting redemption are not given on the basis of merit earned, but are God's gratuitous gifts to humankind. No one is excluded; no one is turned away.

GOD AND GLORY: RETRIBUTION VS. RESTORATION

Don't the results of restorative justice bring God more glory than the results of retributive justice? Think about it. One the one hand, we read plenty in the Old Testament about vengeance, retribution, and the destruction that follows. Very seldom do the people conquered by divine acts of vengeance reconcile with God. Very seldom do we see those relationships restored. God, or those acting in God's name, destroy the alleged offenders so that the relationship never stands a chance of reconciliation or restoration. On the other hand, when we read about God forgoing retribution in favor of restoration, we also see people reconciling with God and restoring their relationships with each other. Look at Romans 3. In the first half of the chapter, Paul explains that the law condemns all people. No one escapes the punishment demanded by the law. It's basically built upon retributive principles. You sin, you die. I love the second half of the chapter. But God's grace and righteousness reverse the law of retribution and redeem us through Jesus Christ. Justice doesn't come through divine punishment; it comes through divine restoration (32). We especially observe this in the life of Jesus.

What would have happened if Jesus, in terrible pain on the cross, had commanded an army of angels to come and wipe out his persecutors? What would have happened if Jesus had bought into the violent response of Peter when the Romans came to arrest him? Violence, bloodshed, death, maybe even war, right? But instead, Jesus responded in the opposite way. He commanded Peter to put away his sword and he spoke words of forgiveness from the cross. In so doing, he broke the cycle of violence and reconciled us to God so that we could spend an eternity celebrating and enjoying our restored relationship with a God who loves us. Which brings God more glory—retribution or restoration? I think the answer is obvious.

6

An Economy of Forgiveness

For as the heavens are high above the earth,
so great is his steadfast love toward those who fear him;
as far as the east is from the west, so far he removes our transgressions
from us.

—Psalm 103:11–12

. . . under the new covenant the forgiveness instead of the punishment
of enemies has been enjoined on all [Christ's] disciples in all cases
whatsoever.

—Leo Tolstoy, *The Kingdom of God is Within You*

In the world, violence is met with counterviolence; in the Kingdom
[of God] it is met with forgiveness.

—John D. Caputo, *After the Death of God* (63–64)

On the day we discussed forgiveness as it related to the cross, Josh, as usual, pushed back a bit when I mentioned that penal and satisfaction theories of atonement compromise the nature of forgiveness. He commented: "How does the fact that God needed Jesus to pay our debt or satisfy for our sin weaken or hinder true forgiveness? If Jesus pays God and Jesus *is* God, then God pays God back for sin and then forgives *us*. God pays *and* forgives."

That's one way to soften the idea that God requires someone to take the hit for sin before God can forgive it. And that explanation satisfies many of us. At the same time, however, we need to consider what these conceptions of atonement and forgiveness say about God. They seem to leave us with a God who puts on a violent charade. And it's not a harmless charade. An innocent man dies a heinously violent death. And think about Judas, whom God used to betray Jesus. He also dies a terrible death. Then there's Jesus' mother. What grief she must have felt watching her beloved son die, beaten, bleeding, in anguishing pain. All because God had to make a show of God paying God? What kind of God would invent such an economic fiction that results in such atrocious suffering? Additionally, if we think that God must punish sin or get paid back for sin, or somehow needs the divine order restored before God can forgive sin, what image of God are we promoting? What are we saying about God's character? What are we saying about the nature of divine forgiveness? In order to answer these questions and address Josh's comment, let's first take a look at the nature of true forgiveness.[1]

FATHOMING FORGIVENESS

The justice we discussed in the last chapter works hand in hand with the forgiveness we'll discuss in this chapter. Forgiveness flows naturally from restorative justice. One produces the other, for without forgiveness there can be no reconciliation; and without reconciliation there can be no restoration; and without restoration justice means nothing. The need to forgive implies a breach in relationship, a need for both reconciliation and restoration. Without forgiveness we couldn't have a relationship with God, and often we wouldn't have very satisfying relationships with others. But what is forgiveness, exactly? Why is it necessary?

The need to forgive implies a wrong done to us by someone. So before we even think about forgiving someone, that someone must do something that offends, hurts, disrespects, or deceives us. For example, I was talking to my son about getting registered for classes in the fall. He got irritated with me and spoke a bit disrespectfully (and all my sons know better!). My son's talking back to me put a damper on our relationship. For a few moments, he alienated himself from me even though, because I love him, my forgiveness was there for him to receive when he was ready for it. Not too long afterward, he realized he had done wrong and apologized. Since both of us were willing to reconcile, our relationship was restored. So when we talk about forgiveness we need to remember that forgiveness itself already implies a wrong done by someone or by some community to another person or community.

My falling-out with my son is small-scale forgiveness, but think about our relationship with God. Through our sin, we wrong God and ruin our relationship. Sin stands between us and a right relationship with God. But out of love for us God first forgives our sin and desires to reconcile with us as soon as we are ready to receive divine forgiveness (Rom. 5:8). But what exactly has God done by forgiving us? What does divine forgiveness entail? Let's look at some of the most frequently used metaphors that explain God's forgiveness.

Wipe Out

When we think of sin as a barrier that keeps us separated from God we can also imagine forgiveness as the means for taking that barrier out of the way or wiping it out. God forgives us and eradicates the relational and spiritual wall keeping us apart. To forgive means to wipe the sin out, to remove the sin and the punishment.[2] The Bible often speaks of God removing our sin when people pray and ask for forgiveness. The psalmist tells us that God removes sin even as far as the east is from the west (Ps. 103:12). Isaiah expresses praise because God has cast his sins behind God's back (38:17). And Micah tells all of us that God will cast all our sins into the depths of the sea, thereby removing them far from us (7:18–20).

Of course the image of the scapegoat in Leviticus 16:22 offers us one of the most significant examples of God removing human sin. In this passage, the yearly Day of Atonement required the priest to take a goat, lay hands on it to symbolize transferring the sins of the people onto the goat, and let it go into the wilderness. The goat symbolically represents divine forgiveness by taking the sins away from the community into a barren wilderness where they will be seen no more (we'll discuss the other goat in the next chapter).

According to the prophet Jeremiah, God doesn't only wipe out or take sin away; God goes the extra mile and actually forgets about it (Isa. 43:25; Jer. 31:34; Heb. 10:17). The psalmist asks God to forget his sin in keeping with God's steadfast love and goodness (Pss. 25:7; 79:8). In contrast, most human beings may forgive a sin, taking it out of the way so we may reconcile and restore a damaged relationship, but we don't often forget the offense. In fact, I've heard people say, "I'll forgive but I certainly won't forget!" I'm glad God's forgiveness doesn't imitate ours.

By way of illustration, we can compare forgiveness to taking out the garbage and setting it on the curb for the truck to come take it away. We never see it again and we completely forget about past trash that we've already discarded. Or, we can use the analogy of a chalkboard. During one class session I usually cover the chalkboard with writing, erase it, write all over it again, and erase it again. If I wipe out the writing too soon, students will cry out, "wait! I'm not finished copying it!" They know that if I erase it before they've taken their notes, they'll forget what they saw written on the board and will do very poorly on the next exam. Well, God erases the chalkboard before anyone has a chance to write it all down. So it's wiped out and forgotten.

Clean Up

Probably the most significant understanding of forgiveness in the Bible deals with the idea of cleansing or purification. God's forgiveness cleanses and purifies us, so "though [our] sins are like scarlet, they shall be like snow; though they are red like crimson, they shall become like wool" (Isa. 1:18). Of course we know that snow and wool are white— the color that in ancient Middle Eastern cultures symbolized cleanliness and purity.[3] God decontaminates us like God did for Isaiah by touching his lips with a burning coal. God burned away Isaiah's guilt and purified him so he could speak for God (6:7). We see purification as a metaphor for forgiveness specifically in the priestly duties on the Day of Atonement, the holiest day of the year, in Leviticus 16. By sprinkling blood on the tabernacle's mercy seat and altar, the priests purified the tabernacle from contamination and the people from their sin. The idea of purification from sin continues into the New Testament as well in the book of Hebrews (9:22). Here Jesus purifies (forgives) us from all sin with the sprinkling of his blood.

The New Testament presupposes the metaphor of purification from sin in passages that speak of forgiveness through the shedding of Jesus' blood (Matt. 26:28; Eph. 1:7; Col. 1:14). First John 1:9 tells us that by forgiving us God has cleansed or purified us from unrighteousness. So we can compare forgiveness of sin metaphorically to any purifying process. For instance, salt on a wound will draw out all the poisons and purify the injury from contamination. In fact, putting salt on a poisonous snake bite draws out the venom so the victim has a better chance of surviving. In the same way, forgiveness as purification draws the contamination out of us so we can live pure lives in service to God.

Why?

But why does God forgive us? If God considers us enemies (Rom. 5:8–10) and law-breakers (just read Rom. 3:9–20), why would God want to continue in a relationship with us? According to the Bible, God "*longs* to be gracious to you; he waits on high to have compassion on you" (Isa. 30:18 NASB, emphasis mine). God's love, compassion, and mercy impel God to forgive sin. Nehemiah says that even though the people turned from God in disobedience and did all sorts of terrible things, God still sought to forgive out of grace, steadfast love, and mercy (9:17; also Num. 14:19; Dan. 9:9). In fact the psalmist sings God's praises because God forgives out of love even though we don't deserve it (Ps. 86:5).

So God forgives us because God loves us. But that's not the only reason. Luke explains that through the forgiveness of sin, we will see and understand our salvation (Luke 1:77). According to the Bible, the fact that God forgives sin encompasses the message of salvation. Luke makes this clear, saying that "forgiveness of sins is to be proclaimed in [Jesus'] name to all nations beginning from Jerusalem" (Luke 24:47). Peter stood before the people, preaching the good news in the book of Acts. The good news he preached was the forgiveness of sins through Jesus (Acts 2:38; 5:31; 10:43; 13:38; 26:18). The writer of Ephesians proclaims that we have redemption, that is, the forgiveness of sins, through Jesus Christ (1:7; also Col. 1:14). Paul tells us that God reconciled us to God's self. How? By not counting our transgressions against us. In other words, God reconciles and restores us to an intimate relationship by forgiving our sin. Forgiveness *is* the good news! Forgiveness saves us by opening the way to reconciliation with God.

Forgiveness and Reconciliation

In Traditional Theories

My students get tired of hearing me preach to them about theological consistency. Even though I present many varying perspectives on each topic and encourage them to choose what they believe based on the evidence we see in Scripture and tradition, I also tell them that their theology must remain consistent throughout—from God to creation to humanity, sin, and salvation, all the way to eschatology (study of the end times). So if they begin their theological structure with the premise "God is love," I expect them to carry that basic theme all the way through to the end. It's no different with our theories of forgiveness.

With that in mind, we need to expose the theological inconsistencies about forgiveness found in satisfaction and penal theories of the cross. If God is love, which is my starting point, then my thoughts on forgiveness must be consistent with God as love. But because the traditional satisfaction and penal models of the cross make forgiveness hinge upon some sort of economic transaction between Jesus and God, they also imply some harsh images of God that do not harmonize with a God of love. They contaminate authentic divine forgiveness. Think back to our discussion on traditional theories of atonement and forgiveness in chapter 4.

In order to remain consistent with the image of a loving, compassionate, merciful, and just God, we need to rethink our ideas about forgiveness. We might want to surrender our previously held beliefs about Jesus paying God or Jesus suffering our punishment before God will forgive sin. After all, as we discussed in chapter 4, if our debt is paid, satisfied, or punished, then there's nothing left to forgive. The debt's been paid; the sin has been punished. We have God administering retribution through pay back in some form or another. So if God must have God's pound of flesh (literally God's own pound of flesh if we believe Jesus is divine), then what does that say about God? We are left with the imagery of divine forgiveness through violence and injustice that not only permeates our perceptions of God, but that also invades and influences our own behavior. Such disturbing images of God lead us to the search for more consistent models of divine forgiveness that are not founded on retaliation, retribution, or remuneration, but on the basis of creating a new relationship that extends forgiveness without the violent economics of exchange.

For example, the parable of the forgiving father in Luke 15 gives us a relational image that casts doubt on the idea of an economic transaction in order to forgive sin. The father in the story is satisfied merely with his son's return to him. He does not first demand the son repay the money frittered away on careless living. In fact, he refuses to admit to any debt on the son's part at all. He covers him in a loving, forgiving embrace and receives him into the fold.[4] A very unorthodox treatment of a son in those days to be sure. Continental philosopher and postmodern theologian, John Caputo, expresses the liberality of the father's forgiveness: "In the story of the prodigal son, the father does not sit down and calculate just how much suffering he should inflict upon his errant son for his prodigality but is prodigal with forgiveness; indeed, the idea that seeing the son suffer would in some way constitute a pay-back to the father would clearly be abhorrent to the sort of father portrayed in this story."[5]

I love the poem by William Blake, not only because it beautifully expresses my own thoughts, but also because it's good poetry. In one section of the poem "Jerusalem," he covertly chastises those who hold to traditional views of atonement, thereby compromising the nature of divine forgiveness. It's worth repeating here:

"Doth Jehovah forgive a Debt only on condition that it shall
Be payèd? Doth He forgive Pollution only on conditions of Purity?
That Debt is not forgiven! That Pollution is not forgiven!
Such is the Forgiveness of the Gods, the Moral Virtues of the
Heathen, whose tender Mercies are Cruelty. But Jehovah's
        Salvation
Is without Money and without Price, in the Continual Forgiveness
        of Sins,
In the Perpetual Mutual Sacrifice in Great Eternity. For behold!
There is none that liveth and sinneth not! And this is the Covenant
Of Jehovah: 'If you forgive one another, so shall Jehovah forgive
        you;
That He Himself may dwell among you.' (f. 61, 11. 19–26)[6]

In other words (although it's hard to top Blake's words), God forgives
without condition, without payment or satisfaction or suffering or even
repentance. This divine forgiveness actually cancels the debt. It goes
unpaid. God takes the loss. God, through Jesus, sacrifices the right to
get paid back and suffers the loss.[7] With that in mind, let's see how we
can reinterpret forgiveness, making it consistent with our image of God
as loving, compassionate, and merciful.

Forgiveness

We tend to have difficulty accepting the possibility that God forgives
sin unconditionally since, from a human viewpoint, forgiveness of such
magnitude is impossible. Many prefer to cling to human notions of
justice and forgiveness. As Caputo points out, "unaccountable" forgiveness "disturbs our sense of law and order, disrupts our sense of
economic equilibrium, undermines our desire to 'settle the score' or
'get even,' blocks our instinct to see to it that the offenders are made
to 'pay for' what they did."[8] Divine forgiveness does not keep balanced
accounts with strict records of wrongs done and retributive actions to
balance them out.

   We can think of the forgiveness of God as a paradox of the true
gift. God unconditionally gives up payment for our debt, releases us
from debt, and dismisses our debt. Thomas Aquinas comments on
the character of gift giving, which includes forgiving, by saying that
"a gift is literally a giving that can have no return, i.e., it is not given
with the intention that one be repaid and it thus connotes a gratuitous
donation."[9] Thomas continues in this vein, telling us that the basis for

such giving is love—the very love that effects our atonement in the life, death, and resurrection of Jesus.

Only unconditional, non-transactional forgiveness can be a true gift. Receiving a gift is not the same thing as earning a reward. For God to require that we earn our forgiveness or that Jesus earns God's forgiveness for us through death or merit or satisfaction does not meet the standards for a pure gift of forgiveness. If Jesus earns forgiveness for us, then forgiveness is our due in return for his death on our behalf. In that case, by forgiving us God gives us what Jesus has already earned for us. Whatever has been earned cannot be considered a gift according to Aquinas's definition—or mine for that matter.

Caputo says it best in his own words:

> So if the other is to be forgiven only after measuring up to certain conditions, if the other must earn or deserve forgiveness, then to forgive him is to give him just what he has earned, to give him his just wages. But that would not be to give a gift, but to give the other his due, to repay the labor of his repentance with the wages of forgiveness; it would be not a gift but the economy of retributive justice.[10]

Caputo asks the question: "How does God—as opposed to bankers—forgive his debtors?"[11] He takes us to Luke 18:9–14 and, in agreement with the scholarship of A. N. Wilson, interprets the story of the Pharisee and the tax collector as an illustration that serves to show us an act of divine forgiveness and divine gift-giving. In an older version of the story, the Pharisee is a good man, paying his dues to God, and the tax collector is a sinner, who does not pay his dues to God. Both men are the same before God and God forgives them on equal ground, "the sun of whose love and forgiveness rises upon both the good and the bad."[12]

According to Caputo, the emphasis, rather than remaining on the two men, falls upon God who forgives unconditionally, radically "leveling the difference between the Pharisee, who does well, and the tax collector who does not."[13] God does not concern the divine conscience with settling accounts in order to forgive. God does not get caught up in the endless cycle of economic exchange, a tit for a tat, and quid pro quo. Instead, God forgives all human beings unconditionally, with boundless, radical, overflowing, excessive, incomprehensible love. God's forgiveness is a pure gift, a pure fore-giving that gives even before we repent.[14]

The definition of the word "forgiveness" itself leads us to the conclusion that God's forgiveness is unconditional, a pardon of an offense without repayment of any sort. The Greek word for "forgiveness," *aphesis,* means to let go or to dismiss, to set free or to acquit or remit, so that the concept and act of forgiving is the relinquishing of a legitimate reason for complaint, letting go of any offense and the right to demand retribution.[15]

Yet, to ease some of our discomfort, forgiveness does not imply a state of amnesia in which the offense is treated as if it never happened. Instead, forgiveness seeks to restore a relationship in spite of an offense. Although the forgiveness given as a result of Jesus' work of atonement does not entail an economic transaction of any sort between Father and Son, the gift of forgiveness is nonetheless costly.[16] The New Testament story of the forgiving father in Luke 15 hints at the excessive nature of forgiveness. The father is willing to suffer the pain from the wrong done to him by his son and still offer forgiveness. He does not demand that his son return his inheritance to the father, nor that the son beg the family's pardon. Instead he prepares a banquet for his son. Forgiveness, as this father knows, is not merely a matter of words spoken, "I forgive you," or of an embrace given. "It is a creative act, costly and achieved only by the output of energy. It means thinking nothing about one's rights or about abstract justice, but surrendering one's self-concern altogether. It means absorbing the wrong instead of retaliating; giving, and not demanding any *quid pro quo.*"[17] In other words, the father's forgiveness has cost him a great deal. But even so, this father willingly forgave his son. Why? Because, out of deep love for his son, the father desired the reconciliation and the restoration of the relationship.

With Reconciliation

Forgiveness and reconciliation are not the same thing. We cannot reconcile with someone unless we first forgive them, but we don't have to reconcile in order to forgive. Forgiveness first; reconciliation second; restoration third. We can see this in 2 Corinthians 5:19 that says, in Christ, God "was reconciling the world to himself." How did God do that? The rest of the verse tells us: "by not counting their trespasses against them." In other words, God works to reconcile us by first forgiving us.

The Bible tells us that our sin caused a horrific and unfathomable chasm between God and humanity so that our relationship with God is profoundly damaged. Nonetheless, the forgiveness of God reaches out and embraces all of us, even the worst of us. Such boundless love and unexpected forgiveness in the face of our own sin and guilt reveal, as in a mirror, the depth of that guilt. When we expect retribution and receive redemption in its place, we are better able to realize the extent of our sin. Consequently, we repent so that reconciliation and restoration can take place between God and us.[18]

Fortunately, God desires above all else to reconcile with us and to restore our relationship to one of unity and love. The writer of Ephesians describes God's reconciliation. He says that Jesus "is our peace; in his flesh he has made both groups into one and has broken down the dividing wall, that is, the hostility between us" (2:14). At one point in time, we were far away from God and from our neighbors. There was a great distance between us that we could not cross. But the life, death, and resurrection of Jesus have brought us near again—to God and to each other. A separation no longer exists because God in Jesus has broken down the walls that divide us. God has taken away the hostility that kept us apart. How did this reconciliation happen? God first forgave us (2:13–14).

Colossians 1:20 says that reconciling us through Jesus *pleased* God! It satisfied God. It wasn't the horrific, violent death of an innocent man that satisfied God. Rather, it was the love of Jesus, revealed in his life and death, as he sought God's forgiveness on our behalf and effected the way toward reconciliation with all things in heaven and on earth. That pleased God. In fact, God's reconciliation with all creation through forgiveness enables us to stand before God in purity and enter into at-one-ment with God and with each other. That satisfies God.

A real-life story may help drive the point home. On January 21, 1995, international investment banker, Azim Khamisa got a phone call delivering the devastating news that his only son, twenty-year-old Tariq, was shot to death while delivering pizzas. Tariq was a college student whose dreams to become a journalist would never come to fruition. His killer? A fourteen-year-old boy named Tony Hicks, who was trying to impress his fellow gang members. Tony was a young, angry teenager who lived with his grandfather, hung out with a violent gang, and who fell victim to societal forces. So, that same night, Ples Felix, Tony's grandfather, received the devastating news that his grandson had shot and killed an innocent man. Both families, from very different walks of life, thrown together unwillingly by an act of random violence; both completely grief stricken over the senseless loss of Tariq's life and the dim future Tony's life now held.

Azim fell into such despair and depression that he thought about ending his life. He soon realized, however, that allowing circumstances to destroy his own life would make him a victim of the shooting as well. He fought the urge to blame Tony, who he believed was a victim of society. Azim also refused to blame Tony's grandfather, who raised him. So rather than strike out against Tony and his grandfather, Azim, (a Muslim), reached out in forgiveness to Ples (a Christian) and Tony. Azim transformed his grief with forgiveness and his anger with compassion. With Ples, he visited Tony in jail and offered his forgiveness, setting in motion the process of healing and restoration. Through Azim's unselfish act of forgiveness, Tony broke down in tears of remorse and repentance. Azim offered Tony a job and then offered the hand of friendship to Tony's grandfather, Ples (they are still very close friends). The reconciliation among Azim, Ples, and Tony has led to the development of the "Tariq Khamisa Foundation"—an organization committed to "stopping children from killing children."[19] Ples and Azim work together to promote the vision of forgiveness and reconciliation—a vision God extends to us. In forgiving us and reconciling with us, God has entrusted to us the message of reconciliation. "We are ambassadors for Christ," and God is appealing to us to spread the word of forgiveness and reconciliation to all who will listen (2 Cor. 5:20). In fact, we might say that we all belong to the "God in Christ Foundation," and we're looking for new members.

IN A NUTSHELL

One of the most beautiful pictures of justice and forgiveness we see in Scripture is the Year of Jubilee in Leviticus 25:8–17. It occurred every fifty years and memorialized the time of the Hebrew people's slavery in Egypt. When God's people suffered severe affliction, oppression, and abuse, when hope of rescue and redemption from their plight had died, God moved on their behalf and through Moses, liberated them from slavery and brought them out of the land of Egypt into a new land.

After living in the land awhile, those folks who found themselves in debt and couldn't pay it often sold their inherited lands or even went into slavery themselves in order to pay what they owed. But, God instituted the Year of Jubilee in order to memorialize their freedom and to make sure no Hebrew ever suffered under the yoke of slavery or lost their inherited land permanently. Every fifty years would be a year of liberation for them. Slaves were set free and lands sold due to debt returned to the original owner. It was a time of redemption, of rescue, of liberation through the forgiveness of debt. A time of healing from sickness, setting people free, preaching good news, and restoring shalom to the land. In fact, the Year of Jubilee began on the Day of Atonement—the day in which God forgave the sins of all the people.

Interestingly, the very first thing Jesus says about the reason for his coming points us to the Year of Jubilee. While in Nazareth, he stood up in the synagogue and read from the scroll of the prophet Isaiah, saying,

> "The Spirit of the Lord is upon me,
>   because he has anointed me to bring good news to the poor.
> He has sent me to proclaim release to the captives
>   and recovery of sight to the blind, to let the oppressed go free,
> to proclaim the year of the Lord's favor."
>
> Luke 4:18–19

Interestingly, he closes the book and sits down before reading the rest of the passage that says, "and the day of vengeance of our God" (Isa. 61:2). God's vengeance has no place in the Year of Jubilee or in the salvation of the people. So we see that Jesus conceives of his mission in terms of the Jubilee and he begins his ministry not by preaching hell-fire and damnation to the downcast and poor, but by proclaiming the Year of Jubilee in which debts are forgiven or remitted, and the people start with a clean slate; people receive healing, and liberation. This speaks volumes about God's plans for us. Jesus teaches that God forgives debtors their debts, out of mercy, without repayment. With God, every year is the Year of Jubilee.

As we discussed earlier, the New Testament story of the forgiving father in Luke 15 hints at the sacrificial nature of forgiveness. As custom dictated, the father could have demanded much from his son as compensation for the sin against him and for the squandered inheritance. Moreover, the parable takes place in a society that highly values personal honor. The prodigal son had so dishonored his father that some sort of recompense was expected. But the father sacrificed both his honor and his right to seek retribution against his son. He truly forgave him and in doing so gave up the restoration of his honor and of his purse in favor of the restoration of the relationship with this child. As a gift, forgiveness involves selfless sacrifice—the sacrifice of giving up on receiving something in return. In forgiving sin, God in Christ sacrificed receiving the debt we owed God for sin.[20]

God's sacrificial and redemptive justice enacted through forgiveness reveals the nature of atonement as "at-one-ment." Because God forgives us, God opens the way for reconciliation and restoration. The chasm that separated us from God no longer exists. God has removed the boundaries and closed the gap so we can enter into the presence of God, at-one with God in a loving relationship. God answered Jesus's prayer in the garden of Gethsemane that we be one with God just as Jesus is one with God (John 17:11). No atoning bloody sacrifice that appeases an angry God, no punishment of an innocent man that absolves us from guilt. In fact, according to Rita Nakashima Brock, violence never saves, never restores, but only creates something worse, something violent in return.[21] Rather, the restoration of relationship through the power of forgiveness describes our at-one-ment with God. I argue that Jesus did not "make" atonement for our sins; he "did" at-one-ment through forgiving, restorative justice.

In fact, the costly sacrifice of Jesus continues "doing" at-one-ment through unending forgiveness, the repetition of forgiveness that we too are called to "do." Peter asked, "how many times should I forgive?"[22] The answer amounted to saying—repeatedly. Always. Continually. Don't stop. Keep on doing it. Only through loving forgiveness does reconciliation occur. Only through loving forgiveness does at-one-ment with God and others transform a violent world. In so doing, we follow in the footsteps of Jesus' dis-arming love with continual sacrifices of forgiveness, repetitions of reconciliation that dis-arm others. Through the Spirit of God we respond with loving living, not out of an economy of violence for violence, but out of love.

God's imagined violence toward Christ begets human violence toward one another. Rather than a repetition of violence that only begets violence, we embrace the repetition of love that begets love. I dare to dream of a world dis-armed by the reconciling repetition of God's forgiving justice re-enacted in the lives of Christ followers throughout the world. Such extravagant forgiveness, reconciliation, and love serve justice and truly satisfy God. In other words, to serve justice through forgiveness satisfies God—God is satisfied through forgiveness by which justice and mercy redeem creation and fulfill God's promise of restoration for all.[23]

7

The Costly Sacrifice

Nothing but the Blood

For I desire steadfast love and not sacrifice,
the knowledge of God rather than burnt offerings.

—Hosea 6:6

"'To love him with all the heart, and with all the understanding, and
with all the strength,' and 'to love one's neighbor as oneself,'—this is
much more important than all burnt offerings and sacrifices."

—Mark 12:33

Hallow the body as a temple to comeliness
and sanctify the heart as a sacrifice to love;
love recompenses the adorers.

—Khalil Gibran, "Beauty"

TRADITIONAL SACRIFICE

We use the term "sacrifice" to talk about Jesus' death on the cross. Even
though blood sacrifices are far removed from our everyday life, without
cultural counterpart whatsoever, the concept profoundly influences
our theology of the crucifixion today. When we apply the term to the
cross, however, it usually suggests Jesus' need to appease God for sin
through suffering our punishment, to satisfy God so God can forgive,
or to win us back to God. Used in that way, the word "sacrifice" at best
alludes to a transaction or an economic exchange between God and
Jesus. At worst, it hints at the need to manipulate God so that God
will forgive sin and save us from eternal punishment. So our traditional
language about salvation in Jesus turns on the economic, transactional
notions that God wouldn't or couldn't forgive and save without blood
changing hands. It cultivates the idea of buying off God, of giving God
something dead and bloody before God will forgive and save us.[1] In
other words, we don't automatically have God's favor. God needs to be
won over, or worse, bought, through the sacrifice of an innocent life.

While discussing blood sacrifice with a critically minded student,
she shook her head and put her thoughts on the topic into words: "You

113

mean to tell me that God must have blood and death to be pacified enough to forgive us? How is that different from the human sacrifices to Molech that the Bible condemns? And what does God want with a dead bird or with a slaughtered ox, or even a dead son for that matter? It's like God says, 'ok, I'll be able to forgive you if you kill something first. And make it really bloody, please.'"

Important questions to ask. If we hold to the idea of sacrifice as merely the external, literal taking of a life, then we are saying that God needs or wants or requires a bloody death of an innocent man in order to save us. But by thinking in this manner we miss the point of the sacrifice altogether. And worse, we portray God as an angry, vengeful, bloodthirsty, tribal deity, much like the gods so prevalent in the surrounding cultures during biblical times. I don't think that is the message we want to communicate, even though we do so without thinking about it. We believe that God is loving, compassionate, and merciful. So how, then, can we interpret Jesus' sacrifice and still express God in those beautiful terms?

The biblical witness quite clearly talks about Jesus' death as a sacrifice. But so was his life. In fact, Jesus offered an extremely costly sacrifice on our behalf, for our salvation. And his sacrifice greatly pleased God, but most likely not in the way we've been taught to think about it. We need to see sacrifice from a different, yet biblical, perspective in order to find the answers to these questions. Let's begin with a definition.

SACRIFICE IS . . .

We bandy about the word "sacrifice" quite frequently, often without thinking about it. When my husband and I decided to have children, for instance, we *sacrificed* a lot for me to stay at home with them. We didn't have new cars or take lavish vacations or even hire babysitters. In other words, we made a commitment to sacrifice certain material comforts in order to serve our kids in the way we thought best for them. My childhood friend Cindy grew up in a one parent home. Her mother worked three different jobs in order to support her. I spent a lot of time at Cindy's house and remember her mother coming home from one job completely exhausted only in order to change her clothes and head off to the next job. I don't know how she did it, but she *sacrificed* having a life of her own so her daughter could live hers comfortably. Both of us expressed our devotion to serving our children in different, yet fully valid ways. Both of us set our lives apart from other more self-serving activities in order to provide for our children.

Moreover, we describe the commitment of men and women who serve in the military as a sacrifice. They *sacrifice* their lives in the service of our country. In other words, the word "sacrifice" comes into play when we want to express some sort of selfless, freely given service or gift. So it should come as no surprise when the followers of Jesus describe his life and death as a sacrifice. By dedicating himself to God and to us with unselfish love, Jesus *sacrificed* his life for us. He gave up living according to his own desires; he gave up a long life ending with a peaceful, natural death. And according to Philippians 2:6–8, he gave up his place as God's equal in order to live with us as a man who suffered hunger and thirst, insults and rejection, and physical and emotional pain. He probably came down with colds in the winter, had toothaches from improper dental care, and suffered headaches and fatigue, all before he had to endure a painful death on a Roman cross.

But what, exactly, does it mean to say Jesus *sacrificed* his life for us? The term "sacrifice" comes from the Latin word *sacrificium*, a combination of the words *sacer*, which means "to set apart" or "to consecrate" and *facere,* which means "to make." Taken together as the word "sacrifice," they point to a religious act in which something in the common, secular realm is consecrated for use in the sacred or holy realm.[2] In fact, we can translate it as "making something holy." For example, in the days when the Hebrew people built the first tabernacle under the direction of Moses, they took common materials like wood and gold and made them into instruments for use in worship. After crafting them into objects, however, they consecrated them to God—they set them apart from secular use for sacred use in the tabernacle. They became holy instruments. Not only did the Hebrews consecrate certain objects for holy purposes, they also set apart specific individuals such as priests. And applied to Jesus, we can say that Jesus set his life apart from his own desires in order to serve God and us. Some might also say that God set Jesus apart for a very specific purpose—to reconcile us to God.

IN THE OLD TESTAMENT

When we hear the word "sacrifice" we often think about the Old Testament system in which priests slaughtered animals and sprinkled their blood on the altar. But the practice of sacrifice didn't begin with Israel.

For centuries prior to God giving the Hebrew people the Law, along with specific instructions for performing sacrifices, Middle Eastern peoples were offering bloody sacrifices to their gods. These sacrifices were transactions, a way of manipulating their gods to bless them with good crops, fertility, wealth, and position. By offering food or blood or flesh, ancient people hoped to pacify, appease, and motivate their gods to show favor to them. In fact, some Semitic cultures actually sacrificed their infant children to the god Molech in order to appease him and gain his blessings for prosperity.

As products of these surrounding cultural beliefs, some Old Testament writers were content enough to express sacrifice in terms of feeding or appeasing God, or as a substitute for the sinner.[3] So for centuries, Israel's worship centered on ideas of sacrifice as external rituals that placated God for their sin. And as we read the Bible today, we too often interpret the Old Testament sacrifices as a means to appease God or as if somehow the animal received the punishment meant for the Hebrew people.

But we see another interpretation of the theology of sacrifice when we read other Old Testament writers. They focused on the blood sacrifice as a way to cleanse the sinner and the earthly tabernacle. For example, the author of Leviticus describes the blood sacrifice on the Day of Atonement as one that cleanses the people from their sin (Lev. 16:29–30). In fact, the emphasis of the sacrifices in Leviticus largely focuses on the idea of cleansing and purifying. Moreover, biblical scholar Jacob Milgrom agrees with the Levitican author and contends that the Hebrew sacrifices had more to do with purification, cleansing, and forgiveness, and nothing at all to do with substitutionary punishment.[4]

When we read about the sacrifices in Leviticus, for example, we very often see them connected with "atonement." The word we most often translate as "atonement" or "to atone" comes from the Hebrew word *kippur* (*kpr*), which carries with it a deeply significant meaning that unfortunately gets lost in translation. The word *kippur* means "to cover over," "to make disappear," "to wipe away," "to cleanse," or "to purify." The blood of the sacrificial animal, then, cleanses the people from sin, wipes it away, and in so doing, purifies them. To make atonement for sin (*kippur*), then, means to wipe out sin through purification. For example, when Moses or the priests sprinkled the blood on the people or on the altar (see Exod. 24:8 and Lev. 8), they were cleansed and purified, their sins gone. The word *kippur* is sometimes translated as "forgive" or "absolve," revealing to us quite a profound symbolism

(Deut. 21:8; Pss. 65:4; 78:38; 79:9; Ezek. 16:63). Cleansing or purification is synonymous with forgiveness.[5]

So the Hebrew people offered sacrifices to God as a ritual that symbolized the purification from their sin and the forgiveness that follows. It had nothing to do with appeasing God or with the punishment of the animal as a substitute for the people. They either weren't aware or they lost sight of the fact that the external ritual actually symbolized the internal offering of the sacrificer's life to God. Their sacrifices became a hypocritical show of piety without the inward heart condition to back it up. As we'll see in Scripture, the sacrifices meant to please God ended up angering God instead. Later the prophets came along and tried to transform the ideas surrounding sacrifice from an external act of blood shedding and burnt offerings into what they thought God desired them to be in the first place—a symbol for an internal condition of the heart and an external show of devotion.

TRUE SACRIFICE: AN OUTWARD SYMBOL OF AN INWARD REALITY

While the sacrificial system in the Old Testament served the ancient Hebrew community and reflected the religious sensibilities of the surrounding cultures, it seems that the people misinterpreted God's intentions. They focused more on the external nature of the sacrifices and missed the significance of the symbolism lying behind the act. The rituals were intended to reflect an inward heart condition that manifested itself in their outward behavior with acts of charity and compassion. With hearts and minds totally devoted to God, symbolized by their sacrificial offerings, the people would naturally act in ethical ways. But they didn't. They were offering their sacrifices and then living their lives as if God never existed, missing the point of their acts of worship in the temple. In fact, the Hebrew people missed the point so drastically that the prophets spoke out against their sacrifices. The outside ritual didn't correspond with the inward purity the sacrifices were supposed to symbolize.

Proverbs 21:3 expresses this sentiment: "to do righteousness and justice is more acceptable to the LORD than sacrifice." In an even more direct passage, Jeremiah speaks for God saying that God never commanded the Israelites to offer sacrifices and burnt offerings. Instead, God commanded them to obey God's voice, to walk in the way God showed them (Jer. 7:21– 24). But they did not. They offered sacrifices and then lived as they pleased, forgetting God had called them to a life of active devotion and obedience.

We have the same idea expressed in Psalm 50:12–13 where God speaks: "If I were hungry, I would not tell you, for the world and all that is in it is mine. Do I eat the flesh of bulls, or drink the blood of goats?" Of course the answer is no.[6] God doesn't want the flesh of their sacrifices; God wants the love and obedience that the sacrifices symbolized. The psalmist also tells us that God doesn't desire merely sacrifice and burnt offerings, but prefers instead that individuals please God by doing God's will (Ps. 40:6–8). In another passage God tells Hosea that loyalty and knowledge of the divine please God more than burnt offerings (Hos. 6:6). In other words, blood sacrifices in themselves aren't the things that please God.

In fact, Isaiah informs the Israelites that God will look favorably toward those who are "humble and contrite in spirit" and who obey God's word. Obviously the people weren't offering their sacrifices with the inward heart condition that pleases God because Isaiah goes on to say that "whoever slaughters and ox is like one who kills a human being . . . whoever presents a grain offering, like one who offers swine's blood" (a big no-no by the way!) (66:2–3). In other words, without the heart conditions of humility and devotion, ritual sacrifices meant nothing, and actually, they were an abomination to God.

By this point you might be thinking, "Just a second here! Then what do we do with the verses in Exodus and Leviticus that give specific instructions about offering sacrifices, all supposedly from the mouth of God?" We can deal with this supposed inconsistency in Scripture if we take into consideration the message of the prophets about true sacrifice. When God gave the command to offer the blood of animals, the people lost sight of the true meaning of the sacrifices. Apropos to the surrounding culture, they may have mistakenly believed that the external ritual pleased God rather than the most important aspect of sacrifice—the one the blood sacrifices symbolized—the inward condition of the heart dedicated to God. So when God denies ever commanding the Israelites to sacrifice animals, God may be using a bit of rhetorical hyperbole in order to get a point across about the true meaning of sacrifice, that is, an inward surrender and obedience to God (Jer. 7:21–23). God rejected their sacrifices because they offered them without a heart of love and submission toward God that the sacrifices symbolized. In other words, they were being hypocritical.

God then goes on to tell the people that the true sacrifice is obedience. The same set of verses from Psalm 50 that we saw above continues to tell us what God considers a true sacrifice: "Offer to God a sacrifice of thanksgiving, and pay your vows to the Most High. Call on me in the day of trouble; I will deliver you, and you shall glorify me" (50:14). In a psalm attributed to David who had just stolen Bathsheba from her husband in order to have sex with her, David laments and asks for forgiveness. He knows he could offer all sorts of external sacrifices for his sin but he also knows the heart of God and that God's desire for true sacrifice doesn't include spilling the blood of an animal. He says, "for you have no delight in sacrifice; if I were to give a burnt offering, you would not be pleased. The sacrifice acceptable to God is a broken spirit; a broken and contrite heart, O God, you will not despise" (Ps. 51:16–17). He knows that the true sacrifice, the one that pleases God, begins in the heart and ends with a life given totally to God.

The prophet Isaiah speaks for God about the same issue. Decrying the sinful, hypocritical actions of the priestly rulers who pretend righteousness but disobey God in reality, he laments, "'What are your multiplied sacrifices to me?' says the LORD. 'I have enough of burnt offerings of rams, and the fat of fed cattle. And I take no pleasure in the blood of bulls, lambs, or goats. . . . Bring your offerings to me no longer, incense is an abomination to me.'" Instead, "wash yourselves, make yourselves clean; remove the evil of your deeds from my sight. Cease to do evil, learn to do good; seek justice, reprove the ruthless; defend the orphan, plead for the widow" (Isa. 1:11, 13, 16–17 NASB). Isaiah's message reminds us that God doesn't desire the external ritual of shedding blood, but rather the life set apart, given to God for God's purposes—taking care of those in need, seeking justice, doing good. All these actions express the internal heart condition of a sacrificial, life-giving commitment to God.

Micah 6:6–8 gives us one of the most beautiful expressions of true sacrifice, the sacrifice God desires. The prophet announces God's judgment upon the rulers in Judah and Israel for their injustice toward the people. The priests offer sacrifices to God yet they sin greatly against God by oppressing the inhabitants of the land through bribery, cheating, violence, and exploitation of power. In protest over their actions, Micah reproves them, saying: "With what shall I come before the LORD, and bow myself before God on high? Shall I come before him with burnt offerings, with calves a year old? Will the LORD be pleased with thousands of rams, with ten thousands of rivers of oil? Shall I give my firstborn for my transgression, the fruit of my body for the sin of my soul? He has told you, O mortal, what is good; and what does the LORD require of you but to do justice, and to love kindness, and to walk humbly with your God?"[7] Again, the prophet expresses that the true sacrifice is to obey God by doing God-type acts on behalf of others. Throughout the Bible, then, we see that the prophets rejected the sacrificial system, revealing its symbolic nature and God's desire for a deep inward devotion. This idea continues into the New Testament, and is especially revealed in the life, teachings, and death of Jesus.

Jesus and the True Sacrifice

What we've seen so far in the Old Testament is that God tried and tried to get a message across. First God used what the people were familiar with—the sacrificial system in the Old Testament. They didn't fully grasp that, so God sent the prophets along to tell them they had it wrong and to teach them about the kind of sacrifice God really wanted. They still didn't get it. I can sympathize with God here. I would often warn my boys to stop throwing a ball in the living room by shouting down to them from upstairs. After hearing the ball bounce off a wall for the second or third time, I would finally yell down the stairs, "do I have to come down there?!" And usually, I had to go down the stairs and take the ball away. Well, finally God said the same thing to people in Jesus' day: "Do I have to come down there and show you?!" The answer was yes. Only God didn't' come down and take the ball away. God came down and played ball, so to speak. God, in Jesus, came down to earth and lived among us, trying to teach us the way of true sacrifice (Heb. 1:1–3).

In the Gospels, Jesus himself refutes the sacrificial system and its rules governing external behavior. He broke the law when he shared a meal with unclean sinners (Mark 2:16–17) and picked grain to eat on the Sabbath (Matt. 12:1–7). When the Pharisees confronted him with his "sin," which would require a sacrifice offered under the law, Jesus rebuked them, saying that they had no idea about the nature of true sacrifice, for if they had, they would have known what it meant when God said, "I desire mercy and not sacrifice." He communicates the same idea in Mark 12:32–34. Here, Jesus reinterprets the law with his teaching on the greatest commandments—love God and neighbor. An unnamed scribe comes to Jesus and voices his agreement, saying, "you are right, Teacher; you have truly said . . . to 'love [God] with all the heart and with all the understanding, and with all the strength,' and 'to love one's neighbor as oneself,'—this is much more important than all the whole burnt offerings and sacrifices." Jesus praises the scribe for getting it right.

The book of Hebrews also refutes the effectiveness of the external sacrificial system and tells us that it was just a symbol pointing to the sacrifice of Jesus yet to come (Heb. 9:8–9). Echoing Psalm 40, the writer informs the readers that God neither desires nor takes pleasure in blood sacrifices. The better sacrifice that Jesus made was obedience, doing God's will and selflessly giving his life in obedient submission to God. Jesus lived out his life-giving devotion to God by taking care of the sick, feeding the hungry, and speaking out for widows, orphans, and lepers. So we see that true sacrifice includes not just external rituals but total devotion to God.

The Sacrifice of Devotion

We see the inherent quality of sacrifice as devotion and obedience when we look at the meaning of the Hebrew word for sacrifice. *Korban* (*Corban*), commonly translated "offering" or "sacrifice," has no real equivalent in English. So we lose some its true meaning in translation. Unfortunately, our translation of the word often leads us to think of a person bringing something to God in order to satisfy or appease. We somehow think that God not only requires our measly gifts, but also that God is satisfied with them or condescends to forgive our sin because of them.

As if God requires our gifts. God is not enriched by our gifts! So what does the word *Korban* mean in the Hebrew and how does it help us know the character of true sacrifice? The root word actually means "to come near" or "to draw close," in this case, to God. In every step of the process the people brought sacrificial offerings in order to show that in their hearts and minds they desired nothing more than to have a close, intimate relationship with God. In drawing near to God the people come close enough to touch, see, and know God.[8]

The blood sacrifices also symbolized the desire of a person's heart to find union with God—which goes along well with the meaning of "offering" as "to draw near to God." These sacrificial offerings were not given to appease God, but to provide the people with the opportunity to unite themselves with God. One rabbi comments, "Let no one think, therefore, that God requires offerings to feed or appease Him. The Eternal One has no needs that man can satisfy—no needs at all, for everything is His and nothing is beyond His power!"[9] Instead, according to the rabbi, purification by blood translated into purification by giving a person's life to God, which the blood merely symbolized. Blood sacrifice points not to death, but to life. Just as the blood is the life, so the blood symbolizes the giving of life, "a symbol of God's inward purifying and regenerating baptism by the forgiveness of sins"[10] So let's discuss the blood and its meaning for true sacrifice.

WHAT'S BLOOD GOT TO DO WITH IT?
BLOOD IS THE LIFE!

It's written into our liturgies and claimed in our prayers. We sing glorious hymns of praise about it, and we hear it preached from pulpits in churches across the world. What am I talking about? "Nothing but the Blood of Jesus."

> What can wash away my sin?
> Nothing but the blood of Jesus.
> What can make me whole again?
> Nothing but the blood of Jesus.

I always prayed the blood of Jesus over my four boys every day before they went off to school in the morning. I invoked it like it was a talisman against the attacks of the devil or a force field that would supernaturally protect them from harm. But is it? What does that mean? How do we actually apply the blood of Jesus to our lives? We don't have the physical blood to smear all over us, to cover us like a blanket of protection. In fact, I don't think the actual blood of Jesus ever washed over anyone at all, literally speaking.

So what do we mean when we sing, preach, praise, and invoke the blood of Jesus? What's blood got to do with Jesus anyway? And what does it have to do with a saving sacrifice? Let's begin our search for the significance of the blood in order to give a more complete picture of its relevance for us today.

Blood and the Bible

Leviticus 17:11explains blood as the life force. In this verse we are told that "the life of the flesh is in the blood, and I have given it to you on the altar to make atonement for your souls; for it is the blood by reason of the life that makes atonement" (NASB). This means that the flesh lives only because the blood gives it life. No blood, no life. Blood, therefore, symbolizes life. In fact, medieval Jewish rabbi, Rashi, comments that interpreting the blood as a symbol for life is a well-known Jewish tradition that goes back literally centuries.[11]

Additionally, in the Hebrew sacrificial system we see that the blood of animals somehow atoned for sin. God required the blood *because* the blood is life. Blood, therefore, is connected with atonement as the symbol for *life*. It is the *life* (life that the blood brings) that atones for sin—the offering of life that makes atonement. Blood stands for life and represents the life given to God. That life, given to God in devotion, atones, cleanses, purifies, and brings about forgiveness of sin. *Blood* equals *life* and must be offered as atonement for sin.[12] The next question we might ask is: what is atonement?

We get the word "atonement" from the sixteenth-century Protestant reformer William Tyndale (1494–1536). He defined it literally as *at-one-ment*, to describe the double act of God's cleansing our sin and reconciling us into union with God. We often see the word "atonement" in the English translations of the Old Testament, especially in the book of Leviticus. Leviticus gives the people instructions on how to offer animal sacrifices to God. In order to atone for sin, the priest must sprinkle the blood of the lamb or goat on the altar. This sprinkling of blood, as a symbol of the offerer's life given to God, cleanses him of sin. The cleansing is analogous to forgiveness.

It's important to remember that killing the animal and sprinkling its blood on the altar to atone for sin has nothing to do with punishing the animal in place of punishing the people. It has everything to do with blood as the life force that cleanses and purifies the people. The priest kills the animal for its blood—for the *life* that the blood symbolizes. In fact the Hebrew word for "to sprinkle" is closely connected to the act of forgiveness—to sprinkle blood, then, points to the act of God forgiving sin.

For the Hebrews, the blood of an ox or goat symbolized *life* or, when offered, the giving of *life* to God. Remember the scapegoat that took the sins of the people far away on the Day of Atonement? Well, the blood of the other goat sacrificed on that same day symbolized the purification of the people and the gift of their lives to God. The blood served as an outward symbol of an inward reality—the life of the worshiper forgiven *by* God and given *to* God—set apart for God's purposes. As the worshiper offers his life, as symbolized by the blood, he is purified and stands before God forgiven, with a clean slate.[13]

The blood points to the costly nature of life and the personal investment entailed to develop and maintain close relationships with God and with others. So now whenever we read the word *life*, just know that I am talking about the *life* that is in the blood. Whenever you see the word *blood*, think "life." That will help us to understand the cross and the impact of the shed blood of Jesus.

Okay, before we move on to applying what we've seen to the life of Jesus, let's outline what we've discussed so far:

- True sacrifice is the act of setting a person apart for God's purposes, a selfless relinquishing of control in order to be used by God.
- True sacrifice is an inward condition of the heart offered to God. The Israelites performed blood sacrifices as an outward symbol of giving their own lives to God.
- The blood symbolizes the life of the worshiper given in devotion to God.
- The true sacrifice, the giving of a life in devotion to God, cleanses the worshiper from sin. We'll see how the sacrifice of Jesus cleanses us, as we read on.
- The manifestations of a true sacrifice as symbolized in the giving of blood/life are outward acts of love, kindness, mercy, justice, and compassion.

FORGIVENESS AS THE ULTIMATE SACRIFICE

When Jesus submitted to death on a cross, he bled. We see him in paintings throughout history dripping blood and bloody sweat. And because of our traditional theories of atonement, we seem to believe that nothing can satisfy God's anger but to see innocent blood flow. But that blood, the blood we sing about, include in our prayers for protection, and in our worship liturgies, symbolizes the selfless *life*

Jesus lived on our behalf. During his time on earth, while he lived as a man in the form of a servant (Phil. 2:7), Jesus revealed God to us, showed us by example how to live a God-pleasing life, exposed our deeds of darkness—the very ones that put him to death—forgave us our sin, and disarmed us with God's disarming love. A costly sacrifice indeed! All symbolized with the blood, which stands for his very life lived among us.

We might say, and we'll discuss this more in the next chapter, that the sacrifice of Jesus Christ on the cross was acceptable to God not because of the external offering of Christ's body with its dripping blood, but because of the internal disposition with which it was offered. In giving himself in death, Jesus turned over his heart, his soul, and his love to God and others. He said, "I have come to do your will, O God," revealing an inner condition of love and submission to the will of God in total self-surrender (Heb. 10:7).[14] The actions of true sacrifice reveal an inward condition of the heart that loves and pleases God (Heb. 11).[15]

But that's not all there is to it. Jesus selflessly, sacrificially gave his life to God and to others, but in doing so, as a human being he sacrificed the right to take vengeance on those who killed him, and as God he sacrificed the right to receive payback for sin. In other words, Jesus forgave sin, gave up getting paid back for the debt sin incurred, pardoned the offense without remuneration of any sort. Quite a selfless, life-giving sacrifice.

We don't usually think of forgiveness as a sacrifice. But it actually is one of the most costly, difficult, and agonizing sacrificial acts anyone can do. We know from our own experience how hard it is to forgive. We want revenge, restitution, vindication. We don't want to let an offense go unanswered or unchastised. But forgiveness won't allow that. Forgiveness means we let the offense go, sacrificing our right to exact punishment, settle the score, or balance the accounts. We give up the pleasure of getting even. We sacrifice getting paid back. I know how often I've agonized over trying to forgive someone. If they would just recognize how much they hurt me. If they would at least apologize! But forgiving means we sacrifice our desire for remorse or for an apology or even for the pleasure of telling the person off. It costs us. But we do it because God asks us to forgive those who sin against us; we do it because that's what a heart submitted to God in love and devotion does—it sacrifices self for sake of love.

We saw in chapter 6 that the story of the forgiving father in Luke 15 hints at its costly nature. If ever a father had the right to feel hurt, to take offense, and to be angry at a son, this father does. His son asked for his inheritance before the father was even dead. When I visit my mother I'll often see a piece of jewelry I like and tell her I would like that "someday." It makes her feel like I'm just waiting for her to die so I can have her possessions. The father in our parable must have felt worse—his son didn't just want a piece of jewelry, he wanted his entire inheritance right then—a younger son at that! Enough to make a father's blood boil, right? Not this father. Not only did the son get his inheritance, but he also squandered it away on loose women and intoxicating drink. When he does decide to slink home with his tail between his legs, he expects the worst. But we've seen that his father, probably a distinguished land owner, humiliates himself by running to meet his wayward son. He doesn't ask for an apology. He doesn't demand his son pay him back. He doesn't take his son over his knee and spank him or ground him for the rest of his life. He sacrifices the right to receive payback. The accounts are never balanced. The father forgives the son sacrificially.

The example of the forgiving father has a lot to teach us about sacrifice and forgiveness. 1 John. 1:7 helps explain it for us: "If we walk in the light as he himself is in the light, we have fellowship with him and the blood of Jesus his Son cleanses us from all sin" (NASB). So the blood of Jesus, or, rather, the life of Jesus given up for us, cleanses us, purifies us, from all sin. But let's take it a bit deeper. Hanging from the cross, his blood pouring out, sprinkling the ground below him, Jesus cried out, "Father forgive them, for they don't know what they are doing." Remember, the sprinkling of blood in the Old Testament connects to "forgiveness." Jesus gave his life and forgave us for ours. That forgiveness cleanses us, purifies us—just as the word *kippur* that we translate "atonement" indicates. So when we receive Jesus as savior we tap into his life, symbolized by the shedding of his blood. We receive God's forgiveness, symbolized by the sprinkling of his blood. And that forgiveness cleanses us, *kippurs* us if you will.[16]

This brings us to the verse in Hebrews that says: "without the shedding of blood there is no forgiveness." We also read in Hebrews 9:22 that "[i]ndeed, under the law almost everything is purified with blood, and without the shedding of blood there is no forgiveness of sins." Remember, the Hebrew word we translate as "to sprinkle" points to the purifying act of forgiveness. In the verse I quoted above, we who give our lives to God as a sacrifice have our hearts and consciences sprinkled and therefore washed and purified. Without giving our lives to God as a living sacrifice, we wouldn't be aware of the washing and purifying power of God's forgiveness. God's forgiving, purifying love is symbolized by the blood as an element of abundant life. The washing and purification power enables us to realize God's forgiveness. With that in mind, we might amplify and paraphrase Hebrews 9:22 and say, without the giving of your life as a living sacrifice, as symbolized in the Old Testament by the shedding of life blood, you will not understand being washed clean; you will not know the blessings of God's purifying forgiveness—a forgiveness symbolized and apprehended by the shed life-blood of Jesus. A cleansing, purifying forgiveness that Jesus prayed for from the cross. We now live our lives in that forgiveness and are at-one with God through Jesus.

OUR INNER SACRIFICE

This idea of blood sacrifice as a symbol for giving a life to God carries over into the New Testament and our life in Christ. We shouldn't take Paul too literally, as we talked about before. He was trying to reach the common people, so he took the conventional ritualistic ideas and transformed them into expressions of worship, submission, and spiritual growth. We see this clearly in Romans 12:1: "I appeal to you therefore, brothers and sisters, by the mercies of God, to present your bodies as a living sacrifice, holy and acceptable to God, which is your spiritual worship." When Paul talks about a living sacrifice, he is trans-lating the language of the Old Testament blood sacrifice from external ritual, which doesn't please God, into the internal condition of the heart, which does please God.

There is nothing in these verses about blood sacrifice. Paul puts forth the message that God wants our *lives*, not our literal blood. Remember, the blood in the Old Testament sacrificial system symbolized *life*—the lives of the worshipers offered to God. The true sacrifice, the one that God desires, is not the death of an animal with its blood smeared in the temple. No, the sacrifice God desires is symbolized by the Old Testa-ment sacrifices and is in reality a softened heart, a spirit that loves God and that offers praise and thanksgiving no matter the circumstance. This is worship! And Jesus offered this life to God *and* to us as a saving sacrifice and godly example.

Just as Jesus offered his life to the world during his entire life all the way to his death on the cross, Romans 12:1 exhorts us to offer our lives to the world on God's altar. That doesn't mean we cut our throats and sprinkle our blood on the church altar. It means we give our lives to God. We model our lives on that of Jesus. Interestingly, when we commit our lives to following Jesus, God sets us apart for God's holy purposes. We become a sacrifice—a living sacrifice set apart for God's service.

We present our entire body, mind, and soul to God and submit our lives to God. The symbolism of the blood, revealed to the ancient Hebrew people through the familiar symbolic rite of sacrificing animals, finds its fulfillment first in Jesus, who gave his life to God and for us in obedience. It then finds fulfillment in us as we tap into the cleansing blood or life of Jesus and give our own lives to God. We give our lives as a living and holy sacrifice, and by doing that, we worship God.

THE OUTWARD SIGN OF INWARD SACRIFICE

So we have sacrificed our lives upon the altar of God. How do we practically live out that sacrificial life-giving? The Bible doesn't leave us stranded with commands but no instructions. It tells us it all starts in our minds by saying, "Do not be conformed to this world, but be transformed by the renewing of your minds, so that you may discern what is the will of God—what is good and acceptable and perfect" and "let us hold fast our confession of our hope without wavering, for he who promised is faithful; and let us consider how to stimulate one another to good works" (Rom. 12:2; Heb. 10: 23–24, NASB). Basically, then, we think with the mind of God. If we have the mind of God, we will live Godly lives (1 Cor. 2:16). As we love God and others and work to spread that love around the world, we give our lives as living and holy (set apart) sacrifices to God. In so doing, our lives themselves are a form of worship. Let's see a couple of examples of sacrifice in action.

Commands from the book of Hebrews shed light on the essence of this sacrifice symbolized by the shedding of blood: "Pursue peace with everyone" (12:14); "provoke one another to love and good deeds" (10:24); love each other and entertain strangers (13:1–2); remember those unjustly imprisoned (13:3). These actions reflect sacrifices that give life rather than take life. Such selfless giving is expressed by the sacrifice of praise, sharing our possessions, and doing things that benefit others (13:15–16).[17]

Just think about the poor widow in Luke 21. She owns next to nothing, maybe just the clothes on her back. She has no one to take care of her. Yet she ambles into the temple, waits her turn in line, probably hearing all the loud clanging of coins as those in front of her drop in handfuls. Then it's her turn. She drops two small coins, equaling around a penny, into the treasury box. They probably make a tiny little tinny sound as they hit the bottom of the box. But, she gave *all* she had—just like Jesus did. And Jesus praises her for her life-giving sacrifice—I say life-giving because she could have bought food or drink with that money. Giving all she had symbolized a life given to God. Her sacrifice cost her much.

In another instance (Luke 18), two men went to the temple to offer prayer—one a Pharisee and the other a tax-gatherer. Now remember, tax-gatherers were considered the scum of the earth back then because they often cheated people and bled them dry. But this tax-gatherer, with downcast eyes, beat his chest, confessed his sin, and begged God for mercy. The Pharisee, on the other hand, prayed with self-righteous pride and thanked God that he was better than dirty swindlers like the tax-gatherer. He even told God that he gives a tenth of his income, fasts twice a week, and we can guess that he offers the required blood sacrifices, too. Well, God is not impressed. Jesus makes it clear that what counts is the giving of a life, the sincerity of a person's heart toward God. Love counts. Jesus praised the man with the contrite spirit, the one who sacrificed pride and self-esteem and came humbly, and I dare say lovingly, before God. That's the nature of true sacrifice.

Ok, one more—although there are many more. You've all heard about the rich young ruler (Mark 10:17–27). He wanted to inherit eternal life. Jesus didn't tell him to sacrifice a lamb or an ox in order to procure God's forgiveness. No. Jesus told him to sell all he had and give it to the poor. He told the man to sacrifice his life's work in order to take care of the poor. That's a costly sacrifice for someone with a lot of money. Can you see Donald Trump giving away everything he owns in order to follow God? I'm not saying God requires everyone to give away their wealth or that wealth keeps a person from intimacy with God. But wealth is the sacrifice Jesus asked this particular rich man to make in order to show his heart was completely God's. He couldn't do it. I wonder if the sacrifice was just too costly. If his heart belonged to something other than to God. And we have seen the sacrifice God requires—our heart and mind and soul (Matt. 22:37–40;

Luke 18:18–27). In other words, the greatest sacrifice is to lay down our lives, to sacrifice our lives to God. We experience a mystical sort of death. We die daily as Paul tells us—daily because sometimes we have to keep reminding ourselves of the sacrifice we've made in giving our hearts totally over to God (1 Cor. 15:31).

The New Testament describes the continual process of mystical death in the words of the apostle Paul who says, "I die daily." In another well-known passage, the mystical death is further explained: "I have been crucified with Christ; and it is no longer I who live, but it is Christ who lives in me. And the life I now live in the flesh I live by faith in the Son of God, who loved me and gave himself for me" (Gal. 2:19–20). Now we don't actually nail ourselves to crosses and hang until dead. Of course not. Death, like shedding blood, is symbolic for the giving of our lives to God. We give up living our way in order to live the way Jesus lived. Through the sacrificial offering of our lives, we offer our entire life, physically, mentally, and spiritually to God. Again, a costly sacrifice indeed.

Philippians tells us the reason for such a sacrificial way of life: "I want to know Christ and the power of his resurrection and the sharing of his sufferings by becoming like him in his death, if somehow I may attain the resurrection from the dead" (3:10–11). So we sacrifice our lives to God, in the Romans 12:1 sense of the term, so that we may know God and be restored to God forever. Philippians also exhorts us to "do nothing from selfishness or empty conceit, but with humility of mind let each of you regard one another as more important than himself; do not merely look out for your own interests, but also for the interests of others. Have this attitude in yourselves which was also in Christ Jesus" (Phil. 2:3–5 NASB). A life of sacrifice, therefore, is a life that cares for others and treats others with love as we "bear one another's burdens and thus fulfill the law of Christ" (Gal. 6:2 NASB). We "make" (*facere*) our lives "set apart" (*sacer*) for God's purposes. It's a life just like Jesus' who made a very costly sacrifice by asking God to forgive us our sins (Luke 5:17–26; 7:36–50; 23:34; John 8:11).

Our exploration into the atonement so far has raised some very important questions. If Jesus wasn't punished for our sin, if his death didn't somehow satisfy God's honor, if God didn't require Jesus to pay the debt for our sin in order to forgive, then what did Jesus actually accomplish on the cross? How are we "saved"? Read on. The next two chapters will present an alternative theory of atonement built upon what we've discussed so far.

8

Re-Tuning At-one-ment

In Christ, God was reconciling the world to himself, not counting their trespasses against them . . . .

—2 Corinthians 5:19

He who understands the cross aright—this is the opinion of the reformers—understands the Bible, he understands Jesus Christ.

—Emil Brunner, *The Mediator*

God is not revealed in the New Testament as an infinite Shylock demanding his pound of flesh before he will exercise mercy.

—W. T. Conner, *The Gospel of Redemption*

Our discussion of forgiveness and the connections between "blood" and "life" leads us to other tough questions. Let's assume that divine justice hinges on mercy and that God forgives all of us, before we repent, without the need for some sort punishment or payback or satisfaction. Yet, by dying on the cross Jesus gave himself as a costly sacrifice and saved us. But how was his death a sacrifice? What exactly happened when Jesus died on the cross? What did he accomplish?

We need to remember that when we speak of the cross or the passion event (as some label it), we really include the incarnation as a whole. In other words, when we discuss salvation and the salvific nature of Jesus' sacrifice, we mean to say that the sacrifice makes up the entirety of his life, from the manger to the grave to the resurrection to the ascension. So let's pull it all together and construct an alternative theory of atonement that incorporates all of the above questions and then some. We'll use various metaphors and focus on God as loving and nonviolent. We'll include true forgiveness, restorative justice, incarnation, the blood of Jesus, sacrifice, re-creation (or transformation), and at-one-ment.

WHAT DID JESUS ACCOMPLISH? THE BIBLICAL LANDSCAPE

The Hermeneutical Hurdle

Theologians and biblical scholars throughout the ages have constructed a myriad of theories about what Jesus may or may not have accomplished on the cross. The Bible itself uses many metaphors to explain the work of Jesus on our behalf. As we discussed in chapter 2, these historical metaphors emerged out of the everyday experiences of the common people during those times. So the problem with interpretation occurs when we try to take any of these metaphors literally or when we try to apply them according to our own, contemporary understanding of the language without examining the culture in which the metaphors arose. Phrases such as "Jesus paid the debt sin incurred" or "Jesus bore the punishment for my sin" or "Jesus paid the ransom for me" are metaphorical ways of speaking about an event that's otherwise very hard to explain. Think about it. In what manner do you explain, even to yourself, how the life and death and resurrection of someone who lived over two thousand years ago can save us today? In fact, that question itself kept me from becoming a Christian before I turned twenty-six. I didn't understand what the fuss was all about until a friend of my mother's told me that my sin ruined my relationship with God. She said my sin had to be punished, so God sent Jesus to suffer the penalty for it so I could be restored to God. Yes, the metaphor of the penal substitution theory of atonement along with the scary terrors of hell brought me into the kingdom of God! It takes all kinds of stories to reach all kinds of people. Still, let's keep in mind that as we talk about what Jesus accomplished on the cross, we are talking metaphorically. And most of the time we are using metaphors from a tradition and culture separated from us by over two thousand years, across one or more continents, and through two or three different languages. I call these interpretive separations the "hermeneutical hurdles."

Even though our traditional theories of atonement have successfully furthered the kingdom of God, we have seen in the first chapter that they may also have contributed to the violence and abuses condoned and committed by the church for at least the last 1,700 years. While earlier Christians thought that penal substitution and satisfaction theories perfectly expressed salvation through Christ, some of us now believe these theories have their dangers. Actually the theories are a bit like asbestos. Way back in the middle of the nineteenth century until sometime in the 1940s, we hailed asbestos as a wonderful substance for insulation. We used it for everything imaginable from pipe insulation, to brake shoe padding, to fire retardant in a plethora of products, to flocking for our Christmas trees. We thought it was great stuff. But we now know that asbestos is a major cause of cancer. In December 2003 the government banned its use completely.[1] We found out the hard way that its extreme danger to the human body far outweighs its benefits. We could say the same thing about penal and satisfaction theories of atonement. The implicit violence of the theories, and the danger that the violence presents to the world, far outweigh their benefits as metaphors for explaining salvation. The inconsistencies and tyrannical image of God they espouse have turned untold thousands away from the love that God offers through Jesus. Although I can't prove this with absolute certainty, the history of Christian violence seems to bear witness that for centuries these traditional theories have played a part in instigating our own violent behavior toward those we consider our (and therefore God's) enemies. So, it's time to reinterpret and to suggest alternative theories that reveal the God of Jesus, who desires the salvation of all people (2 Tim. 2:4).

Restorative Justice

In chapter 5 we discussed the differences among various traditional theories of atonement based upon more retributive notions of justice. We pointed out their inconsistency with a God who desires all people to be saved and who longs for a restored relationship with all creation. As we consider another theory, the one I construct in these next two chapters, we will see how it harmonizes with restorative rather than retributive justice and with the metaphors the Bible uses to speak of the atonement. So, as we move forward through this section, think about the following questions as they relate to justice: What exactly did Jesus accomplish on the cross? And how might we think about justice in light of the cross?

Jesus Transcends the Law

We often read Old Testament law through the lens of divine retributive justice that demands that the wrongdoer pay a penalty of some sort. And we do see retributive aspects of the law, especially in passages such as Deuteronomy 28, in which God tells the Hebrews that if they don't obey the law they'll suffer all sorts of horrible curses and catastrophes. The problem arises when we apply the same sort of retributive justice to God's actions in the cross event. We have built our doctrines of atonement around this idea of retribution, of pitting justice against love and grace. In so doing, we've made retributive justice the ruling attribute of God, subordinating love to justice. Ironically however, the book of Colossians tells us that the legalistic, retributive way of dealing with sin was nailed to the cross, taken out of the way (2:13–14). Rather than seeking retribution for sin, God reveals in the life, death, and resurrection of Jesus a higher type of justice that gives hope, liberates, and redeems. In other words, Jesus shows us divine justice as restorative and by so doing exhorts us to live according to the same standard.[2] Jesus fulfilled the law and gives humanity the divine Spirit of grace and love (Matt. 5:17; 2 Cor. 3:1–18).

Actually, we might say that sin condemned and punished through retribution is sin condemned without hope for redemption. But sin exposed through righteousness, with the intent to restore the sinner to God, is grounded in the hope of salvation. So instead of saying that God inflicted the pain of the cross on Jesus as a penalty for our sin, we can say that the horrific nature of the cross exposed and condemned the gravity of our sin. After all, human beings are the ones who put Jesus to death, not God.

And remember, Jesus never said anything about coming to receive punishment for sin, but he said quite a bit about forgiving it. The righteousness of God in Jesus transcended the retributive aspects of the law and brought about our forgiveness—think about Jesus' prayer for our forgiveness from the cross. In this manner, Jesus gave us his life and revealed to us the law of love that restores us to God and to each other. The Bible tells us that no greater love exists than this (John 15:13).

The law did not fully reveal God to us. The New Testament tells us that the life, death, and resurrection of Jesus reinterpreted the old law and revealed something new about God. It tells us that Jesus fulfilled the law, broke down its barriers that, due to sin, separated us from God. Jesus set us free from its legal constraints, and showed us a better way to God—a way that walks in love, forgiveness, and grace. Jesus summed up the law with two commandments—to love God and to love others (Matt. 5:17; 22:37–40; John 1:17; Acts 13:39; Rom. 3:20–28; 5:1–2; 7:4–6; 8:2; 10:4; 13:10; Gal. 2:15–20; 3:13; 5:14; Eph. 2:15–16; Heb.

7:19; 10:1–9). So we see that the law of retributive justice plays no part in the work of Jesus. Instead, mercy and grace transcend the law of retribution in favor of forgiveness.

The law cannot save because it doesn't bring forgiveness. We also see that the law demands some sort of retributive action against wrong-doers. Whereas the law condemned sin, the grace and love of God forgave sin through Jesus. But the Bible tells us over and over again that God forgives sin. We see Jesus, the revelation of God, forgiving sin during his ministry and right before his death while hanging on the cross—which indicates to us that God's forgiveness through Jesus was available to us even before he went to the cross (Matt. 9:1–8; Mark 2:1–12; Luke 5:17–26). This fact also reveals that God didn't limit the salvific work of Jesus only to wiping out sin or to dying on the cross. God sent Jesus to show us the *way* to live a transformed life, to show us the *truth* about what that new way encompasses, and to reveal the *light* that we will shed on the world as we live as Jesus lived.

Jesus Bears Our Burden

The Bible makes it clear that Jesus bears our burden. And if we believe that the Old Testament foreshadows the coming and the work of Jesus, we see burden-bearing even there. For instance, we can rejoice with the psalmist, singing, "Blessed be the Lord, Who bears our burdens and carries us day by day, even the God Who is our salvation! *Selah* [pause, and calmly think of that]!" (Ps. 68:19 AMP). Or we can lament with Isaiah over the pain of an innocent man and recite, "Surely he has borne our infirmities and carried our diseases; yet *we accounted* him stricken, struck down by God, and afflicted" (Isa. 53:4). Remember, just because *we* thought God struck him down doesn't mean God really did.

In the New Testament we see that Jesus "bore our sins in his body"—after all, in our sinfulness, we nailed him to the cross! (1 Pet. 2:21–24). We can say with the writer of Hebrews that Jesus "offered [himself] once to bear the sins of many" (9:28). Jesus carried the burden of our sin by allowing us, in our sinfulness, to put him to death. And we can almost feel his compassion for us as he says, "Come to me, all who are weary and are carrying heavy burdens, and I will give you rest" (Matt. 11:28). But what does all this mean? How does Jesus bear our burden?

A couple of years ago, a friend of mine shaved his head and only ate very small bits of food for two months. I didn't understand these drastic measures, so I asked him why he did it. Come to find out, one of his close friends was diagnosed with cancer and had to undergo chemotherapy. That friend lost all of his hair and was so nauseated most of the time that he could only eat little bits of food. And my friend Joseph decided to share his sick friend's burden by standing in solidarity with him, shaving his own head and adjusting his own diet to match his friend's. In essence, he "took on" the consequences of his friend's illness, and he "suffered" a measure of his friend's pain and grief as a show of love and compassion. Joseph hoped that by sharing his burden, his friend would know he wasn't alone in his misery. Now, I know that Joseph isn't Jesus, but this analogy still helps us to understand a bit what Jesus did by bearing our burdens.

As the embodiment of God's love, and true to the nature of that divine love, Jesus entered into our miseries. He took upon himself all the burdens of our human condition and suffered in solidarity with us and, out of love and compassion, identified with our sufferings, adversities, pains, and evils. He plunged himself into the depths of all our misfortunes, brought upon us and upon him by our sin.[3] Jesus reveals that he shares our burdens by spending his life healing and working miracles on behalf of the downtrodden. He takes on our infirmities and bears our sicknesses (Isa. 53). He partook of our sins by bearing the consequences for them—consequences we inflicted on him.

These metaphors do *not* mean that he literally took on our sin or our infirmities as a mysterious imputation or had our punishment transferred to his person and, consequently, by his suffering satisfied the justice of God. That kind of penal suffering would only satisfy the very worst injustice. And think about it. If Jesus did take on the punishment for our sin, why would anyone need to suffer in an eternal hell? According to the penal and satisfaction theories, Jesus suffered for all humanity. He paid the price, satisfied the debt, and said "it is finished." So it would be a grave injustice if God required two punishments for sin—one paid by Jesus and one paid by eternal suffering. Instead, Jesus took upon himself our sinning enmity by bearing all the abuse we handed out to him. He was painfully burdened by our fallen and broken condition, and he agonized with us in the most profound way possible—he suffered on account of our sin.[4] Jesus knows how to treat his enemies—he suffers with them (us) as a friend. He suffers all our wickedness in order to win us with his love.

Jesus took the burden of our sin, the heavy weight that sin incurs, as he suffered our sinful wrath on the cross—not God's wrath, our wrath! Ephesians 2:3 calls human beings "children of wrath." We've most often interpreted this verse backwards, as "we are sinners who will suffer God's wrath." But if we read it in context, we see that the wrath applies to us—it is our wrath toward each other (and even toward all creation), our wrath that works itself out through violence. Yes, as much as we don't like to admit it, we are children of wrath who resort to violence whenever the opportunity or the whim strikes us. We aimed our violence at Jesus. And we sinned by killing him. Our sin put him there. Our sin cursed him to suffer an unjust, horrific death. Out of love he did so (Gal. 3:13). He died in order to reveal the greatness of God's grace, love, and desire to save us from the sin that executed him. By exposing sin, Jesus redeemed it. By loving us, Jesus forgave it. By submitting to it, Jesus stands in solidarity with all who suffer—he bears our burdens in a redemptive way—by exposing and hindering the cycle of sin and violence.[5]

Jesus exposes the nature of human brokenness and our inclination to resort to violence at every turn. He let human beings execute him. He didn't run away; he didn't call down myriads of angels to smite the Romans or the Jewish leaders; he didn't fight back with his own sword or let Peter lop off anyone's head. He even fastened a slave's ear back on after Peter's first attempt and told him to stop the violence. He "fought" back with peaceful protest and allowed himself to be killed by the world's wrath—by the children of wrath. In doing so, he exposed the heinous nature of our sinfulness and forced us to come face to face with the gravity of our own sin.

By analogy, let's think of it in this way: During the civil rights movement in the 1960s, black men, women, and children suffered terrible violence at the hands of prejudiced white people. A white man could kill a black man without too much fear of being held accountable for taking a life. The black community "fought" back with peaceful protests at lunch counters and on busses without much chance of success. But on September 15, 1963, a number of Ku Klux Klan members hid a bomb under the steps of the Sixteenth Street Baptist Church in Birmingham, Alabama. The bomb exploded just as a group of children were making their way down the steps to Sunday School. The explosion killed four young girls. Interestingly, the sermon that morning was titled "Love that Forgives."

In the aftermath of the bombing, one newspaper editorial commented that "[f]or the rest of the nation, the Birmingham church bombing should serve to goad the conscience. The deaths . . . in a sense are on the hands of each of us."[6] In the days after the killings, many people, strangers to the victims, paid visits to the grieving families to express their sorrow and shame. Thousands of people from all different races attended the funeral service. It took the violent death of four innocent children to expose the profound injustice and horrendous wickedness involved in the persecution of black people. In other words, these killings exposed the abysmal nature of human sin. When faced with the gravity of their sin, the American people reached out to the black community in remorse and shame, increasing sympathy for the cause of civil rights. Finally, ten months later, on July 2, 1964, President Johnson signed the Civil Rights Act of 1964 that established equal rights for African Americans according to the law. We might say that those four young girls carried the burden of our sin and suffered death so that many others might live in freedom with the civil rights due to all human beings.

Similarly, through Jesus, God carried the burden of our sin. I love this quote by Horace Bushnell; it aptly expresses the character of God's love toward us and helps us understand the burden of sin Jesus carried for all creation: "God's eternal character has a cross in it, a sorrowing, heavily burdened mercy for his enemies, a winning and transforming power. . . ."[7] In our transformed, newly created state, we feel the burden Jesus carried. His horrific death and the forgiveness Jesus extended in the midst of it brings us face to face with our vile and violent ways to the point that many of us, in remorse and shame, respond to the forgiveness and reconciliation available to all humanity through his life, death, and resurrection.

Jesus Won the Victory over Sin and Death

The Bible tells us about the victory Jesus won over death and sin. By rising from the dead, Jesus conquered death. The *Christus Victor* theory of atonement builds its case on this idea. 1 Corinthians says it like this: "Death has been swallowed up in victory" (15:54). In other words, he put death to death! Taken in context with the verses before it, we can assume that because Jesus did away with death, we will all trade in our mortal bodies for immortality someday. Yes, our bodies still die— everyone's does unless you're Elijah or Enoch. But we no longer need to fear our death. Why?

Jesus also took away the "sting" of death, which according to 1 Corinthians 15:55–56, is sin. Sin no longer holds us in death's grip. It says,

"'Where, O death, is your victory? Where, O death, is your sting?' The sting of death is sin, and the power of sin is the law. But thanks be to God, who gives us the victory through our Lord Jesus Christ." Sin gave death its sting. Just as a bee stings us and it hurts, albeit temporarily, sin makes death sting us and makes death's permanence something to dread. When Jesus puts death to death, he takes away the sin or the sting of death. It is no longer a permanent death. We not only have the hope of future resurrection and life everlasting with God in Christ, but we too have the victory over sin if we live according to the will of God, that is, loving God and others.

Jesus died on account of sin—in our sinfulness, we executed an innocent man (Gal. 1:4). And Jesus died on our behalf so that we could see the depth of our profound distance from God and turn away from our wrongdoing (Rom. 5:6, 8).

Jesus Gives Life

We can use a big theological word to describe how Jesus gives us life: recapitulation. In the second century, the church father Irenaeus used the term to describe a "great reversal" in which Jesus is the second Adam. We (humanity) were dead in our sins. But God is life. So when the "the Word became flesh," that is, human, Jesus brought the life of God into human flesh and in so doing, he restored life to us and brought us back into communion with God (John 1:14). In giving humanity God's life, the incarnation broke the stranglehold that death had over us. Consequently, we can all have communion with the God of eternal life because that life is now in us through the human Jesus. Not only did he break the strangle hold of death, but because Jesus defeated sin in the flesh, he also liberated us from the slavery of sin through forgiveness and passed on to us the power to defeat sin (see this logic in Rom. 5:12–21; 1 Cor. 15:21–22). In other words, through the first Adam, all humanity suffered the propensity to sin and remained captive to sin's deadly hold on us. Like Adam, we all sin, which makes us the slaves to sin and the spiritual death that goes along with it. But Jesus, the second Adam, defeated sin and death. Through him and the life of God in the flesh, we inherited the power to defeat sin and death as well. Jesus passed his righteousness on to us. So, like a new cosmic Adam, Jesus presents to God the totality of the universe restored to unity in him. By descending to us (as a human being), Jesus lifts us to God (as divine).[8] Of course the incarnation and our participation in it as the body of Christ on earth profoundly influences the way we should live our lives.

Through a life of love lived in total obedience to God, including the fact that he saw it through to the end by dying on the cross, Jesus reversed the fallen path that Adam started us on. Not only that, Jesus reclaimed all of humanity and all of creation and put it all back on the path toward fulfilling the purpose for which it was created—namely union and communion with God. Where Adam brought death, Jesus brought the reverse—life. Jesus' obedience displaced Adam's disobedience. Adam had to die because he had sinned, but Jesus didn't sin and therefore didn't have to die. But by voluntarily taking on our human condition (including all of its consequences) and rising from the dead, he broke the hold of sin and death. He brings life to all who love him. Consequently, Jesus has overcome all of the results of Adam's sin for all creation, for all time and eternity.[9]

Jesus also gives us life through his life, death, and resurrection when we think of him as the Passover lamb. It's important to remember that the sacrifice of the lamb was in no way penal—it did not take on the punishment for the people's sin. Its death did not satisfy God in any way. On the contrary, the Passover lamb symbolized the giving of *life*. The lamb sacrificed in Egypt brought life to the people. Those who did not show proof of the life of the lamb on their doorposts died. The blood of the lamb gave them life. And as the Passover lamb of the New Covenant, Jesus gives us life as well. He gives us the eternal life of God through the incarnation. When we eat and drink of the bread (body) and the wine (blood) in the eucharistic celebration, which many of us call Communion, we give thanks to God for the life we have through Jesus.[10] In some traditions we actually partake of the life (in the body and the blood) of Christ by eating the eucharistic meal.

We see this same concept carried over into the New Testament. In the book of John, Jesus says he is the bread of God, "which comes down from heaven and gives life to the world." (John 6:33 NASB) He promised that "if any one eats of this bread, he will live forever; and the bread also which I shall give for the life of the world is my flesh" (John 6:51 NASB). Partake of Jesus (God in human flesh) and you will live.

Jesus Acts as Our Mediator

To act as a mediator for someone means to intervene on their behalf or to stand in the middle and harmonize both sides of an argument. A mediator helps bridge the gap between estranged and conflicting parties in order to reconcile them and restore their relationship. Jesus does this for all creation. He mediates between God and humans by reconciling us and restoring our relationship (1 Tim. 2:5–6). In the book of Hebrews we're told that Jesus is the mediator of a new covenant, a covenant of peace and reconciliation between God and all creation. How did he mediate? He shed his blood (think *life*) in a manner that speaks a better word than the blood of Abel (Heb. 12:24). Now what in the world does *that* mean?

Abel's death was anything but reconciling and it brought condemnation down on his brother Cain for killing him. Although Jesus and Abel might have been murdered for similar psychological reasons (anger, retribution, fear, jealousy), Jesus' life brought life. It revealed to us the way to reconciliation and restoration between God and all creation. Although Abel's blood cried out from the ground for vindication and retribution, Jesus cried from the cross, "Father, forgive them!" So in the face of torturous injustice Jesus doesn't call out for vengeance. He loves his enemies so extravagantly that he acts as the mediator and asks God to forgive them, us—the human race.

Forgiveness

In addition to restorative justice, Jesus accomplished forgiveness on the cross (remember, when speaking of the cross, I include the entirety of Jesus's life, death, and resurrection). What does the forgiveness of God through Jesus mean for us? What (and who) does it include?

Jesus Reconciles Us

We've talked quite a bit about reconciliation but haven't really defined it in terms of Jesus and the cross. What does it *mean* to say that through Jesus we are reconciled to God? First of all, according to the *Oxford English Dictionary*, "reconciliation" indicates "the action or an act of bringing a thing or things to agreement, concord, or harmony." It is what restores estranged parties back to friendship. Jesus has done just that for us (and for all creation).[11]

Amazingly, Jesus reconciled us to God *while we were still enemies!* We up and decided to do our own thing against the wishes of our creator and as a result made ourselves God's enemies. Even though God sought us, forgave us, and longed for a loving relationship with us (Isa. 30:18), we continued to flaunt our freedom (or should I say slavery to sin?) and live apart from the will and the friendship of God. But through the life of Jesus, God sought to bring us back into harmony, to reconcile us.

Romans 5:10–11 puts this in words for us: "For if while we were enemies, we were reconciled to God through the death of his Son, much more surely, having been reconciled, will we be saved by his life. But more than that, we even boast in God through our Lord Jesus Christ, through whom we have now received reconciliation." We see that through the *life* of Jesus, we receive forgiveness from and reconciliation with God. By allowing sinful human beings to kill him publicly, Jesus revealed to us the fathomless, extravagant love of God. He stood in solidarity with us as sufferers and as sinners. He plunged himself into the depths of human despair and forgave us. As we tap into that life of love that Jesus extends to us, we reconcile with God and with each other.

We see this reconciliation again in 2 Corinthians:

All this is from God, who reconciled us to himself through Christ, and has given us the ministry of reconciliation; that is, in Christ God was reconciling the world to himself, not counting their trespasses against them, and entrusting the message of reconciliation to us. So we are ambassadors for Christ, since God is making his appeal through us; we entreat you on behalf of Christ, be reconciled to God. For our sake he made him to be sin who knew no sin, so that in him we might become the righteousness of God" (5:18–21).

I love these verses. Through Jesus, God reconciles us. How? By not counting our sins against us—in other words, by *forgiving us*! Reconciliation comes through forgiveness. We who were once estranged from God are brought into harmony with God, repairing the breach that once separated us.

The same idea is expressed in Colossian 2:13–14, in which God forgives us by actually erasing the debt that sin held against us. To erase it means the debt was there and then it wasn't. There's no balancing of accounts; no one had to suffer our punishment in order to make restitution. Just like I erase my chalkboard, God simply erased the debt. God forgave it. He nailed it to the cross. What we see in full measure from the cross is love, the love of God revealed fully through Jesus. Jesus expressed this love by saying, "Father, forgive them, they don't know what they are doing." Not, "Father, release them from the debt now that I've paid the price for it." Not, "Father, now you don't have to punish them because you've punished me." But, forgive them. While they are still enemies. Before they repent (Rom. 5:9–10). You get the picture!

Through the love and forgiveness of God, revealed and realized through the life, death, and resurrection of Jesus, two estranged parties, God and humanity, are brought back into harmony (John 15:14). Additionally, as if that weren't enough, Jesus brought peace through reconciliation.

Jesus Brings Peace

Reconciliation through forgiveness brings peace between formerly conflicting parties—in this case, God and humanity. The book of Ephesians tells us that Jesus proclaimed peace to those of us who were far from God and to those who were nearer to God (2:15–20). And Jesus proclaimed this peace by something that speaks louder than words— by his actions. Even though he suffered because of our sinful actions in putting him to death, Jesus sought to forgive and to reconcile us to God, bringing peace, love, and restoration not only between God and humans but among those in conflict with each other—Jews, Gentile, male, female, slave, and free. Peace all the way around! But isn't that what the angels declared at the birth of Jesus—peace on earth, goodwill to all people?

We get the same message in Colossians 1:20: "And through him God was pleased to reconcile to himself all things, whether on earth or in heaven, by making peace through the blood of his cross." Yes, through the life (blood) of Jesus—a life of love for all things, human and not human, for all creation—we have peace with God. That peace brought unity to what formerly existed in disunity (Col. 1:21–22). What's more, peace *with* God gives us the peace *of* God that passes all comprehension (Phil. 4:7–9).

Jesus Redeems Us

My mother used to collect S & H Green Stamps. This was forty to fifty years ago when grocery stores used to give a certain number of stamps per dollar spent. She pasted them in a little Green Stamp book. When she filled all the pages and collected a big bunch of filled books, she loaded my brothers and me into the car and took us to the Redemption Center to trade the stamps in for merchandise—an iron or a blender or a soup pot, for instance. The "Redemption Center"—an interesting name for a stamp trading joint!—was a place where people traded one thing for another.

When theologians speak about the atonement, they often use the language of redemption. As we discussed in chapter 2, it's important to remember that the writers of the Bible used metaphorical language to talk about the atonement. And that's the case with the words usually translated "redeem" or "redemption" in the New Testament. They serve as metaphors that give us the image of Jesus delivering us, liberating us, rescuing us from lives lived apart from God, and reclaiming us as God's own possession (Col. 1:13). Sometimes the word conveys the idea of making good on a loss or making amends.[12] Another way to look at it is to say that Jesus, as the good shepherd, brought us back into the sheepfold, or that Jesus procured our adoption into God's family (John 10:1–16; Rom. 8:15–17). We could also assert that we have a new owner (Rom. 7:4; Gal. 3:29). Or, like the Green Stamps, we might analogize that Jesus traded death for life, slavery for freedom, sin for righteousness, disobedience for obedience. By becoming human, he exchanged sinful humanity for the righteous humanity that characterized our nature before sin entered the world. He exchanged the old nature for the new nature in the life of God (2 Cor. 5:17). And he invites us to share in that life and all it entails.

Although some biblical scholars believe that the word indicates an economic transaction of some sort, others believe that the word in the New Testament speaks of the *fact* of our delivery from sin rather than of the *means* of that delivery.[13] In this case the metaphor points to our delivery from sin but shouldn't be taken literally as "Jesus paid the price for our deliverance." Taking redemption in the literal sense raises too many problems that theologians have struggled with for centuries, such as: Who did Jesus literally pay? The devil? Many object to this theory because they can't believe God would have to submit to the devil in any way—God pays the devil?! Did Jesus pay God? Then what does that say about the nature of forgiveness? We've discussed this problem in chapter 6.

If we say that Jesus' sufferings were not penal but redemptive, then Jesus couldn't have paid God or the devil or anyone else in order to rescue, deliver, liberate, or reclaim us. The important piece here is that through the incarnation, Jesus did rescue and liberate us from slavery to sin. He did deliver us from spiritual death. And in so doing, he reclaimed us for the kingdom of God.

Jesus Purifies Us

We spent chapter 7 talking about sacrifice, blood, and purification. But let's expound on it a bit here so we can fit it into the alternative theory in chapter 9. We know that the Bible tells us Jesus "takes away the sin of the world" (John 1:29). He "cleanses us from all sin" (1 John 1:7). And his blood will purify our consciences so that we can serve the living God (Heb. 9:14). Through his blood (read *life*) we are "sprinkled clean from an evil conscience and our bodies washed with pure water" (Heb. 10:22). And finally Jesus "freed us from our sins in his own blood" (Rev. 1:5). Good news, right? And it's probably what most of us have always believed. But I'm just not sure that the ways we've always interpreted these verses are true to the biblical concept of the cleansing blood of Jesus.

We often use the word "propitiation" to explain how the blood of Jesus effects salvation. And we entangle our interpretation of the word with ideas of substitution and some sort of transaction in which the blood of Jesus "buys" our way out of hell or purchases God's favor for us. But the Greek word we translate "propitiation" takes us back to the "mercy seat" that sat on top of the Ark of the Covenant in the Old Testament.[14] The priests would take blood into the holy of holies once a year on Yom Kippur—the Day of Atonement (the Day of Purification) (remember the meaning of *kippur*, p. 116, from the last chapter?)—and sprinkle it on the mercy seat, cleansing the entire nation and making all the people pure for another year. In the New Testament, Jesus is the mercy seat where our cleansing took place (Rom. 3:25; 8:3). So, in essence, we can equate Jesus with the means by which Israel believed its sin-caused impurity could be cleansed. Among the many metaphors Paul uses to explain the atonement, he is telling us that Jesus is the *new* mercy seat and with the sprinkling of his blood (life) the community is purified. In other words, the blood of Jesus acts as a cleanser.[15]

The blood is life, "the sacred, mystic, new-creating touch of life."[16] Remember that under the law, death is unclean and people who touch a dead body must go through a purification process. Life, symbolized by the blood of Jesus, cleanses. The cleansing and purifying action of the blood (life) of Jesus is intimately connected to forgiveness. We might even say that the cleansing symbolizes forgiveness. We see this in the book of Hebrews: "Indeed, under the law almost everything is purified with blood, and without the shedding of blood there is no forgiveness of sins" (Heb. 9:22). Or, we could say that without the cleansing and purifying power of blood (life), there is no forgiveness of sin. Jesus selflessly gave his life, symbolized by his shed blood, in order to lead us to God, to forgive our sins. We see this life-giving forgiveness that cleanses us when, from the agony of the cross, he beseeches God to forgive humanity its sin—in other words, "cleanse them God!" And God did (Luke 23:34).[17]

We can interpret the many passages of Scripture that talk about the blood of Jesus in light of its cleansing and purifying power, washing away the stain of sin through forgiveness. We must remember, however, that when we invoke the "blood" we really do so as a symbol for "life." So for verses such as: "this is the blood of my covenant, which is poured out for many," we could say instead, "this is my life, which has been given for many" (Matt. 26:28; Mk. 14:24). Or ". . . the church of God that he obtained with the blood of his own Son" (Act. 20:28), might mean that God obtained the church through the life of Jesus that brought forgiveness of sin. We could interpret the verse "through him God was pleased to reconcile to himself all things, whether on earth or in heaven, by making peace through the blood of his cross" (Col. 1:20) to mean that through the cleansing purification of forgiveness, God reconciled all creation through the selfless, life-giving, sacrifice of Jesus. How about this one? "Therefore Jesus also suffered outside the city gate in order to sanctify the people by his blood. Let us then go to him outside the camp and bear the abuse he endured" (Heb. 13:12–13). We might say that by the life of Jesus, we are cleansed, purified, and forgiven. Because of that, we must live selflessly, giving our lives for the benefit of others even if their sin causes us to suffer as Jesus did.

Jesus Reveals and Imparts Love

Through his life, death, and resurrection Jesus not only reveals God's love to us, but he also imparts that love to us. In John 15:13, Jesus tells us that "no one has greater love than this, to lay down one's life for one's friends." And Jesus did just that. Medieval theologian Peter Abelard believed that God's love as revealed in Jesus is the foundation for our salvation.[18] First, Abelard reminds us that God's love for us motivated God's sending the Son to redeem humanity from sin. In order for us to realize the profound depth of divine love, Jesus willingly lived and died, giving us both the revelation and the example of God's love. And in order for God to show the depth of God's love for us and to convince us that we must love God in return, Jesus willingly submitted himself to our sinful actions and allowed us to execute him on the cross.[19] Abelard explains the purpose of the cross: "'[T]o the showing of his justice'—that is, his love—which, as has been said, justifies us in his sight. In other words, to show forth his love to us or to convince us how much we ought to love him who 'spared not his own Son' for us."[20] So the cross gives us profound knowledge and genuine assurance of the love God has for us and the extravagance of forgiving grace.

Second, Abelard also believes that Christ's passion not only reveals the depth of God's love, but also that through this love, God saves us. Abelard writes, "through this righteousness—which is love—we may gain remission of our sins. . . ."[21] For Abelard, then, love is the motivation behind the cross; the revelation of the cross is love; the source of forgiveness and, therefore of salvation in the cross is love. The cross symbolizes divine love, the revelation of God's love for us and for all creation. The extravagant depth of divine love led Jesus to the cross as a willing sacrifice of love. In fact, the cross enables us to understand the extent of God's love and inspires us to love God in return.[22]

Jesus did not die in order to win God's love for us, but to win us over with God's love. God's love went to the limit for us, dove into the depths of the human condition, suffered the consequences of our sin by dying a terrible death as an innocent man. And in the midst of that suffering love, Jesus revealed the greatest love all—forgiving his enemies and praying to God to do the same. Through the incarnation, God took on human flesh and gave human flesh the life of God. But how? In the next chapter I will construct an alternate theory, maybe just a thought experiment, for you to consider. So read on.

9

An Alternative View

He has abolished the law with its commandments and ordinances, that
he might create in himself one new humanity in place of the two, thus
making peace, and might reconcile both groups to God in one body
through the cross, thus putting to death that hostility through it.
—Ephesians 2:15–16

Before we can begin to see the cross as something done for us, we have
to see it as something done by us.
—John Stott, *The Cross of Christ*

You are not likely to err practicing too much of the cross.
—Alexander Whyte, in *The Pilgrim's Progress*

HOW DID JESUS ACCOMPLISH SALVATION?

So far we've talked about what Jesus did when he lived and died and
rose again, but we've yet to undertake a complete theory of atonement
that incorporates all of these things into a unified whole. We want to
know how Jesus did it. We want to get down to the nitty-gritty, the
theory that beats all theories.

Well, I can't promise that. After all, theologians have tried for centuries to piece together a theory of atonement that perfectly lines up
with everything Scripture says about the life, death, and resurrection of
Jesus and how it applies to our salvation. But I will offer a theory that
I believe best harmonizes with my main image of God—a God of love
who desires nothing more than to restore us into an eternal relationship
with God and with all creation. But as we move forward let's keep in
mind that we speak metaphorically. Jesus did this; Paul did this; the
great theologians of the Christian tradition did this. We get in trouble
when we take the metaphors literally. If we do, we end up with the
rigid dogma of absolute certainty that eliminates the need for faith.

That said, our faith still seeks to understand God and the work
of God through Jesus. We construct theories and develop doctrines
and write creeds and confine our separate communities to those who

believe as we do. If we hold our beliefs with a bit of humility, knowing we could be wrong, however, we may learn to disagree in a spirit of love rather than blast our so-called heretics with mean-spirited, bombastic derision. After all, the Bible does exhort us to clothe ourselves "with compassion, kindness, humility, meekness, and patience," and above all to clothe ourselves with love (Col. 3:12–14). So in that spirit, let's combine everything we've talked about so far into an alternate theory that will leave us with an image of God in harmony with the revelation of God through Jesus Christ.

Incarnation

The Western theological tradition doesn't emphasize the importance of Jesus' incarnation (literally, "in the flesh") for salvation. The Eastern Orthodox tradition, however, makes an essential link between the incarnation and atonement. Because of the incarnation, something tangible happens on a cosmic level to change our relationship with God and with each other. In the words of Cyril of Alexandria, "God made human flesh his own."[1] Or, in other words, regardless of the way we might think about the divinity of Jesus, God descended into the human condition by becoming one of us with a human body and mind. But there's a bit more to it. In Jesus, two natures were united—human and divine. And since the son has taken on humanness, the two natures are united in Jesus. So he took what belonged to him—the life of God—and gave it to us. And he also took to himself what belonged to us—humanity—and healed it, restored it, and transformed it into what God created us to be. What a sweet gift. Jesus participated in humanity and in the process healed and reconciled it so that humanity could participate in God. In other words, he lifted human nature into the Godhead (Eph. 2:6). We could say that God descended to us in our humanity so we could then ascend to the life of God.[2]

Substitution

A number of theologians that oppose penal substitutionary theories of atonement prefer to eliminate the language of substitution altogether. I do not. Although I see it somewhat differently than the traditional view, substitution plays an important role in how Jesus saves us. Paul uses different ideas about substitution, and not all of these ideas harmonize with one other. So what are we to make of substitution?

Let's look at how the people before and during the lives of Jesus and Paul might have understood substitution. In 4 Maccabees 5:1–6:30, a book in the Apocrypha accepted by the Roman Catholic Church as canonical Scripture, we have a story about Eleazar, a priestly leader during the Maccabean revolt. The tyrant king, Antiochus, knowing that the law forbade Jews to eat pork, commanded Eleazar to eat a pig. Of course he refused. So Antiochus tortured him by flogging him until his flesh hung in bloody strips from his body. He kicked Eleazar and beat him, burned him with fire, and poured horrid liquids into his nose. Finally Eleazar spoke his last words before dying. He lifted his eyes to God and said: "You know, O God, that though I might have saved myself, I am dying in burning torments for the sake of the law. Be merciful to your people, and let our punishment suffice for them. Make *my* blood *their* purification, and *take my life in exchange for theirs*" (6:27–30; I added the italics).

What did Eleazar mean? In essence he's suggesting that his suffering substitutes for those who come after him, that his shed blood purifies them, and his life is given so they don't have to give theirs. Finally, we see that "the tyrant [Antiochus] was punished, and the homeland purified—they (Eleazar and other martyrs) having become, as it were, a ransom for the sin of our nation. And through the blood of those devout ones and their death as an atoning sacrifice, divine Providence preserved Israel. . . ." (4 Macc. 17:21–23). Now this does not mean that Eleazar paid the price for the sin of the nation, or that he was punished in the place of the people. The writer used the metaphor of substitution and ransom in order to communicate an important truth. The deaths of those like Eleazar exposed the violence and sin of the oppressors and led to their downfall, cessation of sin, and violence against the people. His suffering (and other martyrs like him) helped to stop the suffering of people in the future. By exposing the cycle of violence in those times, he helped to end it. In essence, he died so that many others didn't have to.

Think, too, about Martin Luther King Jr. or about those four girls killed in the Birmingham church bombing we discussed earlier. What Eleazar has in common with them is that they all died substitutionary deaths that in some way redeemed the future. Each one of these martyrs exposed the evil of oppression, abuse, and violence. They enabled their communities to see human sin at its worst and in so doing, brought the horrific nature of these evils to light, forcing the guilty to confront the atrocities they committed.

I am not saying that God willed these deaths, in fact the opposite. These deaths occurred because of sinful persons acting outside of God's will. These martyrs exposed sin. In uncovering the sin of the abusers, their deaths served not only as wake-up calls but also as catalysts that set the wheels of peace-making rolling. Their deaths worked to stop the flow of violence. They suffered so others after them didn't have to. Mark Thiessen Nation puts it aptly, saying that "[s]ome of us may never have truly known the depth and breadth of racism without the extraordinary lives of King, Perkins, Rosa Parks, Fannie Lou Hammer and countless others."[3] We might say that their suffering served as a substitute for all those who might have died horrible deaths at the hands of wrongdoers had the martyrs not died instead. Their deaths provide vicarious salvation from further violence.

We apply this idea of substitution to the life, death, and resurrection of Jesus as well. Of course, one of the passages from which we get our doctrines of substitution is Isaiah 53:4–12. We need to remember that Isaiah is part of the Hebrew Scriptures written by Jewish authors. Jewish scholars do not interpret these verses as referring to Jesus at all. Christians have adopted the Hebrew Scriptures as their own Old Testament and believe many of its passages point to Jesus—like this one in Isaiah 53. So let's explore this passage briefly through a Christian rather than Jewish lens. Here are the verses that indicate substitution in some form:

53:4 "Surely he has borne our infirmities and carried our diseases; yet we account him stricken, struck down by God, and afflicted." Jesus bore the infirmities and diseases that we laid on him. Yes, Jesus suffered the consequences of our sickness—our seemingly incurable disease called sin. We thought God did this to him (as our traditional theories of atonement suggest). But people during those times thought everything came from the hand of God. We know better now. Some of the worst evils come from our own hands, not God's.

53:5 "But he was wounded for our transgressions, crushed for our iniquities; upon him was the punishment that made us whole, and by his bruises we are healed." However, God did not do it to Jesus. We did. He died *because of* our sinfulness. In our sin, we put him on the cross. His death was a crime committed by sinful humans. Jesus died in order to expose and to stop the cycle of retributive violence so that many others after him wouldn't have to suffer the same fate. Through his suffering, if we live the kind of life Jesus lived and tap into the life he gives, we are healed and liberated from this endless violence.

53:6b ". . . and the LORD has laid on him the iniquity of us all." Jesus came to do God's will, which was to show the way to life. To reveal the extravagance of God's love for all creation by living a human life and suffering the consequences of sinful humanity. In this way, the sin of humanity was laid on Jesus' shoulders. When Jesus took on human flesh, he also took the weight of sin on his shoulders. Human sin led to his horrific death. When he asked God to take away the cup he had to drink in the Garden of Gethsemane, Jesus was really asking God to deliver him from having to live his human life to the end, including all the consequences (Luke 22:42). It's like Jesus prayed, "Lord, please don't let me have to complete this journey, this mission to show the extravagance of your love to all humanity. This path will lead to horrific suffering." So we can't say God wanted Jesus to die on the cross—that wasn't the "cup" Luke spoke of. The "cup" God asked Jesus to drink was to live among us and to reveal the ways of God to us—the way of life, and of love. That way of love led to his death on a cross.

53:8 "By a perversion of justice he was taken away. . . . For he was cut off from the land of the living, stricken for the transgression of my people." Did you catch that? By a perversion of justice Jesus was killed. Can we actually believe that God required a perversion of justice? He was executed (stricken) because people are sinful and kill those who rock the boat. He was stricken *because of* our transgressions.

53:10a "Yet it was the will of the LORD to crush him with pain." Again, God willed that Jesus live among us, just like God wills that we live our lives here in the human community on earth. What are the consequences of Jesus living among sinful humans? We crushed him, beat him, crucified him. God willed that Jesus come and live among us. By living among us Jesus naturally had to suffer all the consequences of living in a human community. We willed that Jesus die on the cross.

53:12b ". . . because he poured out himself to death, and was numbered with the transgressors; yet he bore the sin of many, and made intercession for the transgressors." Jesus bore our sin—he died because we are sinners who use violence to accomplish our agendas. But what did Jesus do while hanging on the cross, while his enemies were killing him? He interceded on our behalf. He prayed and asked God to forgive them! And I think God did just that.

So, Jesus saves us from living life shrouded in the darkness of abuse by suffering that darkness and abuse himself. By exposing the human tendency to rationalize unmitigated violence upon another person, race, or nation, Jesus opens the way for us to change. He transforms us not only by a sweet replacement of sinful human nature with the pure nature of sinlessness in which we were created but also through his example. He transforms the world by exposing the horrendous nature of sin. He transforms those who suffer by standing with them in solidarity as a fellow sufferer. In fact, one of the ways to talk about vicarious suffering is to see it as suffering *with* rather than suffering *instead of*. We can call this "inclusive place-taking," which means "sharing" the place of others. Jesus included himself with us in our suffering the consequences of sin. This "place-sharing" reaches to the center of our being as we take on the life of Christ.[4] Because Jesus endured horrendous suffering because of us and on our behalf, we can entrust our grief to him. We can cast our cares upon him. We can exchange our heavy burden for his lighter one—because he carries ours.[5] But that's not all. Because Jesus gives us life as the second Adam and the incarnation of God, he lifts us up into the Godhead so we too can share the life of God, by living the life of Christ, exposing violence and loving others by living peacefully. In other words, we live Jesus' incarnational life—we are the incarnation of the life of Jesus now on earth.

At-one-ment

Although the Bible uses many different metaphors to describe what happened when Jesus lived, died, and rose again, we can affirm with Paul the following: "For I handed on to you as of first importance what I in turn had received: that Christ died for our sins in accordance with the scriptures, and that he was buried, and that he was raised on the third day in accordance with the scriptures. . . ." (1 Cor. 15:3–4). So we see that even Paul, who tries elsewhere to explain the salvific nature of Jesus's work on earth, here boils it all down to: (1) Jesus died; (2) Jesus was buried; and (3) Jesus rose again. In other words, the most important thing for Paul to know and to explain and to preach is that through Jesus, God provided not only for our salvation, but for the redemption of the entire creation (Rom. 8:19–22). By studying the various biblical metaphors that communicate God's salvation, we see that through Jesus, God deals with the sin problem and draws us into a forgiven, reconciled, and restored relationship not only with God but with each other.

However we unpack it, whichever way we interpret it, something of cosmic, concrete significance happened that opened the way for us to enter into God in a new kind of life. The result of the significant "something," is at-one-ment with God. Jesus had this at-one-ment in mind when he prayed for us in John 17. He intercedes to God on our behalf: "I ask not only on behalf of these, but also on behalf of those who will believe in me through their word, that they may all be one. As you, Father, are in me and I am in you, may they also be in us . . ." (John 17:20–21).

Early church fathers in the East spoke of at-one-ment as union with God or as *theōsis*. And Eastern Orthodox Christians still believe that Jesus was made human so that humans could be made divine. Now, the Orthodox Church doesn't teach that humanity will actually be God or be equal to God—that idea would not have passed muster with the Church at large. But it does teach that we will become so like Jesus, so united, so at-one with God, that we will be one, relationally speaking. In Jesus, who descended to us, we ascend to God. We unite with God and participate in the love relationship with the Father, the Son, and the Holy Spirit. Through our unity with Jesus our human nature is re-made into its original beauty, reborn to new life. "So if anyone is in Christ, there is a new creation: everything old has passed away; see, everything has become new! All this is from God who reconciled us to himself through Christ . . ." (2 Cor. 5:17–18). Through the perfect unity of the divine and human in Jesus, God participates in the life of humanity. Through that perfect union in Jesus, we also participate in the life of God.[6]

The metaphor of participation, of God participating in our human-ness and we participating in God's divinity, illustrates the beauty of reconciliation and the restoration of our relationship with God. We actually participate in God's nature and God in ours. As 2 Peter 1:4 tells us, we become partakers of the divine nature, liberated from our corrupt nature through the work of Jesus. Jesus, then, acts as the true mediator between God and humans (and all creation, actually) by uniting the human and divine into one, so that we are "at-one." At-one-ment gives new meaning to "Immanuel," God with us. God in us. One with us—never forsaking us because we are at-one.

The at-one-ment of God's nature and ours through Jesus means that God's heart becomes ours; God's desires, God's purposes, and God's kingdom vision are ours as well. For us, at-one-ment means that to live is Christ (Phil. 1:21). No longer do we live, but Christ lives within us (Gal. 2:20). This is the nature of at-one-ment. Sprinkled with the life-giving shed blood of Jesus Christ we are cleansed, purified, forgiven, and made at one with God so that we too, in imitation of Christ, can offer our own lives as living sacrifices acceptable to God. This is the nature of true worship!

Liberation from the cycle of Violence

Traditional theories of the atonement buy into the idea of redemptive violence. Jesus' violent death on the cross redeems us. But as we discussed in the chapter on justice, violence, in God's eyes, doesn't bring peace. It keeps the cycle of retribution in motion and gives birth to continued violence—and God considers that violence a sin. But then what do we make of the violence of the cross and Jesus' reaction to it?

Traditionally, we've been taught that Jesus could have called legions of angels down on his persecutors and saved himself from suffering a tortuous death, not to mention giving himself the satisfaction of seeing the angels smite his enemies in one fell swoop. People passing by the cross as he hung dying taunted him saying, "he saved others; he cannot save himself. Let the Messiah, the King of Israel, come down from the cross now, so that we may see and believe" (Mark 15:29–31). But he didn't. Jesus stayed there on the cross, and rather than call down an army of angels, he prayed for our forgiveness. The opposite of retribution and its ensuing violence.

By asking God to forgive us, he revealed the heart of God. He showed us that the way to God is not a war-path, but the way of peace, forgiveness, and reconciliation. Jesus exposed and interrupted the cycle of violence that we never seem able to escape on our own. Through Jesus, God entered into our world, suffered the consequences of our attachment to violence and reversed the retributive cycle of violence into a cycle of forgiveness, reconciliation, restoration, and peace. Theologian Mark Heim states it beautifully: "God was willing to be a victim of that bad thing we had made apparently good, in order to reveal its horror and stop it."[7] With our traditional theories of atonement, in which God requires violence in order to bring peace, we have made violence a good thing, a redemptive thing. In opposition to that way of thinking, Jesus reveals the horror of the violence and dies trying in an effort to put a stop to it once and for all.

ONCE UPON A TIME

Okay, now for the alternate theory I promised all laid out and incorporating everything we've talked about so far. I'll put it in story form.

Once upon a time a loving God created a universe filled with planets and stars. In that universe God created a planet called Earth and populated it with all sorts of living creatures. God created living beings, called people, to live and to love freely just like God does. God deeply and passionately loved the people and enjoyed an especially intimate and satisfying relationship with them. God participated in their lives and they participated in God's. But the people, who had once freely loved their creator, decided to strike out on their own. They forgot how to live the way God had taught them. They forgot how to love the way God loves. They started killing and abusing one another in order to get what they wanted. Soon they became enslaved to a life of anger, violence, oppression, and every sort of wrongdoing. Now, they could no longer enjoy the freedom that comes from the love of God and from living the way God had taught them. Instead, they created for themselves a life that enslaved them to cycles of violence and sin.

So God knew something had to be done to save them from their life of slavery to sin. God had to rescue them, bring them back into an intimate participation in God's life, and teach them how to love all over again. Well, what better way to do that than to walk among them, speak to them, live as an example to them, and fully participate in their lives by taking on their humanity. What better way to bring them back into the life of God than by loving and forgiving them, and finally to reconcile and restore them? So that's what God did. Jesus came and lived among them as "God with us."

Jesus loved the people and taught them how to love God and each other. He showed them how to live a life of peace and told them that they were all equally loved in God's eyes. He fed them and healed them and rejoiced with them and wept with them. He told them that they could be free from the anger, violence, oppression, and wrongdoing that made their lives so miserable. He told them that they could be one with God and receive God's eternal life as their own. And many people listened and followed Jesus. Great crowds gathered to hear him speak and to see him heal the sick. He loved the people like no one ever had before. He told them that if they followed in the way he lived and taught, they would have abundant life, that they would have an intimate relationship with God that leads to new life, just like he did.

But the rulers and the leaders of Earth feared his influence and didn't like the way he taught the people about freedom and equality. They feared that the great crowds gathered to listen to Jesus would turn against them. So they decided to kill Jesus. They did it in the worst possible way for that day and time. They nailed him to a cross. And even though they put him through terrible beatings, and spit upon him, and drove nails into his hands and feet, leaving him hanging to die, he never uttered one single word of hatred or anger. He didn't threaten them with vengeful invectives or retribution. Instead, he let them execute him like a common criminal. He took upon himself their sinful actions toward him and suffered because of their sin. He let them crush him and destroy him. You'd think that God at least would have sent thousands of angels to get back at them, to kill them because they killed Jesus. But God didn't. Even though God grieved at the sight of such horrific abuse, God let Jesus finish out the life he committed himself to live on Earth—which ended with a horrible death at the hands of the people. Despite the fact that God didn't need or condone such a terrible execution and hated the evil that prompted it. Instead, God interrupted the cycle of violence with good. God created something good in spite of the wickedness of human sin.[8]

It happened that through the death of Jesus, other people saw the injustice of what happened and decided to live differently, to make up their minds to change their evil and violent ways and to live the way Jesus taught them. The death of Jesus comforted others who suffered at the hands of violent people and they knew that Jesus was somehow there suffering with them, understanding their pain and their sorrows and the burdens they carried because he suffered the same things. Such a public death revealed to all people the extravagance and limitless depth of true love—love of God and love for God.

But what truly amazed the people is what Jesus said while he was dying. Instead of cursing the people who killed him in such a terrible, unjust way, Jesus looked up to heaven and prayed for them. He prayed

for them, asking God to forgive them. As the representative of humanity, it's as if Jesus prayed for all the people God ever created and asked
God to forgive them for every sin they ever committed. And those who
knew Jesus realized that he was such a righteous man that God certainly would answer his prayer and forgive all the people of the Earth
(Jas. 5:16). And God did—God forgave them all, including all of us as
part of the human race, and opened the way for reconciliation and the
restoration of our relationship. In forgiving, God also lifted us up into
the life of God. God became human flesh so that cleansed and forgiven
human beings could participate in the eternal life of God.

A few days later, some of the women went to the tomb to anoint
Jesus' body with herbs for burial. But his body was gone! They went
and told all the people that loved Jesus that he had disappeared. They
ran to see for themselves and sure enough, the tomb was empty. It
wasn't too many days, however, when Jesus appeared to them, cooked
them breakfast, let them touch him, and told them all about the new
life that they could have if they would follow his way of love as newly
cleansed, newly created people of God. Many did and still do today.

REHASHING THE POINTS

As simple as this story seems, its tenets form the basis for our faith.
Let's emphasize the points of the story concerning our at-one-ment
with God.

First, Jesus emptied himself of the right to live selfishly and gave his
life in service to all of God's creation. He did so for better or for worse.
He took it upon himself to endure whatever life brought his way, to
suffer the sinful actions of those he met on his journey. Second, he died
at the hands of sinful people. This is how he took on our sin. This is
how the iniquities of us all were laid upon him and how he was crushed
for our transgressions. He suffered the consequences of human sin. In
essence all humanity is guilty of sin and therefore of the death of Jesus.[9]

Third, by asking God to forgive humanity its sin, Jesus sacrificed the
right to receive payback or satisfaction for sin on God's behalf. God,
out of great mercy and compassion, answered the prayer offered sacrificially by God's son and forgave us all of our sin. The blood of Jesus,
or in other words, the life of Jesus "kippurs" us, covers our sin, cleanses
us, and symbolizes God's forgiveness. This forgiveness reaches all of
humanity on a cosmic, objective level. We play a part in reconciling

with God by acknowledging and receiving that forgiveness. Some might call it repentance.

Fourth, Jesus undid the damage the first Adam did and brings us into new life (through faith) with God as the second Adam. The work of Jesus brings salvation to us on a cosmic, objective, concrete level. As the second Adam, Jesus recreated us, recapitulated the damage done by the first Adam, and made us alive together with him before God (Eph. 2:4–10). Just as through Adam's unrighteousness we all fell into unrighteousness and needed salvation from sin, through Jesus' righteousness we all are made righteous and are saved from sin and death (Rom. 5:12–17). Just as we participated in the sin of Adam, we now participate in the righteousness of Christ. Just as the incarnation of Jesus lifts us into the Godhead to share in the divine life, the Church lives now as the incarnate body of Christ on earth. And God invites us to participate in the eternal life of God through Christ. It is no longer we who live, but Christ who lives within us (Gal. 2:20). We are at-one and at-peace with God.

Fifth, through his life, death, and resurrection, Jesus reveals to us the incomprehensible love of God toward us and toward all creation. As partakers of the divine nature, God calls us to be ministers of reconciliation, a sweet aroma of Jesus everywhere we go (2 Cor. 2:15; 5:18–19; 2 Pet. 1:4).The point is this: while Jesus hung dying on the cross he prayed and asked God to forgive those who murdered him. This prayer, uttered in a state of intense suffering, expresses a desire for forgiveness rather than for retaliation from God, pardon rather than a balancing of the books. While the evil of humanity reached a climax in crucifying Jesus, he himself reached out and sought the reverse of revenge. Instead of another chapter in the long human history of eye-for-an-eye justice, the great injustice of the cross culminated in compassionate restoration, a loving embrace that brought shame to the human structures of life.[10] God granted this forgiveness on a cosmic level. In other words, God forgave all people universally, without condition and without exception. It is something objective and concrete that applies to everyone. When we embrace that forgiveness, we are reconciled with God. We are at-one and we go forward to live as the incarnation of Jesus on earth.

Jesus revealed to us and gave us God's restorative justice. Since the death of Jesus occurred as the result of human sin, because he, as the "second Adam" represented all of humanity to God, and since he overcame death for all humanity, Jesus' prayer was a prayer for God to forgive all humanity.[11] Theologian Dorothee Sölle says that "prayer

summons God into this world."[12] Jesus' prayer for forgiveness from
the cross revealed God's gracious desire to transform the violence of
human existence into compassion, love, and forgiveness. God's act of
forgiveness reveals to us the true nature of divine justice as merciful,
reconciling, and restorative. The love of God discloses to us the greatest
of sacrifices that forgives humanity its sin without condition and without keeping accounts. God in Jesus sacrifices the right to vengeance or
punishment. God suffers the loss by forgiving us the debt. God truly
was "in Christ reconciling the world to himself" by "not counting [our]
trespasses against [us]" (2 Cor. 5:19). This divine forgiveness gives
expression to the antiviolent nature of God who seeks to save those
who are trapped in strictures and structures of injustice often justified
by mistaken notions of God and the atonement.

In other words, Jesus made a very costly sacrifice because of us and
on our behalf. The death of Jesus, orchestrated not by God but by
human beings, does not detract from the sacrifice. Remember, Jesus
shed his blood, that is, Jesus gave his life for us and to us out of love.
Thomas Aquinas clearly considers the sacrifice of Jesus a sacrifice of
love. He writes that "on the part of those who put Jesus to death, the
passion was a crime; on the part of Jesus, who suffered out of love, it
was a sacrifice."[13] The active ingredient, therefore, that made the passion of Jesus a sacrifice was the internal condition of Jesus' heart and
mind, his willing love, not the material elements of death such as the
pain, the shed blood, or the nails through his hands and feet.[14] The
violence of the passion did not please or satisfy God and was considered a crime. The true sacrifice of Jesus lies not in the literal shedding
of blood but the inward condition of his heart of love revealed by the
outward giving of his life, symbolized by his blood.[15] Jesus, therefore,
did sacrifice something; his life and death were a sacrifice offered both
to God and to humanity. With a heart freely offered to God and to
humanity in love, he sacrificed the right to take his pound of flesh; he
sacrificed receiving back (as God) what was owed by humanity for the
offense of sin.

What Jesus offers, therefore, is the sacrifice of love and obedience by
completely identifying with humanity and the consequences of human
sin as he suffers in solidarity with the oppressed and abused throughout
time. Theologian Paul Fiddes says that Jesus "plumbs the bitter depths
where broken relationships run out into desolation and nothingness.
He hangs on the cross at the end-point of human sin, at the focus of all
human self-destruction."[16] Through his loving obedience, sacrificial in

both life and death, Jesus integrates us into the kingdom of God, "re-socializes us, that is to say, makes us citizens of his kingdom."[17]

It takes one to forgive and two to reconcile. Although God freely forgives all of us without condition, we can choose to enter fully into the equation in order for reconciliation with God to happen. And this reconciliation takes place as we turn back to God. God lifts us up into the life of God and we participate joyfully in the new life we have in Christ. We can interpret the cross of Jesus as at-one-ment that deconstructs notions of a violent God bent on retributive justice. We see that the justice of God is love and that love forgives, transforms, and seeks to create new and harmonious relationships. Through the forgiveness of God, a way is opened up for the transformation of all humanity (all creation, to be exact). Through the cross of Jesus, we are forgiven without condition, accepted as we are. Through repentance we are reconciled with God and transformed into those who live in the power of divine love.

Divine justice, therefore, is the act of loving and forgiving, a bottomless, endless, profoundly absurd forgiveness that reaches out in love to all humankind. Our response-ability is to receive it, to enter into the forgiveness of God, reconciled and restored. If, that is, we have eyes to see and ears to hear:

> Yahweh is tender and compassionate,
> slow to anger, most loving;
> his indignation does not last for ever,
> his resentment exists a short time only;
> he never treats us, never punishes us,
> as our guilt and our sins deserve.
>
> —Ps. 103:8–10 Jerusalem Bible

Afterword

I appreciate readers keeping in mind the fact that this book is written for a general audience—a genre completely foreign and difficult to comprehend for many academics! It is not an exhaustive academic treatise on atonement theory with endless endnotes and apologia ad infinitum for my construction of an alternative view of the passion event. I have not cited all of the works consulted but have included those texts that offer support for various statements, interpretations, and quotes in the text. I have, however, attempted to keep those at a minimum so as not to overwhelm the curious, intelligent, and engaged lay reader.

In my research for this book, I found a very helpful work by Euan Cameron titled, *Interpreting Christian History: The Challenge of the Churches' Past* (Malden, MA: Blackwell Publishing, 2005). Cameron outlines the history of the church, its doctrines, and the cultural, social, economic, and political shifts that take place and that profoundly influence the direction and focus of theology. I believe another shift is taking place as we strive for peace in a world ripped apart by religious violence. We must find ways to focus on theologies of peace and love for our enemies, or we may totally destroy ourselves. So, as Cameron's book states, Christians have the "constant tendency to stress one feature of the Christian message over another." I hope to stress the message of love, peace, goodwill toward all creation, and the good news of salvation, transformation, and unity with God through the love of God in Jesus.

To those readers who may have found the content of this book questionable, I submit the following questions: what could be more questionable than the abuses, massacres, wars, tortures, bloodshed, and violence already committed by those who call on the name of Jesus? What could be more questionable than an image of God who tells us to love our enemies but tortures God's own enemies in hell for all eternity? What is so questionable about focusing on a message of love and compassion? Which festival of atonement is more questionable given Jesus' gospel of salvation through forgiveness—the celebration of atonement as divine revenge or the celebration of reconciliation through grace and love?

In *The Jesus Driven Life,* Michael Hardin provides us with a great analogy to the divine "choose-me-or-I'll-send-you-to-hell-forever" mentality that our tradition proudly espouses (85). He tells the story of a young man who is completely smitten with a young women. He doesn't think she even knows he's alive, so he loves her from a distance. One day she comes to him and expresses her deep love and devotion for him. She tells him that she wants to be with him always. He is the reason she exists. Wonderful! Dream come true, right? But not knowing how he feels for her, she continues on, saying that if he doesn't love her in return, she's going to make his life a living hell forever. He'll never get out from under her wrath and indignation. She will punish him and torture him and make him pay for his unrequited love. He would probably run for his life! And not turn back! He might even contact the authorities and have a restraining order issued. But isn't this what we've been saying about God for centuries? God says, "I love you with all of my heart and want to be with you forever. Love me back or you'll suffer in hell for all eternity, always separated from me." Yikes! Should we get a restraining order against God?!

My message of the cross, then, refutes the message of an angry father or a dissed lover who must exact retribution, who finds satisfaction in the horrific death of an innocent son, who must have his pound of flesh before he can forgive sin. I focus on the message of a loving God who sacrificially gives up receiving a payback for sin, who is satisfied by a justice that reconciles and restores relationships, who sees to it that mercy triumphs over judgment, and whose love for enemies works to win them over with grace, mercy, and compassion.

Notes

Introduction

1. See Julie Shoshana Pfau and David R. Blumenthal, "The Violence of God: Dialogic Fragments," in *Cross Currents* 51 (summer 2001): 183.

2. See Joanne Carlson Brown, "Divine Child Abuse?" in *Daughters of Sarah* (summer 1992): 25–28; Margo G. Houts, "Atonement and Abuse: An Alternate View," in *Daughters of Sarah* (summer 1992): 29–32; Joanne Carlson-Brown and Rebecca Parker, "For God so Loved the World?" in *Christianity, Patriarchy, and Abuse: A Feminist Critique* (New York: Pilgrim Press, 1989), 2. See also Julie Shoshana Pfau and David R. Blumenthal, "The Violence of God," 183.

3. For centuries Anabaptists have interpreted the Bible through the lens of Jesus, including the Old Testament stories that portray God as violent. For a contemporary work on the topic of interpreting Scripture through the life, teachings, death, and resurrection of Jesus see Michael Hardin, *The Jesus Driven Life: Reconnecting Humanity with Jesus* (Lancaster, PA: JDL Press, 2010).

Chapter 1: God Gone Bad? Religion Gone Bad?

1. See *The Poseidon Adventure*, directed by Ronald Neame Twentieth Century Fox: 1972).

2. *Alan Colmes Show*, June 2, 2009. He gets this from many of the Psalms, but in particular Psalm 35, in which David asks God to kill his enemies. See also Psalms 7, 55, 58, 59, 69, 79, 109, 137, and 139.

3. http://web.archive.org/web/20071013102203/http://relevantmagazine.com/god_article.php
Here is the entire quote: "There is a strong drift toward the hard theological left. Some emergent types [want] to recast Jesus as a limp-wrist hippie in a dress with a lot of product in His hair, who drank decaf and made pithy Zen statements about life while shopping for the perfect pair of shoes. In Revelation, Jesus is a prize fighter with a tattoo down His leg, a sword in His hand and the commitment to make someone bleed. That is a guy I can worship. I cannot worship the hippie, diaper, halo Christ because I cannot worship a guy I can beat up." See also B. Keith Putt, "*Depravatio Crucis*: The Non-Sovereignty of God in John Caputo's Poetics of the Kingdom" in *Peace Be with You: Christ's Benediction amidst Violent Empires*, eds. Sharon L. Baker and Michael Hardin (Telford, PA: Cascadia Publishing House, 2010), 169–170.

4. Matthew White, *The Great Big Book of Horrible Things* (New York: W. W. Norton and Company, 2012), 99–112. Don't let the title of this book fool you. White has done his homework here and has generated a well-respected historical work.

5. Richard Dawkins, *Guardian* (Sept. 12, 2001). See also Douglas John Hall, "Against Religion" in *Christian Century* (January 11, 2011): 33.

6. Evelyn Mullally, *The Deeds of the Norman in Ireland* (Dublin: Four Courts Press, 2002), 102.

7. Richard W. Kaeuper, *Holy Warriors: The Religious Ideology of Chivalry* (Philadelphia: University of Pennsylvania Press, 2009), 22.

8. Cheryl A. Kirk-Duggan. *Violence and Theology* (Nashville: Abingdon Press, 2006), 2, 19–20.

9. For other instances of God's violence see the stories in the Old Testament about Noah's Ark (Genesis 6), the killing of Egypt's first born and drowning the Egyptian army in the Red Sea (Exodus 11–15:21), killing all of Korah's family (Numbers 16), wiping out the residents of Canaan (Deuteronomy 7:2; Joshua 1–13) to name just a few. Throughout the book I make quite a few references to the violence of the Old Testament and the peace-focused nature of Jesus' teachings. I am not leaning toward Marcionite theology here in the least. I don't believe that we should nix the Old Testament in favor of the New, or separate the Jewish God from the Christian God (both testaments are largely Jewish texts after all). I do suggest later on, however, that we need to interpret the violent passages in the Old Testament in light of the teachings of the very Jewish Jesus and in their own context. After all, the Old Testament speaks volumes about the *hesed* and *raham* of God and the divine everlasting grace, mercy, and love.

10. For an interview with Philip Jenkins, author of *Jesus Wars* see http://www.npr.org/templates/story/story.php?storyId=124494788. Jenkins compares the Bible and the Qur'an and argues that the Bible is actually more violent. He contends that the Qur'an "is far less bloody and violent" and that the laws laid down in the Qur'an are quite humane. See also *Jesus Wars* (Harper Collins E-books, 2010).

11. Jack Nelson-Pallmeyer, *Is Religion Killing Us? Violence in the Bible and the Quran* (Harrisburg, PA: Trinity Press International, 2003), 20. Nelson-Pallmeyer thinks religion is indeed going to kill us if we keep on the way we're going. He would diminish the importance and authority of the sacred texts in order to keep peace. I would rather maintain a higher view of scriptural authority and reinterpret it through a peaceful or Jesus lens.

12. Anthony Bartlett, *Cross Purposes: The Violent Grammar of Christian Atonement* (Harrisburg, PA: Trinity Press International, 2001), 96; Rita Nakashima Brock and Rebecca Ann Parker, *Saving Paradise: How Christianity Traded Love of This World for Crucifixion and Empire* (Boston: Beacon Press, 2008), 252.

13. Kaeuper, *Holy Warriors,* 116–117, 120, 129. See also John Bossy, *Christianity in the West 1400–1700* (Oxford: University of Oxford Press, 1985), 72.

14. http://necrometrics.com/pre1700a.htm.

15. Kaeuper, *Holy Warriors*, 21–22.

16. Bartlett, *Cross Purposes*, 67–69.

17. Kaeuper, *Holy Warriors*, 16–17. Although priests criticizing the violence of war in the name of Jesus and under the sign of the cross wrote and preached during these centuries, their calls to peace remained a much ignored (at best) and often persecuted (at worst) voice.

18. Brock and Parker, *Saving Paradise*, 271, 289.

19. Kaeuper, *Holy Warriors*, 120.

20. Kaeuper, *Holy Warriors*, 7. See also Norman Housely, *Fighting for the Cross: Crusading to the Holy Land* (New Haven: Yale University Press, 2008), 75, 184–186.

21. Brock and Parker, *Saving Paradise*, 270. Even though "peace by the blood of the cross" is a biblical idea, these war-minded Christians (a minority, but very dangerous to those who got in their way) misinterpreted it from "peace with God through the forgiveness of sin, by the blood Jesus shed on the cross" to "temporal peace with the empire through killing those who disagree with our doctrine."

22. Bartlett, *Cross Purposes*, 95.

23. Brock and Parker, *Saving Paradise*, xi, 274. Brock and Parker write that "life-size images of the Crucifixion appeared in churches throughout Northern Europe [10th c] to remind the faithful of their crime of killing Christ and to teach them fear of God's judgment." Gazing upon the crucifixion also reminded them that if they didn't lay down their lives in battle just as Jesus laid down his life for them on the cross, God would judge them harshly for all eternity (258).

24. Rita Nakashima Brock and Rebecca Ann Parker, *Proverbs of Ashes: Violence, Redemptive Suffering, and the Search for What Saves Us* (Boston: Beacon Press, 2001), 41, 44. See also Brock and Parker, *Saving Paradise*, 224, 297, 311–312; Kaeuper, *Holy Warriors*, 119. The churches in the Byzantine east continued to emphasize the resurrection more so than the crucifixion. To my knowledge, there aren't any icons depicting soldier-saints and there is not a single Eastern Orthodox person sainted for being a soldier as there are in the Western, Latin churches.

25. Brock and Parker, *Saving Paradise*, 262–265.

26. Brock and Parker, *Saving Paradise*, 310. You can see some of this artwork in the Gothic section of the Museu Nacional D'Art Catalunya in Barcelona, Spain. See also Euan Cameron, *Interpreting Christian History: The Challenge of the Churches' Past* (Malden, MA: Blackwell Publishing, 2005), 73–79 and Edward Peters, ed., *The First Crusade: "The Chronicle of Fulcher of Chartres" and other Source Materials* (Philadephia, PA: University of Pennsylvania Press, 1998), 32. These stories may have been hyperbolized and exaggerated over the centuries— but we don't really know for sure.

27. Kaeuper, *Holy Warriors*, 13; See also Brock and Parker, *Saving Paradise*, 256–257. Of course, we don't want to minimize the sacrifice of those who suffer

for the sake of Jesus through no choice of their own. But I do want to point out that traditional interpretations of the cross have motivated and encouraged unnecessary violence in various forms. Much of this is violence executed in the name of Jesus and under the sign of the cross—egregious violence that I don't think God wills or sanctions. Many innocent saints have been victims of terrible pain, torture, suffering, and death and they are the heroes of the faith. But they didn't purposefully go looking for ways to suffer, to take up their own cross, for the sake of piety. As they tried to embrace their new life in Christ, the suffering found them and they endured it as Jesus endured the cross.

28. The exact numbers of people killed during the crusades and the various inquisitions is not known, although there are widely ranging estimates. Taking into account the crusades and the inquisitions alone, the estimated number of deaths range between 3,000,000 and 10,000,000. These numbers don't include the estimated millions who died in religious wars throughout the centuries, the massacre of Native Americans, or the various witch hunts. No matter how we look at it, that's a lot of people killed in the name of Christ and under the sign of the cross. See the following website for a detailed breakdown by Matthew White. This scholar has done his homework: http://necrometrics.com/pre1700a.htm; Matthew White, *The Great Big Book of Horrible Things: The Definitive Chronicle of History's 100 Worst Atrocities* (New York, NY: W. W. Norton and Company, 2012).

29. Matthias Beier, *A Violent God-Image: An Introduction to the Work of Eugen Drewermann* (New York: The Continuum International Publishing Group, Inc., 2004), 220–221. Beier, who quotes the German theologian Eugen Drewermann, writes, "Jesus did not want to die on the Cross and he never thought to declare inhumanity and torture to be signs of a true trust into God. To the contrary: he lived so that humans would receive back their dignity as creatures of God, so that they would regain their innocence and uninhibitedness in relation to God, and so that the unceasing suffering which afflicts humans because of God [as portrayed] in the religions of human history would find an end. Precisely for that reason people who understood him called him *the life*: because what he spoke allowed them to live and brought them to life. Exactly for that reason they called him *the way*: because thus they found direction and perspective in their life. Exactly for that reason they called him *the truth*: because through him their life and all things around them found again their true *gestalt*. Because they could live in him as they were actually meant to and created to they call him *Son of God* (John 14:6)" (223–224). See also Hardin, *The Jesus Driven Life*, 28–29.

30. Brock and Parker, *Saving Paradise*, 238. The Roman Catholic Inquisition ended in 1860 even though the last act of violence against a person was in 1858 in Bologna when officials removed a six-year-old boy from the home of his Jewish parents. Of course, at that late date, the action generated a major public outcry, which contributed to antipapal feelings on an international level. Fortunately, by then, times had changed a bit.

31. Beier, *A Violent God-Image*, 12.

32. Brock and Parker, *Saving Paradise*, 49. (I added the italics.)

33. Kaeuper, *Holy Warriors*, 6–9.

34. For a great treatment tracing the history of this switch, see Brock and Parker, *Saving Paradise*. For an English translation of the *Heliand* see *The Heliand: The Saxon Gospel*, translated by G. Ronald Murphy (New York: Oxford University Press, 1992).

35. Douglas John Hall, "Against Religion," 32.

36. Boyd. C. Purcell, *Spiritual Terrorism: Spiritual Abuse from the Womb to the Tomb* (Bloomington, IN: AuthorHouse, 2008), Kindle loc. 711–724. See also Charles Swindoll, *Grace Awakening* (Dallas, TX: Word Publishing, 1990); Elizabeth A. Johnson, C.S.J., "The Word Was Made Flesh and Dwelt among Us," in *Jesus: A Colloquium in the Holy Land*, ed. Dorothy Donnelly (New York: Continuum International Publishing Group, 2001): 158–160; and Jacquelyn Grant, "The Sin of Servanthood and the Deliverance of Discipleship," in *A Troubling in My Soul: Womanist Perspectives on Evil and Suffering*, ed. Emilie M. Townes (Maryknoll, NY: Orbis Books, 1993): 208–210.

37. Brock and Parker, *Proverbs of Ashes*, 22. This text is filled with stories of how those in power over another person use the cross to justify violence and to keep women and children in bondage to it. See also Kirk-Duggan, *Violence and Theology*, 72; James N. Poling, "The Cross and Male Violence," in *Cross Examinations: Readings on the Meaning of the Cross Today*, ed. Marit Trelstad (Minneapolis: Fortress Press, 2006): 50–51. Poling makes a direct connection between theories of atonement and male violence toward women. For another example, see Mary J. Streufert, "Maternal Sacrifice as a Hermeneutics of the Cross," in *Cross Examinations: Cross Examinations Readings on the Meaning of the Cross Today* (Minneapolis, MN: Fortress Press, 2006), 68.

38. Poling, "The Cross and Male Violence," 53–54.

39. Kirk-Duggan, *Violence and Theology*, vii–viii.

40. Streufert, "Maternal Sacrifice as a Hermeneutics of the Cross," 65. See also Nelson-Pallmeyer, *Is Religion Killing Us?* 15, 19.

41. Beier, *A Violent God-Image*, 3.

42. Beier, *A Violent God Image*, 7, 24–25; Cameron, *Interpreting Christian History*, 38. For more on the topic of hurtful ways of being Christian and the struggle of one woman who found her way out of fundamentalist evangelicalism, read Rachel Held Evans, *Evolving in Monkey Town* (Grand Rapids, MI: Zondervan, 2010). This is easily one of the best books I've read in a long time.

43. Kirk-Duggan, *Violence and Theology*, 29. Most of us misinterpret Matt. 10:34 in which Jesus says he comes not to bring peace but a sword. Here Jesus is warning that persecution comes to Christians and that truth will divide people against one another. In other words, Jesus knew we would kill one another over religious issues.

Other Sources

Deacy, Christopher and Gaye Williams Ortiz. *Theology and Film: Challenging the Sacred/Secular Divide*. Indianapolis: Wiley-Blackwell, 2008.
Purcell, Boyd C. *Spiritual Terrorism*. Bloomington, IN: AuthorHouse, 2009.

A thirteenth-century illumination in the British Library, Harley 3244 (folios 27b, 28), depicts a knight sitting on a horse. At the top of the page we see the words: "Militia est vita hominis super terrram" (human life on earth is militia). Militia means "hard struggle," "fighting," or "knighthood." The religious validity of knighthood is obvious from this painting. His fighting equipment is given pious meaning. The armor of God from Ephesians 6, the knight seated on the *Christian Religion*, his saddle resting on a blanket labeled "humility." The sword in his hand is the Word of God; his lance is labeled with the words "steadfastness or perseverance." The corners of his shield depict the names of the Trinity with the lines converging in the center as *Deus* or the Godhead. The parts of the horse are assigned various religious meaning: the rump is "goodwill." An angel above descends with a crown of victory won by the knight in battle and holds in her left hand a banner from 2 Timothy 2:5 that declares only the one who fights the good fight wins a crown. The angel also holds the beatitudes from the Sermon on the Mount, promising holy warriors the kingdom of heaven. They shall inherit the kingdom, they shall be comforted, filled, have mercy, see God, and be called sons of God. The battle-ready knight is waiting to be festooned with streamers, recalling the virtues of mercy, peace, and forbearance. For a copy of the illumination and a full explanation see Kaeuper, *Holy Warriors*, x–xi, 1–4.

Chapter 2: Truth in Metaphor

1. For a great book on metaphor and its function in everyday life see George Lakoff and Mark Johnson, *Metaphors We Live By* (Chicago: University of Chicago Press, 1980). In *A Glossary of Literary Terms*, M. H. Abrams mentions that "after twenty-five centuries of attention to metaphors by rhetoricians, grammarians, and literary critics—in which during the last half-century they have been joined by many philosophers—there is no general agreement about that way we identify metaphors. . . ." Similes and analogies, although often treated as separate figures of speech within figurative language, are forms of metaphor and I will treat them as such in this chapter.

2. Colin Gunton, *The Actuality of Atonement: A Study of Metaphor, Rationality and the Christian Tradition* (Grand Rapids: Eerdmans Publishing Company, 1989), 27.

3. Aristotle, *Poetics*, 1457b 7–8. You can find this text online at http://classics.mit.edu/Aristotle/poetics.3.3.html. Aristotle offers four types of metaphor: (1) from genus to species; (2) from species to genus; (3) from species to species;

(4) from analogy. Some of these types are considered metonymy or synecdoche in today's language—still metaphors, yet under a different name! Why am I thinking about roses?!

4. Janet Martin Soskice, *Metaphor and Religious Language* (New York: Oxford University Press, 1985), 44.

5. G. B. Caird, *The Language and Imagery of the Bible* (Grand Rapids: Eerdmans Publishing Company, 1980), 152. Richard Boyd argues that the use of metaphor "is a task of accommodating language to the causal structure of the world" (Boyd, "Metaphor and Theory Change: What Is 'Metaphor' a Metaphor for?" in *Metaphor and Thought*, ed. A. Ortony [Cambridge: Cambridge University Press, 1979]), 358.

6. In Caird, *Language and Imagery*, 145.

7. Soskice, *Metaphor*, 22, 44.

8. Some linguists argue that when a metaphor becomes common usage or makes its way into the dictionary, it is a dead metaphor. I disagree. It's still a metaphor even though its buried under layers of constant use.

9. Caird, *Language and Imagery*, 152

10. Soskice, *Metaphor*, 89–90.

11. Caird, *Language and Imagery*, 154. Scripture references for the metaphors are as follows in order: Jer. 15:18; Hos. 5:12, 14; Ps. 84:11; Deut. 32:11; Luke 13:34; Isa. 64:8; Pss. 96:10, 13; 47:2, 7, 8; Deut. 32:16; Matt. 7:9–11; Hos. 11:3–4; Heb. 12:9; Mal. 1:6; Eph. 3:14; John 15:9–12; 1:29; Rev. 7:17; John 6; John 15; John 10:11; Luke 6:46; John 1:1; Isa. 53; Matt. 8:19; 1 Cor. 9:7–12; 1 Cor. 9:23–27; Phil. 3:7–9; 1 Thess. 5:1–8; Eph. 6:10–17. Most biblical scholars do not attribute all the New Testament books claiming Pauline authorship as original works from Paul himself. For the sake of simplicity, I will just write "Paul" to indicate all the books attributed to him, while at the same time acknowledging in this note the validity of the biblical scholarship on the topic.

12. 1 Cor. 7:23; 2 Cor. 5:19–21; Col. 2:14–15; Heb. 9:26; Heb. 9:24–25; Matt. 20:28. See also Stephen Finlan, *Problems with Atonement* (Collegeville, MN: Liturgical Press, 2005), 5–9; Mark Heim, *Saved from Sacrifice: A Theology of the Cross* (Grand Rapids, MI: William B. Eerdmans Publishing Company, 2006), 213. Heim believes that some images of God may be harmful to our health—so true. The same cross carried on banners in the Crusades is the same cross hanging in hospitals, places known for healing, love, and compassion.

13. Caird, *Language and Imagery*, 156.

14. Gunton, *The Actuality of Atonement*, 46.

15. Peter Schmiechen, *Saving Power: Theories of Atonement and Forms of the Church* (Grand Rapids: William B. Eerdmans Publishing Company, 2005), 5.

16. Vincent Taylor, *The Atonement in New Testament Teaching* (London: The Epworth Press, 1958), 184–215. In this section Taylor argues that the New Testament atonement metaphors work in tension with one another.

17. See Jürgen Moltmann, *The Crucified God: The Cross of Christ as the Foundation and Criticism of Christian Theology*, trans. by R. A. Wilson and John Bowden (Minneapolis: Fortress Press, 1993).

18. Gunton, *The Actuality of Atonement*, 53–59.

19. Stephen Finlan argues that by using so many different metaphors to explain the atonement Paul is telling us: "Keep all these metaphors in mind, because if you settle on just one, and take it too literally, you will be missing the point." Stephen Finlan, *Options on Atonement in Christian Thought* (Collegeville, MN: Liturgical Press, 2007), 32.

20. Caird, *Language and Imagery*, 157–159.

21. Caird, *Language and Imagery*, 158.

22. Gunton, *The Actuality of Atonement*, 86–87. I think it's important to note that this theological turn to a legal transaction on God's part did not take hold in the East.

23. Gunton, *The Actuality of Atonement*, 128.

24. Gunton, *The Actuality of Atonement*, 93–94. See also Caird, *Language and Imagery*, 153; and Schmiechen, *Saving Power*, 58–119. Caird talks about the "impossible literality" when discussing atonement metaphors and the irresponsibility of interpreting them literally, 188.

25. Gunton, *The Actuality of Atonement*, 120–125.

26. Finlan, *Problems with Atonement*, 35.

27. Caird, *Language and Imagery*, 157. Gunton, *The Actuality of Atonement*, 123–124. Finlan, *Problems with Atonement*, 39ff., argues that because winning converts to Jesus was Paul's main objective, he used metaphors that worked for the people rhetorically. In other words, Paul used metaphors that his listeners would understand in order to make the Gospel more marketable, so it could be "all things to all people" (1 Cor. 9:22).

28. Gunton, *The Actuality of Atonement*, 143.

29. Gunton, *The Actuality of Atonement*, 61–64.

30. Finlan, *Options on Atonement*, 125. Finlan believes that theologians have taken Paul's metaphors much too literally and have missed the main point of Jesus's death. He argues that the main message of Jesus, as seen in his life, death, and resurrection, is that God participates in human suffering, that the cross not only reveals the senselessness and powerlessness of violence but it also reveals our complicity with violence against social victims. Violence is our default mode, but in Jesus, God transforms us and makes love our default behavior. See Finlan, 4.

31. Finlan, *Problems with Atonement*, 62. For a very helpful treatment of how the Christian community has reinterpreted and reconstructed the language, metaphors, and symbols of our faith see Crystal L. Downing, *Changing Signs of Truth: A Christian Introduction to the Semiotics of Communication* (Downers Grove, IL: InterVarsity Press, 2012). This is also an excellent treatment of how cultures reinterpret their metaphors and the necessity and practice of doing so by Christians throughout history. See also Paul Ricoeur, *The Rule of Metaphor: Multidisciplinary Studies of the Creation of Meaning in Language*, translated by Robert

Czerny with Kathleen Mclaughlin and John Costello, SJ (Toronto: University of Toronto Press, 1977).

Chapter Three: Traditional Doctrines—the Good, the Bad, and the Ugly

1. Peter Schmeichen, *Saving Power*, 5.

2. Many of the church fathers held to a form of *Christus Victor* or Ransom theory, including Irenaeus, Origen, Athanasius, Basil the Great, Gregory of Nyssa, Gregory of Nazianzus, John of Damascus, John Chrysostom, Ambrose, Augustine, and Gregory the Great. Each of these early theologians tweaked the theory a bit differently. Irenaeus thought of it in terms of recapitulation in which all fell into sin through the first Adam and all were rescued from sin through Jesus, the second Adam. Gregory of Nyssa thought of the theory in terms of a ransom paid to God. Jesus served as the ransom—God gives the devil Jesus in exchange for humanity. But little did the devil know: Jesus was really God in the flesh. Unable to bear the presence of God's son, he spewed him out and Jesus took all humanity with him in victory over sin and death. Jesus acted as the bait on the fishhook that the devil swallowed whole. For instance, see L. W. Grensted, *A Short History of the Doctrine of the Atonement* (Eugene, OR: Wipf and Stock Publishers, 2001); Inna Jane Ray, *The Atonement Muddle: An Historical Analysis and Clarification of a Salvation Theory*, vol. 15 (The Center for Women and Religion, 1997). For a contemporary theological view on the victory of Christ theory see J. Beilby and P. R. Eddy, eds., *The Nature of Atonement: Four Views* (Downers Grove, IL: InterVarsity Press, 2006), 23–49. See Joel B. Green and Mark D. Baker, *Recovering the Scandal of the Cross: Atonement in New Testament and Contemporary Contexts* (Downers Grove, IL: InterVarsity Press, 2000), 116–125.

3. For a more detailed treatment of the *Christus* Victor theory of atonement see Gustaf Aulén, *Christus Victor: An Historical Study of the Three Main Types of the Idea of Atonement* (Eugene, OR: Wipf and Stock Publishers, 1931) and J. Denny Weaver, *The Non-Violent Atonement* (Grand Rapids: Eerdman's Publishing Company, 2001).

4. See the many works by theologian Walter Wink such as *Engaging the Powers* (Minneapolis: Fortress Press, 1992) and *The Powers That Be* (New York, NY: Three Rivers Press, 1999).

5. Other verses that support *Christus Victor* theories of atonement are: Rev. 12:11; Matt. 20:28; Eph. 3:10–12.

6. See Brock and Parker, *Saving Paradise* for a nice historical treatment of the theory. See also J. Denny Weaver, *The Non-Violent Atonement*.

7. What Anselm first systematically conceived and constructed, other thinkers took and tweaked. For instance, Thomas Aquinas, disagreeing with Anselm's notions of necessity, reconceived the theory to suit his ideas about God's sovereignty and providence, nuancing and softening the necessity of God acting in any certain way to redeem creation. In addition, Colin Gunton makes the point that although the feudal system was the common form of government

in Anselm's day, he did not liken God to an arbitrary or oppressive ruler as we sometimes think about feudal lords—just the opposite. God, as with feudal lords, maintained order, civil rights, and civil obligations so that society could function satisfactorily. See *The Actuality of Atonement*, 89. For a very good treatment of the honor/shame, retributive mindset of people living during Anselm's time see Philip Jenkins, *Jesus Wars*, 28–31. Of course, as with all scholarship, there are historians who do not believe that Anselm was all that influenced by his cultural surroundings and that he constructed his theory of atonement based upon his reading of Scripture alone. I think this is a naive perspective that fails to realize that we are always influenced by our culture. I'm not saying that theologians didn't also pray, read Scripture, and interpret according to how the Spirit led them at the time. I am saying, however, that our perceptions, perspectives, and consequent theological constructions develop out of the society and culture into which we are thrown. In other words, our contexts and our reading of Scripture and tradition work together to form our theology.

8. Two of the most excellent treatments I've found on this subject are Stephen Finlan's two works: *Problems with Atonement* (Collegeville, MN: Liturgical Press, 2005) and *The Background and Content of Paul's Cultic Atonement Metaphors* (Atlanta: Society for Biblical Literature, 2004). Another great source is Peter Schmiechen, *Saving Power*, especially pages 5–55.

9. Abelard, "Exposition of the Epistle to the Romans, 3:21–23," in *A Scholastic Miscellany: Anselm to Ockham*, Eugene R. Fairweather, ed. (Philadelphia, PA: The Westminster Press, 1954), 278–279. Cf., Colin Green, "Is the Message of the Cross Good News for the Twentieth Century?" in *Atonement Today: A Symposium at St. John's College, Nottingham*, ed. by John Goldingay (London: SPCK, 1995), 223; Bernard McCullagh, "Theology of Atonement" in *Theology* (September 1988), 399. See also Abelard, *Exp. in Epist. ad Rom.* i.i quoted from Richard E. Weingart, *The Logic of Divine Love: A Critical Analysis of the Soteriology of Peter Abelard* (London: Clarendon, 1970), 75–76; See also Abelard, *Exp. in Epist. ad Rom.* ii.iii and Prol as quoted in Weingart.

10. In his commentary on Romans 3:19–26, Abelard writes: "Indeed, how cruel and wicked it seems that anyone should demand the blood of an innocent person as the price for anything, or that it should in any way please him that an innocent man should be slain—still less that God should consider the death of his son so agreeable that by it he should be reconciled to the whole world!" See Abelard, "Epistle to the Romans, 3:21–23," in *A Scholastic Miscellany* 283.

11. See Paul S. Fiddes, *Past Event and Present Salvation: A Study on the Christian Doctrine of Atonement* (Louisville: Westminster/John Knox Press, 1989), 145. Abelard, *Rom.* ii.i. in Weingart, 159 states: "In the new life in the Spirit the believer lives in love; he is now a son of God, related to him not in fear of his judgment but in love and gratitude, freely worshipping and serving him"; Abelard, *Exp. in Epist. ad Rom.,* ii.iii: "Therefore our redemption is that supreme love within us, through Christ's suffering which not only frees us from slavery to

sin, but also wins for us the true liberty of sons of God, so that we do all things out of love rather than fear," quoted in Weingart, 159. Quinn, "Abelard on Atonement," 289, argues that "it remains to be seen how the passion of Christ actually works to implant or produce this love in us." For him, therefore, the appropriation of the salvation through the love of Christ depends upon the subjective rather than an objective reality. Abelard himself tells us that the love of God is expressed by the Holy Spirit through feelings in our heart due to which we "sigh for love," and "whoever persists in the love of God must be saved"—a truly subjective appropriation of the love of God and, therefore, of salvation. But even Abelard cannot quite explain exactly how the Spirit infuses us with love. He awkwardly states the process by saying that "God is said *in some way* to go out from Himself to His creatures" (emphasis mine). Peter Abelard, *The Christian Theology,* ed. by J. Ramsay McCallum (Oxford: Blackwell Publishing, 1948), 49, 88; Peter Abelard, *Ethics,* ed. by D. E. Luscombe (Oxford: Clarendon Press, 1971), 91. Cf., Abelard, "Epistle to the Romans," in Fairweather, 279 (love remits sin). See also Weingart, 124, 159, 161. See also Abelard, "Epistle to the Romans," in Fairweather, 278. Abelard gives a prominent place to the Holy Spirit in human apprehension of the divine love in Rom. 2.3 and in *Sermo. xvii.* See Weingart's treatment of Abelard's notions of the Holy Spirit's activities in *The Logic of Divine Love,* 153–156. Abelard too speaks of justice in harmony with mercy and with love. He says that "justified [forgiven] for free means that you are justified not because of your outstanding achievements or gains but thanks to God's mercy who was the first to love us" and "in the time of mercy it is God's justice that he gives us and through which we are justified and the name for it is love." Abelard makes clear that the justice of God, through love and in mercy, results in the forgiveness of sin without condition or compensation (Abelard, "Epistle to the Romans" [3:22, 24], in Fairweather, 275–277). Abelard equates divine justice with divine love. Divine love forgives human sin. See Weingart, *The Logic of Divine Love,* 121, 275–277.

12. John Calvin, *Institutes of the Christian Religion,* translated by Henry Beveridge (Orlando, FL: formatted for Kindle by Signalman Publishing, 2009), 2.1.4 and 2.1.8. Calvin asserts that human sin, beginning with Adam, was so great that it "provoked God to inflict such fearful vengeance on the whole human race" (2.1.4).

13. John Calvin, *Institutes of the Christian Religion,* 2.16.

14. John Calvin, *Institutes of the Christian Religion,* 3.21.7.

15. Beier, *A Violent God Image,* 217.

16. Beier, *A Violent God Image,* 218. See also Roger E. Olson, *Against Calvinism* (Grand Rapids: Zondervan, 2011), 136–154.

17. Gregory Anderson Love, *Love, Violence, and the Cross: How the Nonviolent God Saves Us through the Cross of Christ* (Eugene, OR: Cascade Books, 2010), 32–38. For an excellent treatment on the lack of biblical support for the penal theory of atonement see Finlan, *Options on Atonement,* 27–38 and *Problems*

with Atonement, 39–62 (especially 61–62). Thelma Megill-Cobbler argues that Penal theories of atonement portray God as wicked and cruel—attributes that should, instead, be attached to human beings. See Megill-Cobbler, "A Feminist Rethinking of Punishment Imagery in Atonement," *Dialog*, vol. 35 no. 1 (winter 1996): 18.

18. Elizabeth Malkin, "As Gangs Move in on Mexico's Schools, Teachers Say 'Enough'" in *The New York Times* (http://www.nytimes.com/2011/09/26/world/americas/mexican-teachers-push-back-against-gangs-extortion-attempts.html?ref=world).

19. Because theologians are becoming more sensitive to the explicitly violent and unjust images of God penal and satisfaction models of atonement encourage, the governmental theory of atonement is growing in popularity. While I appreciate and respect the scholarship and theological attempts to soften more violent theories, I don't think the governmental theory, a nuanced form of satisfaction, goes far enough in exonerating God from needing the violent death of an innocent man in order to forgive sin. See Roger E. Olson, *Arminian Theology: Myths and Realities* (Downers Grover, IL: IVP Academic, 2006), 224–41 and http://www.patheos.com/blogs/rogereolson/2012/09/a-neglected-theory-of-the-atonement/.

Chapter 4: The Problem of God in the Atonement

1. Stephen Finlan, *Options on Atonement*, 87.

2. Robin Collins and Rebecca Adams, *Understanding Atonement: A New and Orthodox Theory* (copyright 1995. A work still in progress) http://home.messiah.edu/~rcollins/Philosophical%20Theology/Atonement/AT7.HTM.

3. Peter Schmeichen, *Saving Power*, 51. For a more in-depth treatment of the violence of Mesopotamian and Egyptian cultures surrounding the violence of sacrifice see Scott B. Noegel, "Dismemberment, Creation, and Ritual: Images of Divine Violence in the Ancient Near East," in *Belief and Bloodshed: Religion and Violence across Time and Tradition* (Landham, MD: Rowaman & Littlefield Publishers, Inc., 2007), 17–18.

4. Horace Bushnell, *Vicarious Sacrifice* (Hicksville, NY: The Regina Press, 1975), 60ff.

5. William Placher, *Jesus the Savior: The Meaning of Jesus Christ for Christian Faith* (Louisville: Westminster John Knox Press, 2001), 139. Cf., André Dumas, "La Mort du Christ n'est-elle pas Sacrificielle? Discussion d'objections contemporaines" in *Etudes Thèologiques et Religieuses* 56 (1981): 581–582. Dumas argues, along with Girard, that "this perverse God is suspect of only being the product of human imagination who institutes the magic of substitution. . . . We conceal ethical homicide through a dogmatic theory where it becomes necessary that another one die in our place. . . ." ("[c]e Dieu pervers est soupçonnable de n'être que le produit de l'imaginaire humain qui instaure la magie de la substitu-

tion . . . Nous dissimulons ici l'homicide éthique par une théorie dogmatique, o il deviene nécessaire que quelqu'un meure à notre place. . . ."). See also René Girard, *Violence and the Sacred,* translated by Patrick Gregory (Baltimore, MD: Johns Hopkins University Press, 1972).

6. Doug Frank has written a beautiful book that deals with this issue. See *A Gentler God: Breaking Free of the Almighty in the Company of the Human Jesus* (Menangle, Australia: Albatross Books Pty Ltd., 2010), 106–116, 285. See the essay on "Sacrifice" in *The Anchor Bible Dictionary*, vol. 5, ed. David Noel Freedman (New York: Doubleday, 1992), especially the section on "Prophetic Critique," 881–882.

7. Granted, more and more cities are developing programs that work toward the reconciliation of victims and perpetrators but we still have a long way to go. Horace Bushnell asserts that God getting the suffering and pain for sin from somebody else, other than the sinner, is just plain unjust. Justice as retributive requires that the suffering for wrongdoing come directly from the wrongdoer. He says, "But to remit a punishment or pain deserved, in consideration of a similar punishment or pain not deserved, accepted by an innocent party, so far from being any due support of law, is the worst possible mockery of it. It belongs to the very idea of punishment, that it fall on the transgressor himself, not on any other, even though he be willing to receive it" (Bushnell, *Vicarious Sacrifice,* 493).

8. Friedrich Nietzsche, *On the Genealogy of Morals,* trans. and ed. by Walter Kaufmann (New York: Vintage Books, 1989), 2.7; 2.22.

9. Timothy Gorringe, *God's Just Vengeance: Crime, Violence, and the Rhetoric of Salvation* (New York: Cambridge University Press, 1996), 82.

10. Helen Prejean, *Dead Man Walking: An Eyewitness Account of the Death Penalty in the United States* (New York: Random House, 1993), 124; Gorringe, *God's Just Vengeance,* 11. See also Beier, *A Violent God Image,* 210ff. Beier insists that our image of God as violent not only stems from our own fear, but also motivates us to project our violent tendencies and desires onto God. In other words, we fear possible threats to our well-being in the world so we adopt an image of God as violent and retributive. This image of God enables us then to do violence in order to attack that which threatens us and we do it all in the name of the God who wreaks vengeance and threats on enemies. Our enemies, whom we have just attacked, fear us because we threaten their well-being so they attack back using the same rationale. It's a vicious cycle of violence.

11. See Joanne Carlson Brown, "Divine Child Abuse?" 25–28; Margo G. Houts, "Atonement and Abuse: An Alternate View" in *Daughters of Sarah* (summer 1992): 29–32; Joanne Carlson-Brown and Rebecca Parker, "For God So Loved the World?" in *Christianity, Patriarchy, and Abuse: A Feminist Critique* (New York: Pilgrim Press, 1989), 2.

12. Second Corinthians 5:19; Ephesians 2:16. See Bushnell, *Vicarious Sacrifice,* 41, 46. He doesn't believe the Bible explicitly supports a penal or satisfaction view of the cross. To interpret it as such is too literal a reading.

13. Schmeichen, *Saving Power*, 15.

14. Joel B. Green and Mark D. Baker, *Recovering the Scandal of the Cross: Atonement in New Testament and Contemporary Contexts* (Downers Grove, IL: Intervarsity Press, 2000), 116ff.

15. See Timothy Gorringe, *God's Just Vengeance*, 85–219; Anthony Bartlett, *Cross Purposes*, 56–78; Peter Schmiechen, *Saving Power*, 315.

16. I realize the simplistic nature of this short summary of social cause and theological effect in Christian history. Of course, it is more complicated and many other factors are involved. I use this section of the essay for illustrative purposes only.

17. Jaroslav Pelikan during an interview for the *U. S. New and World Report* (July 26, 1989).

18. T. S. Eliot, *The Four Quartets—East Coker*. Many thanks to Professor B. Keith Putt who first brought this passage to my attention in a philosophy class many years ago.

Chapter 5: What Is Justice?

1. William Shakespeare, *The Merchant of Venice*, IV. I. 106. A small portion of this chapter is published in Sharon L. Baker, "The Repetition of Reconciliation: Satisfying Justice, Mercy, and Forgiveness," in *Stricken by God: Nonviolent Identification and the Victory of Christ*, eds. Brad Jersak and Michael Hardin (Grand Rapids: William B. Eerdmans Publishing Company, 2007). Reprinted by permission of the publisher, all rights reserved.

2. Shakespeare, *The Merchant of Venice*, IV. I. 199.

3. Shakespeare, *The Merchant of Venice*, IV. I. 377.

4. Shakespeare, *The Merchant of Venice*, IV. I. 184ff.

5. See Michael Hardin, *The Jesus Driven Life*, 31–39. See also my book titled *Razing Hell: Rethinking Everything You've Been Taught about God's Wrath and Judgment* (Louisville, KY: Westminster John Knox Press, 2010), 60, 64, 67 on the Jesus lens. See also Hosea 11:3, where we find beautiful imagery of God holding the people in God's arms, healing them, touching them with cords of kindness and with bands of love, feeding them like a mother tenderly feeds her infant children. Or see Joel 2:13 in which God is gracious and merciful, slow to anger and abounding in loving-kindness, who relents from punishing. Many scholars argue that Jesus is violent and uses violence to usher in God's kingdom—I disagree. For a fantastic treatment of the nonviolence of Jesus in the gospels, Acts, and Revelation, see David J. Neville, *Peaceable Hope: Contesting Violent Eschatology in New Testament Narratives* (Grand Rapids: Baker Academic, 2013).

6. Finlan, *Options on Atonement*, 112–114. See also G. B. Caird, *The Language and Imagery of the Bible*, 110–117.

7. For instance, see works by Stephen Finlan, *Problems with Atonement* and *Options on Atonement;* Charles Hodge, *On the Nature of the Atonement;* W. T. Conner, *The Gospel of Redemption*.

8. Christian Smith, *The Bible Made Impossible: Why Biblicism Is Not a Truly Evangelical Reading of Scripture* (Grand Rapids: Brazos Press, 2011), 98, quoting Charles Spurgeon. In *The Jesus Driven Life*, Michael Hardin discusses reading and interpreting the Bible through the life, death, and resurrection of Jesus. He argues that since the work of Jesus fully reveals God to us, especially the three pronged commandment to love God, others, and self, Jesus should be our interpretive matrix. For him any behavior in Scripture that does not line up with the living example of Jesus does not reveal God's behavior to us in any manner (38–39).

9. On conceptual idolatry see Jean Luc-Marion, *God without Being: Hors-Texte,* trans. Thomas A. Carlson (Chicago: University of Chicago Press, 1995), 16–17; Crystal Downing, *Changing Signs of Truth*, 311–312. For more on the Jesus lens see Smith, *The Bible Made Impossible*, 101. Many heavy-weight theologians draw similar conclusions about what I call "the Jesus lens." Consult Martin Luther, Karl Barth, John Stott, G. C. Berkouwer, Geoffrey Bromiley, Donald Bloesch, J. I. Packer, Thomas Oden, and Kevin Vanhoozer, for example. Christian Smith provides a handy and brief synopsis on their thought in this matter (97–109). Berkouwer actually argues that "[e]very word about the God-breathed character of Scripture is *meaningless* if Holy Scripture is not understood as the witness concerning Christ" (Berkouwer, *Holy Scripture* [Grand Rapids: Eerdmans Publishing Company, 1975]), 179 (emphasis added); Donald McKim, ed., *Cambridge Companion to Martin Luther* (Cambridge: Cambridge University Press, 2003), 112. See also Hardin, *Jesus Driven Life*, 39–40.

10. Christian Smith, *The Bible Made Impossible*, 37–48. Smith labels passages of texts that do not fit the reader's interpretive paradigm "leftover" texts. Yet, these "leftover" passages may play a significant role in another interpretive paradigm. For instance, my interpretive paradigm is God is love; divine justice is restorative; God desires to reconcile with all people. The passages that speak of God killing babies and wiping out entire populations function for me, therefore, as "leftover" texts—at least according to Smith. For someone who focuses on God's wrath and justice, however, these texts become primary to their interpretive paradigm and the passages dealing with God's boundless love and forgiveness become "leftover" texts. He says, "In the end . . . different groups of Christians end up invested in different interpretive paradigms, learn to ignore certain potentially threatening leftover texts, and are persuaded that the remainder of leftover texts can be explained away on an ad hoc basis when they are 'rightly understood,' read in proper context, or otherwise 'correctly' interpreted." On Jesus' omission see Finlan, *Options on Atonement*, 113. Gordon Brubacher, "Just War and the New Community: The Witness of the Old Testament for Christians Today, *Princeton Theological Review*, (fall, 2006): 24.

11. Gen. 6:11, 13; 2 Sam. 22:3; Pss. 7:16; 11:5; 72:14; 73:6; Prov. 1:19; 3:31; 10:6, 11; 13:2; 16:29; 21:7; Jer. 6:7; 22:3; Ezek. 7:11, 23; 8:17; 12:19; 28:16; Amos 3:10; Jonah 3:8; Hab. 2:12; and many others.

12. *Anchor Bible Dictionary*, "Righteousness," 731. The Hebrew word *'āśâ* in the phrase "righteousness and justice" indicates the *doing* of the pair. Prov. 2:8–9

also speak of justice as a "good path." In Isa. 59:8–9 justice is absent from the people's path.

13. For example, Pss. 10:17–18; 33:5; 82:1–8; 99:4; Isa. 1:15–17; 30:18–19; 32:1–2; 42:1–4; 61:1–8; Jer. 9:24; 22:3; Ezek. 34:11–16; Hos. 2:19; Zech. 7:9–10; Mic. 6:8. When the word *mishpat* is translated in the English Old Testament, it is done so in a manner that indicates the justice served in a courtroom. Not so in the Hebrew. The word instead implies continuous, repeated actions, *doing* justice rather than exacting justice. Greifswald J. Zobel, *"hesed," Theological Dictionary of the Old Testament,* ed. by G. Johannes Botterweck and Helmer Ringgren, trans. by David E. Green, vol. 5 (Grand Rapids: William B. Eerdmans Publishing Company, 1986), 49.

14. See also Isa. 33:5–6; 51:4–5. Look up Isa. 1:15–17 in which God tells the people to stop shedding blood and do justice, and Job 19:7 in which Job seeks justice and only finds violence. Again, justice is absent in the presence of violence. C.f., Isa. 32:16–18; Jer. 22:15–17; Mic. 3:1–3; 7:2–3; Hab. 1:3–4.

15. See also Pss. 89:14; 101:1.

16. See also Pss. 1:3; 65:9–14.

17. Luke 23:34, 43; Gal. 3:28; 2 Cor. 5:18–19. See also Luke 10:25–37; Matthew 9:9–13; Luke 2:8–14; Matthew 2:1–12.

18. Although the Hebrew word *shalom* most often gets translated as "peace," the word means so much more. Its meaning incorporates the entire range of peace: a state of harmony with God and creation, a total wholeness, completeness, and well-being that infiltrates every aspect of life on the personal, psychological, social, cultural, spiritual, and physical levels. It is a state of wholeness and unity and of restored relationships. See Perry Yoder, *Shalom: The Bible's Word for Salvation, Justice, and Peace* (Nappanee, IN: Evangel Publishing House, 1987), 5,10–15.

19. Fore-giving expresses the notion of "giving beforehand" or giving something *before* a person repents or pays back a debt. Richard Rohr, *Job and the Mystery of Suffering: Spiritual Reflections* (New York: The Crossroad Publishing Company, 2005), 57.

20. C. F. D. Moule, *Forgiveness and Reconciliation* (London: SPCK, 1998), 41–42.

21. Luke 23:34.

22. Moule, *Forgiveness and Reconciliation,* 44–46. Moule states the notion of divine justice well: "The life of Jesus and his death—the inevitable consequence of total dedication to the way of God—and his total aliveness through and beyond (not in spite of) death, all point in this direction, and exhibit the justice of God at its deepest level: 'God in Christ was reconciling the world to himself' (2 Cor. 5:19). No hangover of retributive systems still showing itself in the New Testament can negate this. . . ." See also, e.g., Rom. 3:24; 1 Cor. 1:30; Eph. 1:17; 2:4–6; Col. 1:14.

23. Nelson-Pallmeyer, *Jesus against Christianity,* 295.

24. Based upon a conversation with Scott Holland of *Cross Currents*, Nov. 19, 2006, in Washington, DC. Miroslav Volf emphasizes the importance of victims hanging onto the hope that God will vindicate them in *Exclusion and Embrace: A Theological Exploration of Identity, Otherness, and Reconciliation* (Nashville: Abingdon Press, 1996), 304. For a different perspective on divine justice see Graham A. Cole, *God the Peacemaker: How Atonement Brings Shalom* (Downers Grove, IL; Intervarsity Press, 2009), 71–78.

25. See the story of Otto in my book *Razing Hell*, 115–118.

26. See the following website. There are many stories that tell of victims' and victimizers' transformation through restorative justice. http://theforgivenesspro ject.com/stories/rebecca-demauro-usa/.

27. Kay Harvey, "One Victim's 'Wakeup Call' Produces a Reconciliation," in *St. Paul Pioneer Press* (October 29, 1995).

28. Thomas Aquinas, *Summa theologiae*, Blackfriars edition (New York: McGraw-Hill Book Company, 1964–1966), IIaIIae, q.106, a.2, ad 3; Ia, q.20, a.4, ad 4.

29. Bailie, *Violence Unveiled*, 208–209.

30. Schwager, *Must There Be Scapegoats?* (New York: Harper, 1987), 214. Mark Heim says that "Jesus didn't volunteer to get into God's justice machine. God volunteered to get into ours." See Heim, *Saved from Sacrifice*, 218.

31. Derek Flood, *Healing the Gospel: A Radical Vision for Grace, Justice, and the Cross* (Eugene, OR: Cascade Books, 2012), 10–13. New Testament scholar N. T. Wright argues that the righteousness spoken of in Romans 3:21–26 is justice. He says that righteousness is "the instrument of putting the world to rights—what we might call cosmic restorative justice." See N. T. Wright, "The Letter to the Romans," in *The New Interpreter's Bible: Acts–1 Corinthians*, vol. 10 (Nashville: Abingdon Press, 2002), 400.

Chapter 6: An Economy of Forgiveness

1. I could write an entire book, or maybe two, just on forgiveness. See *Razing Hell*, 39–47, 95–107. In *Razing Hell* I look at forgiveness in general while here we consider forgiveness as it applies to Jesus's life, death, and resurrection and, consequently, to God's forgiveness of our sin.

2. See the *Anchor Bible Dictionary* on "Forgiveness." The context of divine forgiveness in these verses points to a removal of sin: Pss. 32:1, 5; 51:1; Isa. 33:24; Hos. 14:3; Mic. 7:18.

3. See note 5 for chapter 6.

4. See Jer. 33:8. 4. Luke 25:30; Fiddes, *Past Event and Present Salvation*, 101.

5. John D. Caputo, *The Weakness of God: A Theology of the Event* (Bloomington: Indiana University Press, 2005), 232.

6. This poem is in the public domain.

7. Dorothy L. Sayers, "Forgiveness and the Economy," in *The Fortnightly* (April 1941): 380.

8. Caputo, *The Weakness of God*, 208. Billy Graham observes this attitude. During an appearance on the *Today* show he mentioned that he forgives Bill Clinton. His forgiveness created an uproar in the evangelical community. Graham remarked, "I said one word—'forgiveness.' I got all kinds of ugly letters about that." See John Mark Eberhart, "Book Chronicles Graham's Influence," in the Harrisburg, PA, *Sunday Patriot News* (Sunday, September 9, 2007): G7.

9. *Summa theologiae* Ia, q.38, a.2, c. Aquinas, however, applies this notion of forgiveness to humans, but not to God. For him, God forgives only after Jesus satisfies the debt and after the sinner repents (IIIa, q.86, a.2). See also Caputo, *The Weakness of God*, 210–211; John D. Caputo, *The Prayers and Tears of Jacques Derrida: Religion without Religion* (Bloomington: Indiana University Press, 1997), 178. Caputo aptly expresses the notion of forgiveness as a gift: "The question of the gift of giving is inseparable from that of forgiving, that is, of giving 'away' or 'forth' (as in the German *fort*), giving away what is due to come back to us, whether that be a debt or an obligation, real or symbolic. That gift is a give-away. *Le don* is inseparable from *le par-don*. As the gift must not be a secret calculation of a way to get a return for oneself, so it must not encumber the other with a debt. Whatever debts, whatever guilt, the other incurs must be forgiven."

10. Caputo, *The Weakness of God*, 210–211. Caputo criticizes the church for requiring conditions to forgiveness, believing that in actual practice, forgiveness is reserved for *non*-sinners, while the sinners can go to the devil unless and until they shape up and stop sinning. "We forgive non-sinners, who have earned it . . . but not sinners, who really need it."

11. Caputo, *The Weakness of God*, 214.

12. See A. N. Wilson, *Jesus: A Life* (New York: Fawcett Columbine, 1992), 30–31. Wilson asserts that Luke 18:9, 14, the verses framing the story, are later Lukan redactions, reducing the element of Pharisaic pride so that the Pharisee and the tax collector are both on equal ground before God. Cf., Caputo, *The Weakness of God*, 214–215; Matthew 6:43–48.

13. Caputo, *The Weakness of God*, 215; see also A. N. Wilson, *Jesus*, 30–31.

14. Caputo, *The Weakness of God*, 215–218; see also E. P. Sanders, *Jesus and Judaism* (Philadelphia: Fortress Press, 1985), 174, 204, 300.

15. See John Milbank, *Being Reconciled: Ontology and Pardon* (New York: Routledge, 2003), 44. Although I disagree with Milbank's conclusions concerning divine forgiveness I find his research on forgiveness helpful. See also Walter Wink, *When the Powers Fall: Reconciliation in the Healing of Nations* (Minneapolis: Fortress Press, 1998), 16. Wink stresses that repentance does not come before forgiveness; God freely forgives whether or not we repent. In order to be reconciled, however, Wink believes that repentance on the part of the offending party must occur.

16. Moule, *Forgiveness and Reconciliation*, 23–24. Moule suggests that forgiveness includes a type of death to self in that the self gives up or sacrifices the selfish

desire for revenge or retribution; Fiddes, *Past Event and Present Salvation*, 16; Jacques Derrida, *The Gift of Death*, trans. by David Wills (Chicago: University of Chicago Press, 1995); B. Keith Putt, "Prayers of Confession and Tears of Contrition: John Caputo and a Radically 'Baptist' Hermeneutic of Repentance" in *Religion with/out Religion: The Prayers and Tears of John D. Caputo*, ed. by James H. Olthuis (New York: Routledge, 2002), 62–79; B. Keith Putt, "Faith, Hope, and Love: Radical Hermeneutics as a Pauline Philosophy of Religion" in *A Passion for the Impossible: John D. Caputo in Focus*, ed. by Mark Dooley (New York: SUNY Press, 2003), 237–250; John D. Caputo, "Holding on by Our Teeth: A Response to Putt" in *A Passion for the Impossible: John D. Caputo in Focus*, ed. by Mark Dooley (New York: SUNY Press, 2003), 251–254.

17. Moule, *Forgiveness and Reconciliation*, 22. Cf. P. T. Forsyth, *The Cruciality of the Cross*, 2nd edition (London: Independent Press, 1948), 29. Forsyth proclaims that a feeble gospel preaches that God is ready to forgive. A strong and impelling gospel announces the good news that God has already forgiven.

18. Abelard, *Ethics*, 91.

19. http://theforgivenessproject.com/stories/azim-khamisa-ples-felix-usa/.

20. See Gorringe, *God's Just Vengeance*, 60, 78–81. Gorringe addresses the concept of sacrifice as internal, wrought through obedience to God, rather than external through the literal shedding of blood.

21. Rita Nakashima Brock, "The Cross of Resurrection and Communal Redemption," *Cross Examinations Readings on the Meaning of the Cross Today* (Minneapolis: Fortress Press, 2006), 242.

22. Matt. 18:21–22. Thomas Finger also expresses atonement as at-one-ment. See Thomas Finger, "*Christus Victor* as Non-Violent Atonement," *Atonement and Violence*, ed. John Sanders (Nashville: Abingdon Press, 2006), 88.

23. Isa. 61:1–7, 11; 66:17–25; Acts 2:17–21; Rev. 22:1–5.

Chapter 7: The Costly Sacrifice

1. Stephen Finlan, *Options on Atonement*, 29, 31. See also Peter Schmiechen, *Saving Power*, 54–55. One of the roots of atonement lies in the ancient idea of actually feeding the god with the smoke of the burning animal, as we see in the first four books of the Bible (Lev. 21:6, 8; Num. 28:2). We see this idea carried over into the New Testament in Ephesians 5:2 in which Christ's sacrifice is a fragrant offering, smelled and appreciated by God and in 2 Corinthians 2:15–16 in which we are that fragrant aroma of Christ to God. See also Finlan, *Options on Atonement*, 8–9.

2. Henninger, "Sacrifice" in *The Encyclopedia of Religion* (New York: Macmillan, 1987), 544. See also Thachil, *The Vedic and Christian Concept of Sacrifice* (Keralo, India: Pontifical Institute of Theology and Philosophy, 1985), 3–4.

3. I refer indirectly here to the Documentary Hypothesis attributed to Julius Wellhausen in the late nineteenth and early twentieth century. This theory

holds to the idea that the Torah was composed from four independent sources in parallel narratives, later combined by editors into the text we have now. The four sources are the Yahwist (Jahwist) in which we see many anthropomorphic descriptions of God along with the use of the Tetragrammaton (YHWH) when talking about God; the Elohist in which we see the word *Elohim* used for the name "God." The Elohist focuses on prophetic announcements through dreams and visions, the fear of God, and covenant worship; the Deuteronomist in which we see a focus on the law, punishments, rewards, and judgment; and the Priestly source that focuses on God as sovereign creator. It emphasizes ritual, God's presence to those who call on God's name, and the divinely revealed plan for removal of sin. For something other than this extremely brief and inadequate explanation of a complicated theory, see James Kugel, *How to Read the Bible: A Guide to Scripture, Then and Now* (New York: Free Press, 2008). See Leviticus 20:1–5 for God's prohibition surrounding human sacrifice to Molech.

4. See Jacob Milgrom, *Leviticus 1–16*, 254–255 and Finlan, *Options on Atonement*, 10–11.

5. *Kippūr* comes from the root *kpr* (*kāpar*). Some scholars trace its meaning back to an Arabic root for "to cover." Other scholars argue that there is very little evidence for a link between the Hebrew and Arabic words. For a very brief treatment see R. Laird Harris, Gleason L. Archer Jr., and Bruce K. Waltke, *Theological Wordbook of the Old Testament* (Chicago: Moody Bible Institute, 1980). Lev. 4:20, 26, 31, 35; 5:10, 13, 16, 18; 6:7; 19:22; Num. 15:28. Also see Finlan, *Options on Atonement*, 20–21. For an interesting perspective see Brant Pitre, *Jesus and the Jewish Roots of the Eucharist: Unlocking the Secrets of the Last Supper* (New York: Doubleday, 2011), 11–21. See also *"kpr," The New International Dictionary of Old Testament Theology and Exegesis*, vol. 2 (Grand Rapids: Zondervan, 1992); Sylvain Romerowski, "Old Testament Sacrifices and Reconciliation," *European Journal of Theology* (2006): 16–17. Romerowski makes a direct connection between *kippur* and forgiveness—to do one is to do the other. Interestingly, blood and life are connected in most Near Eastern cultures. In fact, even some Native American traditions hold to the belief that the blood is the life of a person.

6. Dennis McCarthy, SJ, argues that the question surrounding sacrifice in Psalm 50 directly admonishes the Israelites for interpreting their sacrifices to God in terms of the old Canaanite ideas of sacrifice. See "Symbolism of Blood and Sacrifice" *Journal of Biblical Literature*, vol. 88 (June 1969): 171.

7. See Raymund Schwager, *Must There Be Scapegoats?* 43–135. Schwager believes that as the Scriptures develop, God becomes less and less violent, with fewer deaths and outright massacres. We may infer from this either a form of progressive revelation or that the world views of the community were changing as knowledge developed.

8. Rabbis Nosson Scherman and Hersh Goldwurm, *Leviticus: A New Translation with a Commentary Anthologized From Talmudic, Midrashic and Rabbinic Sources* (Brooklyn: Mesorah Publications, LTD., 1989), 21ff. See also *Theological*

Wordbook of the Old Testament, #2065. For a good essay on the nature of sacrifice as an inward condition of the heart that mirrors God's own covenant love, see David L. Wheeler, "The Cross and the Blood: Dead or Living Images?" *Dialog* (winter 1996): 10.

9. Rabbis Nosson Scherman and Hersh Goldwurm, *Leviticus,* 31–32.

10. Horace Bushnell, *Vicarious Sacrifice,* 505.

11. Brauch A. Levine, *The JPS Torah Commentary: Leviticus* (Philadelphia: Jewish Publication Society, 1989).

12. Many verses tear down the importance of the sacrificial system, revealing instead the nature of true sacrifice that the blood of animals merely symbolized. See Pss. 51:16–17; 50:12–14; 69:30–31; Prov. 21:3; Isa. 1:11; Hos. 4:8; 6:6; 8:11–12; Amos 5:21–25; Mic. 6:6–8; Jer. 6:20; 7:22–23. Also see Finlan, *Options on Atonement,* 6 and Finlan, *Problems with Atonement,* 40ff. See also Sylvain Romerowski, "Old Testament Sacrifices and Reconciliation," 17–18.

13. See Daniel Stökl Ben Ezra, *The Impact of Yom Kippur on Early Christianity: The Day of Atonement from Second Temple Judaism to the Fifth Century* (Tübingen: J. C. B. Morh/Paul Siebeck, 2003); Roy E. Gane, *Cult and Character: Purification Offerings, Day of Atonement, and Theodicy* (Winona Lake, IN: Eisenbrauns, 2005), 62; See also Dennis J. McCarthy, SJ, "The Symbolism of Blood and Sacrifice," in *Journal of Biblical Literature* 88, no. 2 (1969): 166–176. See also Finlan, *Options on Atonement,* 12–13. See also Andrew Sung Park, *Triune Atonement: Christ's Healing for Sinners, Victims, and the Whole Creation* (Louisville: Westminster John Knox Press, 2009), 35ff—for him, the blood of Jesus symbolizes the suffering, torment, and death of victims everywhere. In shedding his blood, Jesus stood in solidarity with all who shed blood due to violence and oppression. He participates in the agony of their suffering under unjust persecution, exploitation, oppression, and violence (36).

14. Jose Thachil, *The Vedic and the Christian Concept of Sacrifice,* 218–224, 240, 328–330, 362.

15. For a fantastic treatment of the mysteries of the book of Hebrews, its refutation of the external sacrifice, and the message of true sacrifice that it teaches, see Michael Hardin, "Sacrificial Language in Hebrews: Reappraising René Girard," in *Violence Renounced: René Girard, Biblical Studies, and Peacemaking,* Willard M. Swartley, ed. (Telford, PA: Cascadia Publishing House, 2000), 103–119. Hardin argues that in offering himself as the victim of violence, Jesus rejects the sacrificial system that demanded blood in turn for forgiveness. He exposes the inadequacies of violence inherent in blood sacrifice by becoming the ultimate victim and thereby revealing a better way, God's way of a life surrendered to God in obedience, a life of loving God and others. These ideas come from Sh'lah HaKadosh.

16. For an essay on the symbolic nature of blood sacrifices and the connection between purifying and forgiveness see Sylvain Romerowski, "Old Testament Sacrifices and Reconciliation," 16.

17. Hardin, "Sacrificial Language in Hebrews," 115.

Chapter 8: Re-Tuning At-one-ment

1. http://www.govtrack.us/congress/bills/108/s1115.

2. W. T. Conner, *The Gospel of Redemption* (Nashville: Broadman Press, 1945), 95–97. When I read the works of W. T. Conner, I am reminded of the rich Southern Baptist heritage he passed on to his students and, as in my case, students of his students. Conner and his theology exemplify genuine, traditional Southern Baptist beliefs.

3. Bushnell, *Vicarious Sacrifice*, 42.

4. Bushnell, *Vicarious Sacrifice*, 46, 473–474.

5. See Finlan, *Options on Atonement*, 46–47. Although many scholars turn to the curses in Deuteronomy 27 to explain the curse in Galatians 3:13, Finlan argues against this theory. He doesn't believe there is sufficient evidence to warrant such an interpretation of the Galatians passage. In fact, there is no other soteriological formula in Paul's writings that would remotely point to a Deuteronomic reading of the cross. For the interpretation of Ephesians 2:3 see also David B. Miller, "God in the Hands of Angry Sinners: The Misdiagnosis of Wrath in Ephesians 2" in *Peace Be with You*, 234–242.

6. "Nation's Shame." *The Milwaukee Sentinel.* September 16, 1963. http://news.google.com/newspapers?id=RMsVAAAAIBAJ&sjid=wRAEAAAAIBAJ&pg=3102,307586&dq=church+bombing+birmingham+nation's+shame&hl=en.

7. Bushnell, *Vicarious Sacrifice*, 475.

8. James R. Payton Jr., *Light from the Christian East: An Introduction to the Orthodox Tradition* (Downers Grove, IL: InterVarsity Press, 2007), 124ff. Payton, 122–123. Payton makes the point that in the Christian West, we typically understand our sin problem in terms of being guilty or innocent, unrighteous or righteous, deserving of punishment or reward. Jesus is seen as the victim of sin. Eastern Christianity, on the other hand, focuses more on the power that holds us captive to sin and Jesus is seen as the victor over sin. These very different perspectives have helped to shape our theology and doctrines of atonement.

9. Lossky, *Mystical Theology*, 137, 148.

10. Brant Pitre, *Jesus and the Jewish Roots of the Eucharist*, 74–75.

11. See the *Oxford English Dictionary* for etymology and definition.

12. Stephen Finlan, *The Background and Content of Paul's Cultic Atonement Metaphors* (Atlanta: SBL, 2004), 164. See also Finlan, *Problems with Atonement*, 40.

13. Finlan, *Options on Atonement*, 20–21.

14. Finlan, *Options on Atonement*, 21. See also http://ancientroadpublications.com/Studies/BiblicalStudies/MercySeat.html.

15. Day of Atonement is more correctly the Day of Purification (Milgrom, *Leviticus 1–16*, 254–55). For a more detailed account of the Greek word *hilasterion* see Finlan, *Options on Atonement*, 20–21; *Problems with Atonement*, 6ff.; and *Background and Content of Paul's Cultic Atonement Metaphors*, 123–162. The

word never means "expiation," or "sacrificial ritual" as we have so often translated it.

16. Michael Hardin argues that this is the old covenant, which has already been identified as lesser because it cannot lead to the forgiveness of sin (9:9, 12–13; 10:4; 11). "[W]hereas the law required the shedding of blood, it was not yet effective, inasmuch as the blood of bulls and goats cannot take away sin. . . . In the new covenant, sins and lawless acts are forgiven apart from the sacrifice and the shedding of blood. Before sacrifice and apart from sacrifice there is forgiveness" (Hardin, "Sacrificial Language in Hebrews: Reappraising René Girard," 114). In other words, the sacrifice, symbolized by the shedding of blood, is the giving of life—it takes selfless giving of life to forgive.

17. Bushnell, *Vicarious Sacrifice*, 469.

18. Christ's passion is efficacious for those under both the old covenant and the new covenant, although those under the new covenant are given a greater righteousness through the love of God manifested in Christ. Abelard states that, "everyone becomes more righteous—by which we mean a greater love of the Lord—after the passion of Christ than before, since a realized gift inspires greater love than one which is only hoped for." Abelard, *Exp. in Epist. ad Rom. ii.iii.* Quoted from Weingart, 95. For the love of God revealed in Christ's life and death see Weingart, *The Logic of Divine Love*, 123–124.

19. Abelard, "Epistle to the Romans, 3:21–23," in Fairweather, 278–279. Cf., Colin Green, "Is the Message of the Cross Good News for the Twentieth Century?" in *Atonement Today: A Symposium at St. John's College, Nottingham*, ed. by John Goldingay (London: SPCK, 1995), 223; Bernard McCullagh, "Theology of Atonement" in *Theology* (September 1988): 399.

20. Abelard, "Epistle to the Romans, 3:24," in Fairweather, 279.

21. Abelard, *Exp. in Epist. ad Rom.* i.i, quoted from Weingart, 75–76. Abelard, "Epistle to the Romans, 3:26" and Sol., in Fairweather, 277–279, 284.

22. See Michael J. Dodds, *The Unchanging God of Love* (Fribourg, Switzerland: Éditions Universitaires Fribourg Suisse, 1986), 305. See also W. T. Conner, 105ff. Gunton, *The Actuality of Atonement*, 54.

Chapter 9: An Alternative View

1. Cyril of Alexandria, *Commentary of S. Cyril, Patriarch of Alexandria, upon the Gospel of St. Luke*, 2:4.

2. Vladimir Lossky, *The Mystical Theology of the Eastern Church* (Crestwood, NY: St. Vladimir's Seminary Press, 1957), 143–147; Stephen Finlan and Vladimir Kharlamov, eds. Theōsis: *Deification in Christian Theology*, Princeton Theological Monograph Series (Eugene, OR: Pickwick Publications, 2006), 162–164; Christoforos Stavropoulos, "Partakers of the Divine Nature" in *Eastern Orthodox Theology*, edited by Daniel B. Clendenin (Grand Rapids: Baker Academic, 2003), 183–192.

3. Mark Thiessen Nation aptly articulates this form of substitution in connection to the death of Jesus in "Who Has Believed What We Have Heard? A Response to Denny Weaver's The Nonviolent Atonement" in *Conrad Grebel Review* (fall 2009): 17–30, 26. See also Finlan, *Problems with Atonement*, 52–55. He discusses substitution as a "noble death" motif (52–55). See also Elizabeth A. Johnson, CSJ, "The Word Was Made Flesh and Dwelt among Us," in *Jesus: A Colloquium in the Holy Land,* ed. Dorothy Donnelly (New York: Continuum International Publishing Group, 2001), 158–160.

4. See Finlan, *Background and Content,* 178–179.

5. Mark Thiessen Nation, "Who Has Believed?" 23. The passion predictions do not refer to sacrifice, substitution, cleansing, payment, or even attach any saving significance to Jesus's death but refer only the inevitability of his being killed after being rejected by the chief priests and scribes (Mark 8:31; 9:31; 10:33; Matt. 20:18–19; Luke 18:32). Wouldn't Jesus have said something if his death were a payment of some sort? See Finlan, *Options on Atonement,* 39.

6. Bushnell, 523. See also Stephen Finlan and Vladimir Kharlamov, eds. Theōsis: *Deification in Christian Theology,* 1ff. There is so much scriptural evidence for this theory that I'll just list a few here: John 3:6; 10:34; 14:7; 14:12; Rom. 8:16; 8:29; 12:2; Eph. 4:24; 5:1–2; 2 Cor. 3:18; Pet. 1:4; 1 John 3:2; Ps. 82:6; Job 32:8; Phil. 3:21.

7. S. Mark Heim, "Saved by What Shouldn't Happen: The Anti-Sacrificial Meaning of the Cross," in *Cross Examinations: Readings on the Meaning of the Cross Today,* ed. Marit Trelstad (Minneapolis: Augsburg Fortress Press, 2006), 223.

8. For more on this idea, see the first chapter of Jean-Luc Marion, *Prolegomena to Charity,* trans. Stephen E. Lewis (New York: Fordham University Press, 2002). Marion argues that Jesus stops the cycle of violence by not continuing the violence himself. Instead, he absorbs the violence and transforms it.

9. The fact that Jesus, who rebelled against the strictures of institutional religion and oppressive forms of government, suffered a violent death at the hands of the authorities is no surprise. Jesus himself predicted just such a death during his ministry. Thomas Aquinas supports this interpretation of Jesus' passion, labeling the act of putting Christ to death a crime, calling Christ's executioners murderers, and pointing to the leaders of the people as the agents responsible for his death. Abelard, too, denies that the suffering of the cross had any correspondence with violence on God's part or any mercantile relationship to God's forgiveness. See Abelard, *Epist. to the Romans,* 3:36, 282. Cf., McCullagh, "Theology of Atonement," 397–398. According to theologian P. T. Forsyth, the cross, therefore, should not be interpreted as a deflection of God's anger or as a punishment or the transfer of guilt or as some "ledger amount which could be shifted about by divine finance." The cross did not "procure grace, it flowed from grace" (P. T. Forsyth, *The Cruciality of the Cross,* 98). Out of love for humanity trapped in religious structures of violence, Jesus Christ submitted to the religious and secular

powers of that time as a prophetic protest against injustice, oppression, and systemic evil. In so doing, he exposed them and simultaneously both condemned the violence and offered forgiveness. Accordingly, Jesus suffered the cross for us and because of us. See also Craig L. Nessan, "Violence and Atonement," *Dialog*, vol. 35, no. 1 (winter 1996): 31–32. He contends that "[t]he immediate occasion for Jesus' arrest and condemnation to death is a direct consequence of his leadership in the kingdom movement." In other words, Jesus died an agonizing death on the cross because human beings willed it, not God.

10. James 5:16; 1 John 5:14–15; Mark 11:24. The scriptural evidence pointing to the divine will to answer the prayer of God's righteous ones is abundant. The writer of James tells us that "[t]he effective prayer of a righteous [person] can accomplish much" (NASB). 1 John expresses a similar promise of answered prayer, stating: "And this is the boldness we have in him, that is we ask anything according to his will, he hears us. And if we know that he hears us in whatever we ask, we know that we have obtained the requests made of him." In Mark, Jesus exhorts his followers to pray, promising them good results, saying "all things for which you pray and ask, believe that you have received them, and they shall be granted you" (NASB). In other words, throughout Scripture the people of God call out to God in prayer and God answers.

11. In becoming sin for us, as Thomas Aquinas states in reference to 2 Cor. 5:21, Christ's prayer for forgiveness of that sin can be thought to cover all who have sinned. *Summa theologiae* III, q.46, a.4, ad 3. See also III, q.46, a.6, r and ad 2, 3, 4 in which Aquinas writes that Christ was suffering for the sins of all humanity, the very sins that Christ asked God to forgive.

12. See Dorothee Sölle, *Christ the Representative: An Essay in Theology after the Death of God*, trans. by David Lewis (Philadelphia: Fortress Press, 1967), 124, 129. Sölle argues that although Christ's suffering was not a divine imperative, it was not irrelevant. Christ suffered because human agents killed him; he suffered for us by standing with us in our own suffering.

13. *Summa theologiae* III, q.48, a.3, ad 3: "[p]assio Christi ex parte occidentium ipsum fuit maleficium; sed ex parte ipsius ex charitate patientis fuit sacrificium."

14. *Summa theologiae* III, q.14, a.1, ad 1.

15. Abelard, *Ethics*, 97.

16. Fiddes, *Past Event and Present Salvation*, 91. Dumas calls Christ's sacrifice "costly communion," as an act of solidarity through love. Dumas, "The Death of Christ," 590.

17. Sölle, *Christ the Representative*, 118–119. Cf., Moule, *Forgiveness and Reconciliation*, 20. The work of Christ results in reconciliation, which demands the sacrifice of obedience that works itself out in community living. Cf., Gorringe, *God's Just Vengeance*, 77.

Index

Abel, 141

Abelard, Peter
  Anselm's atonement theory compared
    with, 60, 62, 68, 80
  atonement theory of, 60, 62, 68, 80
  and courtly love, 60, 80
  on cross, 23, 147, 174n10, 188n9
  on forgiveness, 175n11
  on God's love, 60, 68, 174–75n11
  on justice, 175n11
  on righteousness, 147, 187n18

Abrams, M. H., 170n1

abuse
  child abuse, 5, 77, 78
  domestic violence, 28, 29, 64, 78
  passive acceptance of, 78
  sexual abuse by ministers, 29
  violence of, 24–26, 78, 169n37

Adam, 52, 53, 139–40, 159, 173n2,
    175n12

Adams, Rebecca, 71–72

African Americans, 137–38

Albigensian Crusade, 13

alternative view of atonement. See
    atonement theory (alternative view)

Ambrose, 173n2

Americas, conquest of, 13, 29–30, 168n28

analogies. See metaphors

anger of God. See wrath of God

Anselm
  Abelard's atonement theory compared
    with, 60, 62, 68, 80
  atonement theory of, 20, 22, 27,
    55–56, 59, 66, 68
  Cur Deus Homo (Why the God-Man?)
    by, 55
  and feudalism, 55–56, 68, 80,
    173–74n7

Thomas Aquinas' atonement theory
    compared with, 173n7

Antiochus, 150

aphesis (forgiveness), 108. See also
    forgiveness

Aquinas, Thomas
  Aristotle's influence on, 80
  atonement theory of, 20, 55, 56,
    68–69, 173n7
  on crucifixion, 58, 160, 188n9, 189n11
  on forgiveness, 106–7, 182n9, 189n11
  on God's sovereignty and providence,
    173n7
  on grace, 97
  on love of Jesus, 68–69
  on repentance, 97–98

Aristotle, 36, 80, 170–71n3

Ark of the Covenant, 145

asbestos, 133

Athanasius, 21, 69, 173n2

"at-one-ment," 10, 14, 112, 123, 153–55,
    161, 183n23

atonement
  definition of, 14
  kippur meaning, 116–17, 126, 145,
    158, 184n5
  origin of term, 123
  questions on, 2–3, 162–63
  See also cross; and other atonement
    headings

atonement metaphors
  Caird on, 172n24
  feminist theologians on, 78, 176n17
  Finlan on, 172nn19, 27, 30
  and God as both just and merciful,
    40–41
  of law, 42–43
  Paul's use of, 172nn19, 27, 30

CPSIA information can be obtained at www.ICGtesting.com
Printed in the USA
LVOW07s2009260415

436025LV00001B/111/P